SMALL
DATA

SMALL DATA

THE TINY CLUES THAT UNCOVER HUGE TRENDS

MARTIN LINDSTROM

Published in Great Britain in 2016 by Hodder and Stoughton.
An Hachette UK company.

1

Paperback ISBN: 9781473634060
eISBN: 9781473630154

Printed and bound in Australia by
Griffin Press

MIX
Paper from
responsible sources
FSC® C009448

The paper this book is printed on is certified against the
Forest Stewardship Council® Standards. Griffin Press holds
FSC chain of custody certification SGS-COC-005088. FSC
promotes environmentally responsible, socially beneficial and
economically viable management of the world's forests.

Carmelite House
50 Victoria Embankment
London EC4Y 0DZ
www.hodder.co.uk

Also available
in ebook

CONTENTS

FOREWORD

CHIP HEATH

CO-AUTHOR OF *MADE TO STICK* AND *SWITCH*

IN TODAY'S BUSINESS ENVIRONMENT, BIG DATA INSPIRES religious levels of devotion and Martin Lindstrom is an atheist.

While many skeptics are bores, Martin is definitively not. Reading his book is like sitting down to dinner with one of those famous explorers of the nineteenth century, Sir Richard Francis Burton perhaps, who has returned from exotic journeys full of striking observations and tall tales. There is a wide, uncatalogued social world out there, and Martin notices everything . . . Russian homes have no mirrors, owners of Roomba robotic vacuum cleaners frequently give them names, American hotel windows never open, cultures as diverse as those in Saudi Arabia and Siberia turn to refrigerator magnets to convey important family values.

Martin is anything but a passive observer. When he arrives at the airport in a new country, he hand-picks a taxicab driven by a nonnative to drive him into town, and spends the trip grilling the driver for observations about the locals. He notes that outsiders often see a culture's idiosyncrasies better than the natives. As an outsider, he visits real people in their homes and watches what they are doing and how they shape their spaces.

Martin did not sit down to write an explicit critique of Big Data. But by showing the virtues of Small Data he throws into stark relief some problems you should be aware of when you consider Big Data. Consider two:

Big Data doesn't spark insight. New ideas typically come from juxtaposition—combining two things that previously haven't been combined. But Big Data typically lives in databases that are defined too narrowly to create insight. When a firm explores Big Data from its online customers, it typically looks only at online purchases. Frequently that database doesn't track purchases customers make at brick and mortar stores (those are in a separate database, jealously guarded by its owners), and neither database is linked to information on the timing of the firm's advertisements. The book describes a breakthrough shopping experience Martin developed for a French retailer that was trying to attract the fickle attention of teenaged girls; Martin's solution arose by triangulating across time diaries, phone records, interviews, personal photo diaries, and mall shopping observations. When psychologist Phil Tetlock studied Superforecasters, people who were far superior in predicting political and economic events, he found that they had a similar tendency to explore across data sources, looking for triangulation. Unfortunately our Big Data databases are not really "Big," they are less like robust cross-trained athletes and more like gawky nerds who have one splinter skill and are mostly ineffective at everything else. They are too narrow to create the juxtaposition that leads to breakthroughs.

Big Data is data, and data favors analysis over emotion. It's hard to imagine data capturing many of the emotional qualities we most value: *beautiful* or *friendly* or *sexy* or *awesome* or *cute.* If data fostered better emotional decisions, then accountants, not poets, would be the cultural prototype for great lovers. Kevin Roberts of Saatchi and Saatchi argued that great brands have two advantages: (1) they evoke *respect* for their technological performance, durability, and effectiveness; and (2) they evoke *love* because, well, . . . we love them. Brands like HP and Duracell are "respect" brands and Big Data can often help make decisions about increasing respect *(Given our history are customers likely to spend 20% more if we make our batteries last 15% longer?),* but brands such as Disney, Cheerios, and Geek Squad are respected *and loved,* and Big Data is pretty incompetent at suggesting how to increase the love.

At one point Martin is asked by the makers of the robotic vacuum cleaner, the Roomba, to help overcome a drop in revenues. Martin focused on Small Data about emotion. He followed Roomba owners into their homes and watched how they interacted with their machines. Surprisingly, owners treated their Roombas like a pet; they named it, they took pride in showing it to their guests (when is the last time you showed off your vacuum cleaner?). When owners stored the Roomba, they didn't stick it in a closet, they left it peeking out from under the sofa, as though it were frozen in mid- action.

Unfortunately, Roomba's leaders had moved away from its initial "cute" factor. Roomba was inspired by R2D2 in *Star Wars*, but over time designs changed, making Roomba look less like R2D2 and more like an appliance. In the first model, the Roomba made sounds; when it accidentally bumped the wall, by accident it said "uh-oh," but at some point the noises were cut by some engineer seeking a simpler design or a manager seeking lower costs. See chapter 7 for Martin's clever advice to the Roomba managers, inspired by the world's cutest automobile, the BMW Mini Cooper, on how to return emotional excitement to their brand.

In sum, Big Data has problems, and Martin is successful at showing how Small Data is essential to overcoming them.

I've talked about the many virtues of the book, so let me also list a couple of cautions. The book should not be read as a work of social science. When Martin quotes statistics, I don't always know when he is serious and when he's pulling my leg (are 60 percent of the tooth-brushes sold in the world really red? Do teenage girls in France really spend *80 percent* of their waking hours mulling their outfits for to-day and tomorrow?). And while Martin is clearly a careful observer, he often extrapolates to grand conclusions that I suspect are bogus (Do Americans have a conflict-aversion that causes us to prefer round cakes to square ones? And does breaking the cake rules by providing a square cake really allow consumers permission to break their diets?). Leaping this far beyond the data would get a masters' student in Anthropology a failing grade.

But Martin is an explorer and raconteur, not a social scientist, so as a reader I am willing to forgive his excesses. And that's easier to do because he so frequently manages to provoke his clients in new directions that are clearly better, as in the Roomba case above.

Here's another of my favorite cases: In the 1990s LEGO's sales were declining and executives were scared by big research studies showing that Digital Natives were increasingly distractible and in search of instant gratification. Swayed by this data, LEGO was considering dumbing down its toys, making the kits simpler and even perhaps increasing the size of its iconic brick. But then Small Data convinced LEGO to do an abrupt pivot, going the other direction completely, after senior leaders visited the homes of their young users and talked to them about hobbies and leisure. In the introduction to this book, you will read about how the critical "datapoint" was an old pair of Adidas worn by an 11-year old German skateboarder. LEGO leaders eventually embraced the aspirational desires of the geeks who wanted kits that were worthy of their talents, and designed larger kits with more complex features.

A few years ago, a 10-year-old family friend proudly showed me his completed LEGO model of the Taj Mahal. It remains the largest set LEGO has ever produced, with over 5900 bricks. When he received the kit, construction commenced immediately. I'm not even sure he waited for the end of his party. The next day he awakened spontaneously at 4 a.m. and worked until school started at 7, and the first thing he did after school at 3:00 p.m. was to head to his room to start again. And he did that the next day. And the next and the next. He finished in 4 days. The price of the kit? $300 at the time. For a kid's toy. And today the kits are collectors' items with prices of $3000 or more. LEGO executives, hearing my young friend's reaction to this complex challenge would suffer from a sweaty brow and dry mouth, thinking about how narrowly they dodged the Big Data–inspired mistake of dumbing down their kits.

Our businesses will not improve through Big Data alone. We need to follow Martin and explore Rich Data. Deep Data. Even if it comes in the form of Small Data.

Our businesses will be better for it.

—*Chip Heath, January 2016*

INTRODUCTION

THE SOLUTION TO LEGO'S PROBLEMS—THE THING THAT may have rescued it from potential bankruptcy—lay in an old pair of sneakers.

It was early 2003, and the company was in trouble, having lost 30 percent of its turnover over the past year. In 2004, another 10 percent vanished. As Jørgen Vig Knudstorp, LEGO's CEO, put it, "We are on a burning platform, losing money with negative cash flow, and a real risk of debt default which could lead to a break up of the company."[1]

How had the Danish toymaker fallen so far so fast? Arguably, the company's problems could be traced back to 1981, when the world's first handheld game, *Donkey Kong,* came to market, inspiring a debate within the pages of LEGO's internal magazine, *Klodshans,* about what so-called "side-scrolling platform games" meant for the future of construction toys. The consensus: platforms like Atari and Nintendo were fads—which turned out to be true, at least until the advent of computer games for PCs launched their wildly successful second wind.

I had begun advising LEGO in 2004 when the company asked me to develop its overall branding strategy. I didn't want the company to move away from what it had been doing well for so long, but no one could deny the increasing everywhere-ness of all things digital. From the mid-1990s on, LEGO began moving away from its core product, i.e., building blocks, and focusing instead on its loosely knit empire of theme parks, children's clothing lines, video games, books, magazines, television programs and retail stores. Somewhere during this same period, manage-ment decided that considering how impatient, impulsive and fidgety mil-lennials were, LEGO should begin manufacturing bigger bricks.

Every big data study LEGO commissioned drew the exact same conclusions: future generations would lose interest in LEGO. LEGOs would go the way of jackstraws, stickball, blindman's bluff. So-called Digital Natives—men and women born after 1980, who'd come of age in the Information Era—lacked the time, and the patience, for LEGOs, and would quickly run out of ideas and storylines to build around. Digital natives would lose their capacity for fantasy and cre-ativity, if they hadn't already, since computer games were doing most of the work for them. Each LEGO study showed that the generational need for instant gratification was more potent than any building block could ever hope to overcome.

In the face of such a prognosis, it seemed impossible for LEGO to turn things around—but, in fact, the company did. It sold off its theme parks. It continued successful brand alliances with the *Harry Potter, Star Wars* and *Bob the Builder* franchises. It reduced the number of products while entering new and underserved global markets.

Still, probably the biggest turnaround in LEGO's thinking came as the result of an ethnographic visit LEGO marketers paid in early 2004 to the home of an 11-year-old boy in a midsized German city. Their mission? To figure out what really made LEGO stand out. What execu-tives found out that day was that everything they thought they knew, or had been told, about late twentieth- and early twenty-first-century children and their new digital behaviors—including the need for time compression and instantaneous results—was wrong.

In addition to being a LEGO aficionado, the 11-year-old German boy was also a passionate skateboarder. Asked at one point which of his possessions he was the most proud of, he pointed to a pair of beat-up Adidas sneakers with ridges and nooks along one side. Those sneak-ers were his trophy, he said. They were his gold medal. They were his masterpiece. More than that, they were *evidence.* Holding them up so everyone in the room could see and admire them, he explained that one side was worn down and abraded at precisely the right angle. The heels were scuffed and planed in an unmistakable way. The entire look of the sneakers, and the impression they conveyed to the world, was perfect; it signaled to him, to his friends and to the rest of the world that he was one of the best skateboarders in the city.

At that moment, it all came together for the LEGO team. Those theories about time compression and instant gratification? They seemed to be off base. Inspired by what an 11-year-old German boy had told them about an old pair of Adidas, the team realized that children attain social currency among their peers by playing and achieving a high level of mastery at their chosen skill, whatever that skill happens to be. If the skill is valuable, and worthwhile, they will stick with it until they get it right, never mind how long it takes. For kids, it was all about paying your dues and having something tangible to show for it in the end—in this case, a pair of tumbledown Adidas that most adults would never look at twice.

Until that point, LEGO's decision making was predicated entirely on reams of big data. Yet ultimately it was a small, chance insight—a pair of sneakers belonging to a skateboarder and LEGO lover—that helped propel the company's turnaround. From that point on, LEGO refocused on its core product, and even upped the ante. The company not only re-engineered its bricks back to their normal size, it began adding even more, and smaller, bricks inside their boxes. The bricks became more detailed, the instruction manuals more exacting, the construction challenges more labor-intensive. For users, it seemed, LEGO was all about the summons, the provocation, the mastery, the craftsmanship and, not least, the hard-won experience—a conclusion that complex predictive analytics, despite their remarkable ability to parse "average" scores, had missed.

Cut to ten years later when, during the first half of 2014, in the wake of the worldwide success of *The Lego Movie* and sales of related merchandise, LEGO's sales rose 11 percent to exceed $2 billion. For the first time ever, LEGO had surpassed Mattel to become the world's largest toy maker.[2]

BELIEVE IT OR NOT, almost every insight I come up with as a global branding consultant happens just this way. I might be developing a new car key for Porsche owners, designing a credit card for billionaires, creating a newfangled innovation for a weight-loss organization, helping reverse the fortunes of a stumbling American supermarket chain or trying to position the Chinese automotive industry to compete globally. There's a well-known quote that says if you want to understand how animals live, you don't go to the zoo, you go to the jungle. And so I do. In nearly every instance, after conducting what I call Subtext Research (which I occasionally shorten to Subtexting), a detailed process that involves visiting consumers in their homes, gathering small data offline and online, and crunching, or Small Mining, these clues with observations and insights taken from around the world, there almost always comes a moment where I uncover an unmet or unacknowledged desire that forms the foundation of a new brand, product innovation or business.

Over the past 15 years, I've interviewed thousands of men, women and children in their homes in 77 countries. I'm on a plane, or inside a hotel room, 300 nights a year. The drawbacks of living a life like this are obvious. I can't really call anyplace home, relationships are hard to sustain, and children and pets aren't an option. Still, there are benefits. Among them is the ongoing opportunity to observe people and the cultures they inhabit from *their* perspectives, and to try to answer questions like: *How do groups of people form? What are their core beliefs? What do they aspire to, and why? How do they create social ties? How does one culture differ from another? Do any of these local beliefs, habits or rituals have a universal significance?*

Not least are the examples of odd behavior, or general truths, I stumble on all across the world. We are afraid, for example, of letting others know more about us than we know about ourselves, fearing most of all that our masks will slip, and we will lose control, letting others see us as we truly are. We are unable to perceive the people we love—husbands, wives, partners, children—aging physically in the same way we notice people we see less often getting older. All humans experience "candy moments"—an internal reward system that takes place while we're working, reading, thinking or focusing, and that divides and re-energizes our routines and re-stimulates our attention. Relatedly, we "reward" ourselves in the wake of completing a big job, just as the generosity we feel toward others around the holidays results in our buying presents for ourselves. And, in a transparent, overpopulated world where we spill our inner lives online, more than ever the concept of "privacy" and "exclusivity" has become the greatest luxury of all.

Why do most of us when we're on our cell phones walk around in a circle as we're speaking, as if somehow to create a moat, or wall, of privacy? Why, when we're hungry or thirsty, do we open the refrigerator door, glance up and down at the contents, close the door and a few moments later repeat this same behavior? Why when we're late for an appointment do we seek out clocks that tell a "better time," thereby justifying our tardiness? Why in an airport or train station or rock concert do we perceive people in crowds as average members of "the masses"—not realizing that they are doing exactly the same with us? Why do so many people get their best ideas in the shower, or in the presence of water?

The people I study and interview could be teenaged girls living in a Brazilian *favela*; merchant bankers in the Czech Republic; housewives in Southern California; sex workers in Hungary; mothers-in-law in India; or sports-obsessed fathers in Geneva, Beijing, Kyoto, Liverpool or Barcelona. Sometimes I go so far as to move inside people's houses or apartments where, with the owners' permission, I make myself at home. The families and I fraternize, listen to music, watch television and eat all our meals together. During these visits—again, with permission—I go through refrigerators, open desk drawers and kitchen cabinets, scour books, magazines, music and movie collections and downloads, inspect purses, wallets, online search histories, Facebook pages, Twitter feeds, emoji usage and Instagram and Snapchat accounts. In the search for what I call small data, almost nothing is off-limits. I've gone so far as to interview consumers through text-messaging—a study shows that people lie less frequently in texts[3]—though I'm far more likely to take people by surprise by inspecting their microwave ovens and glass and plastic recycling cans.

More intriguing than the differences among the men and women I meet and talk to and observe—and the variations of place, and climate, and culture and skin color that I see over the course of a typical year—are the characteristics we all share. (I believe firmly that there are only between 500 and 1,000 distinct types of human being in the world. I'm one of them, and so are you.) I've come to realize, too, that my capacity to link a single observation with another across multiple countries in the course of building or rescuing a brand amounts to a strange skill of sorts. At the end of the day, the apartment buildings in the Russian Far East are fundamentally no different from the gated communities of the American South; and given the extreme climates of both Saudi Arabia and Russia, the behavior of Middle Easterners is in many respects identical to that of Siberians. I've never studied social science, or trained as a psychologist or a detective, but people have told me that I think and behave like all three. I tell them instead I see myself as a forensic investigator of small data, or emotional DNA—a hunter, almost, of desire—a habit that developed by chance when I was a little boy growing up in the farm town of Skive, Denmark, population 20,505.

WHEN I WAS 12 YEARS OLD, doctors diagnosed me with a rare inflammatory form of vasculitis. Henoch-Schonlein Purpura causes bleeding in the small blood vessels of a patient's skin, joints and intestines and can also lead to irreversible kidney damage. I was placed in an isolated hospital room, where for months I wasn't able to move. Apart from a few other patients separated from me by a pair of blue-gray curtains, and a few feet of olive-green linoleum, I was alone.

I woke up every day by 7 a.m. One of the nurses would bring me breakfast and I'd begin my daily regimen of informal surveillance. I'd study my caregivers, my fellow patients, their friends, other family members and, when all those categories were exhausted, as they soon were, myself. I launched this routine as a way of getting through the grueling, boring days of my convalescence. By the time I walked out of the hospital a few months later, I was convinced, in the supercilious way common to some 12-year-old boys, that I understood human beings better than anyone ever had.

What is Patient no. 3 doing now? What will Patient no. 4 do 15 minutes from now? Patient no. 5's voice becomes noticeably hoarser and sicker-sounding when his mother comes to visit, and Patient no. 3 invariably flips his apple juice container upside down when he's done drinking it. I became aware of how the nurse always slid our clipboards back into their slots with such care they made no sound, and how the nurses holding heavier clipboards seemed more self-important, while those without clipboards seemed somehow meeker and more subservient. I made hundreds, even thousands, of observations like these every day as I'm sure anyone imprisoned in a hospital room would. What most people might be quick to dismiss, or roll their eyes at, or forget, I mentally logged, filed and analyzed.

The rest of my stay I spent with a boxful of LEGOs my mother gave me to pass the time. In retrospect it's funny how my hospitalization served to cultivate two of my favorite pastimes and compulsions, namely, LEGOs and people watching.

By the time I left the hospital, I'd gotten pretty good at LEGOs— good enough, in fact, that I got it into my head to construct a mini replica of LEGOLAND in my parents' backyard, which attracted the interest of LEGO Headquarters, as well as two of their patent lawyers. What was the best way to deal with a 12-year-old who loved LEGOs so much that he'd illegally built a facsimile of one of its theme parks? I'm happy to say the company hired me as a model builder and innovator! But that's a story for another time.

What I learned during my hospitalization was more than how to create byzantine LEGO structures. It helped train my eyes and ears to notice, deduce, interpret and, ultimately, make sense of an adult world. Patient no. 5's Pavlovian change of voice reflected his need for maternal care. Patient no. 3 would have done anything to break up the hours he was spending in his hospital bed, and one way to do this was by loudly flipping over his juice container. The nurse who came at night seemed mostly indifferent to her patients, but maybe by being so clumsy and noisy with food trays she was signaling how little recognition she got from her colleagues. No matter how insignificant it may first appear, everything in life tells a story.

As my hospitalization went on, and the staff let me move around more, I remember gazing out the windows at people making their way to their cars and bikes and studying what they wore, and their shoes or sneakers, and what their posture was like, and whether or not they wore any jewelry or wristwatches, and how they behaved when they thought no one else was watching—the young mother combing her hair in a hurry, the businessman reaching back to adjust the heel of his shoe, the teenaged girl preoccupied by the music coming through her earbuds.

How did the mother's manner change when she interacted with other mothers? When her baby cried, how did she calm her? The businessman wore a white, button-down shirt with the tails untucked and wrinkled. Was he aware of this? Was it intentional? Was he showing the world what a rebel he was, or was he just sloppy, or was it self-sabotage? Why did he keep glancing at his watch? Did he hope time would slow down, or speed up? The rubber band he wore on his other wrist—what did that signify? Was he quitting a bad habit, or did it remind him of someone he loved?

It took a childhood disease to give me an outsider's perspective on myself and other people, and to begin to transform the way I looked at the world. I began to register humans as fascinating and alien, which, of course, we are.

Do any of us really know how we come across to other people? Are we aware of the haphazard sequence of small data we leave behind us every day—the rituals, habits, gestures and preferences that coalesce to expose who we really are inside? Most of the time, the answer is No. What we snack on, how we choreograph our Facebook page, what we tweet, whether we chew cinnamon gum or nicotine lozenges—all these slight gestures may at first seem indiscriminate, undirected and too small to have much bearing on our identities. But when we begin to see life through the new and unfamiliar lens of small data, we also come across revealing clues about the people closest to us, including ourselves.

Small data could be inside an oven or a medicine cabinet or inside a Facebook photo album. It could be contained in a toothbrush holder in a bathroom in Tel Aviv, or in how a roll of toilet paper presses up against a bathroom wall in northern Brazil. It could show up in how a family's shoe collection is arrayed in a hallway, or in the scrambled letters and numbers that make up a person's computer password. In the course of doing Subtexting, I dig through garbage cans past squeezed-out toothpaste tubes and ripped candy wrappers and expired coupons, searching for that one thing that will solve the puzzle, or provide the answer I need, even when I'm not sure what the puzzle consists of, or what it is exactly that I'm looking for. A lone piece of small data is almost never meaningful enough to build a case or create a hypothesis, but blended with other insights and observations gathered from around the world, the data eventually comes together to create a solution that forms the foundation of a future brand or business.

My methods may be structured, but they're also based on a whole lot of mistakes, and trial and error, and faulty hypotheses that I have to toss out before starting over again. (I'll go into my 7C methodology in much more detail in the final chapter.) When I enter someone's home, the first thing I do is gather as much rational, observable data as I can. I make notes, take hundreds of photos, shoot video after video. The smallest detail, or gesture, may become the key to unlocking a desire that men, women and children (and, in some cases, the culture itself) didn't know they had. I look for patterns, parallels, correlations and, not least, imbalances and exaggerations. Typically I focus on the contrasts between people's day-to-day lives and their unacknowledged or unmet desires, evidence that can be found anywhere from a Middle Eastern prayer rug laid down on the floor facing in the wrong direction to a chipped hand mirror in a bathroom drawer in Siberia.

After months of observation and research, I set out all my findings on a bulletin board. It serves as both a mural and a time line. What desires lie in the gap between perception and reality, between reality and fantasy, between people's conscious and unconscious fantasies? What are the imbalances inside the culture? What is there too much of, or too little? What desires aren't being fed?

If for no other reason, companies bring me on as a consultant to determine what it is we really want as humans so that they in turn can figure out ways to provide it. My job title may be "branding consultant," but most organizations hire me on as an itinerant sleuth whose mission is to smoke out that foggiest, most abstract of words: *desire*. Desire is always linked to a story, and to a gap that needs to be filled: a yearning that intrudes, agitates and motivates human behavior both consciously and unconsciously.

DESIRE MANIFESTS IN ONE FORM or another hundreds of times a day, in countless faces and guises. It can show up as sexual desire, or in our appetite for food, or for alcohol, or for drugs. It can appear as the desire for money, or for status, or the need to belong to a group, the need to blend in with a crowd or, alternately, to stand out. It can be the desire to become one with another person, or with nature, or with music, or with what's commonly known as "the universe." We crave the security of the past, which is a desire, and the promise of the future, which is another desire. In order to "become" more desirable to others, we buy new clothes, brush our teeth, apply face cream, shave, order a new pair of glasses. (At the same time, as a friend of mine once observed, "The most difficult thing is to look in the mirror and describe yourself.")

Needless to say, desire is elusive. It has a habit of receding once you think you've captured it, only to show up again a few seconds later. All across the world, every culture has its own corridors for desire and escape. Brazilians go to the beach, as do natives of Sydney and Los Angeles. Americans, Middle Easterners and Indians all flock to the movies, or to malls; the English cluster at soccer matches, and at pubs. If you live in Saudi Arabia, escape may involve a trip to Oman. If you live in Oman, escape may be a trip to Dubai. For a Dubai native, escape means London. For a Londoner, escape involves the Andalusian coast of Spain, or the south of France, or California, or Florida. We desire whatever it is—the place, the person, the thing, the period in our lives—we're convinced we're lacking.

The work I do is a sped-up version of ethnographic, or participatory, anthropology, the difference being that instead of spending years in one place observing a tribe of people, I spend weeks and sometimes months in another country. Like any anthropologist—if I can call myself that—I see myself as a neutral amalgamator and observer who pieces together small data, creating a mosaic from which I try to Small Mine a reasonable story line. And like ethnography, my work never really ends. I begin and end my days blindly. I rely on random perceptions and chance revelations. Countries change, after all, and so do the cultural and political mixes of those countries. Technology changes who we are as humans, which causes us to adapt and evolve accordingly.

Over the years, some people have asked how a Danish-born "foreigner" like me is able to travel from one country to the next in an attempt to bring to light desire in areas of the world he doesn't know well. Does it make any sense to bring in a stranger, they wonder, especially one who's there for only a short time? Wouldn't a Frenchman be a better judge of Parisian culture, or an Australian more up-to-speed with what's going on in New South Wales and Queensland? Why not hire a Japanese consulting firm in Japan, a Russian branding company in Russia or an American agency in the United States?

The thing is, I can almost guarantee you that a local team will miss something. The German American anthropologist Franz Boas is responsible for coining the word *Kulturbrille,* or "culture glasses," a term that refers to the "lenses" through which we see our own countries. Our Kulturbrille allow us to make sense of the culture we inhabit, but these same glasses can blind us to things outsiders pick up immediately.

In Japan, for example, the kitchen and the laundry room are the only two zones of the home that only married Japanese women are "allowed" to enter. This isn't a formal law, but an unspoken custom.

How, then, can a Japanese or multinational company go about selling things to women in a nation where three-quarters of Japanese males do the household shopping on behalf of their families, and are unlikely to know what everyday household items their families may need? Most Japanese marketers would lack the perspective or the distance even to notice this. Years ago, in Copenhagen, I went for a stroll with a retail expert who travels as much as I do. "There's no structure in how Danes walk," he said at one point. "They walk all over the place." He was right. I grew up in Denmark, but I'd never noticed this before.

There is a family of freshwater insects known as Gerridae—otherwise known as water bugs, water striders or water skaters—that skim lightly across ponds and lakes. I think of myself as the business equivalent of a water skater. I realize, too, it's both a vulnerability and a strength to enter a country without any fixed ideas. Any outsider risks making generalizations or conclusions that may be incomplete, or naïve, but I've always trusted my instincts—and what are instincts if not experiences and observations accumulated over time that enable a person to make fast conclusions without knowing precisely how?

In-person observation, and a preoccupation with small data, is what sets apart what I do in a world preoccupied by big data. Most of us judge practically everything in seconds, or minutes at most. We've become spontaneous seekers and instant responders. As more and more products and services migrate online, and technology helps us understand human behavior in real time at granular levels, many people have come to believe that human observations and interaction are old-fashioned and even irrelevant. I couldn't disagree more. A source who works at Google once confessed to me that despite the almost 3 billion humans who are online,[4] and the 70 percent of online shoppers who go onto Facebook daily,[5] and the 300 hours of videos on YouTube (which is owned by Google) uploaded every minute,[6] and the fact that 90 percent of all the world's data has been generated over the last two years.[7] Google ultimately has only limited information about consumers. Yes, search engines can detect unusual correlations (as opposed to causations). With 70 percent accuracy, my source tells me, software can assess how people feel based on the way they type, and the number of typos they make. With 79 percent precision, software can determine a user's credit rating based on the degree to which they write in ALL CAPS. Yet even with all these stats, Google has come to realize it knows almost nothing about humans and what really drives us, and it is now bringing in consultants to do what small data researchers have been doing for decades. As one analyst once told me, "Considering that management doesn't know what to do with big data, everyone is searching for what is *post* big data—and the answer is small data."

Millward Brown Vermeer recently initiated Marketing2020, one of the most comprehensive marketing leadership studies ever launched, which included in-depth interviews with more than 350 CEOs, CMOs and agency heads. Not surprisingly, authors Marc de Swaan Arons, Frank van den Driest and Keith Weed found that many marketing organizations have lost their way. In an article published in the *Harvard Business Review,* the authors concluded that if data and analytics fall under the "Think" category, and content, design and production development fall under the "Do" category, then marketers who focus on consumer engagement and interaction belong to the "Feel" category.[8] All three functions are essential, they argue. In short, the integration of online and offline data—that is to say, the marriage of big data *and* small data—is a crucial ingredient of marketing survival and success in the twenty-first century.

This is understandable. We're living in an era in which our online behaviors and communications are haunted by subtext and obfuscation. The German word *maskenfreiheit* can be translated into "the freedom conferred by masks," and anyone who has ever spent time online knows that the ability to customize our digital selves, and our occasional online anonymity, creates personae that bear only a loose resemblance to the people we actually are, and the lives we actually live, when we're offline. You might say that thanks to technology, we are all at least two people, with at least two residences: a bricks-and-mortar home and a home page. Sometimes they overlap, but often they don't.

Nor can we say we are any more "ourselves" when we surf the Web anonymously. Without a name, or a face, or an identity, we become primitive versions of ourselves, a phenomenon some experts attribute to a lack of empathy that comes from communicating laptop to laptop, and that is also familiar to anyone who has ever flipped off a pedestrian, or worse, while driving a car. Empathy, the *New York Times* pointed out last year, is learned two ways. One is by experiencing something distressing ourselves. Another is "by seeing, hearing or even smelling how your action has hurt someone else—something that is not available to those behind a screen and keyboard."[9] (Or, for that matter, behind the wheel of a car.) This is the paradox of online behavior. We're never truly ourselves on social media, and when we communicate anonymously, the result lacks any context that our offline lives might provide and enrich. Online, what we leave behind is largely considered and strategic, whereas the insides of our refrigerators and dresser drawers are not, as they were never intended for public exhibition.

This is why, in my opinion, the best, closest approximation of who we are as humans comes from mixing our online and offline selves, and from combining big data with small data. Considering that 90 percent of what people give off in conversation are nonverbal signals, our truest identities can be found by studying who we are in our real lives, cultures and countries. This amalgamation of gestures, habits, likes, dislikes, hesitations, speech patterns, decors, passwords, tweets, status updates and more is what I call small data.

In the pages that follow, I invite you to fly around the world with me, gathering small data in the course of bringing to light cultural desires necessary to solve puzzles no less challenging, and usually far less straightforward, than the LEGO example. In an information age in which most of us spend all day with our eyes trained on screens, my hope is that this book will inspire you to become even more aware than you are already of the clues around you, and to become conscious of the similarities that exist among all of us. The mission of any brand builder is really no different from that of anyone alive, which is to avoid what mythologist and writer Joseph Campbell once described as the greatest human transgression: namely, the sin of inadvertence—of not being alert, or altogether awake, to the world around us.

CHAPTER 1
FANNING DESIRE

HOW SIBERIAN REFRIGERATOR DOORS AND A SAUDI ARABIAN MALL CREATED A REVOLUTIONARY WEBSITE FOR RUSSIAN WOMEN

PICTURE A MAP OF THE GLOBE, AND YOU'LL NOTICE THAT your perception of the world revolves entirely around where in the world you live. You can't help it, and neither can I. It's automatic. The map of the universe you and I draw, with us inside it, creates an unconscious navigational system, a behavioral GPS, that we follow every day. Our internal map dictates whether we sleep on the right or the left side of the bed at night. It determines where we position ourselves when we walk down the street with a friend or partner. Do we walk to their right, or on their left, nearer to the curb or to the buildings? On a larger cultural level, where we live also determines our timeliness. For example, in Australia, you can be assured that your guests will show up thirty minutes late, often with friends in tow that they haven't told you about. In Switzerland, guests are always on time, and if they plan on being five minutes late, they will let you know. Japanese guests will show up a half hour before they are supposed to, and in Israel, they will be forty-five minutes late.

Our internal maps even determine how we season our food.

Across many parts of the Western world, salt and pepper shakers take up a prominent space on kitchen and dining room tables. As everyone knows, most are uniform in appearance: three pinprick holes on the saltshaker, and a single one atop the pepper. If you live in Asia, however, the number of holes is reversed, with three on the pepper shaker and one on the saltshaker, thanks to the popularity of pepper in Asian countries and the cultural preference for soy sauce.

This observation, and others I've put down into a journal over the years, have made me acutely aware of the placement of objects inside and outside homes. Gardens talk. Footpaths talk. Balconies talk. Mailboxes talk. Needless to say, walls talk. My mission is to decipher what the paved stones and the peonies and the artwork and the stone figurines are telling me about their owners. Why is that painting or poster hung here and not there? What about the owl figurine, the collection of medals, or dolls, or stuffed donkeys, or the wall dedicated to ancestral photos?

We leave these clues to our identities out in plain sight, but they're universal, and in a digital era, they're also indelible. One phenomenon I've noticed brings together the two.

A decade or so ago, when smartphones and tablets achieved mass penetration, it became obvious that men and women over the age of 40 found it challenging to use touch screens. They were used to bearing down on typewriter keys, depressing On and Off buttons, pulling levers and turning knobs. They came of age in a time that required a heavier touch, sometimes a fierce grip. Today, of course, touch is more often than not glancing and ghostly. In airports across the world, one or two generations of men and women stand around helplessly before the touch screen kiosks, not altogether sure of how they work or which key to press. Meanwhile, the five-year-old child beside them navigates the screen with a virtuoso's ease. By studying the number of fingerprinted smudge marks on a phone or tablet screen, it's easy to determine the approximate age of its owner.

The shift from knobs and keys to an increasingly touch-screen world has had several effects. First, thanks to computers and touchscreen note-taking apps we're losing the ability to write things out in long-hand. Second, as a result of supporting the base of their smartphones with their pinky fingers, more and more teenagers have an indentation there. Third, as a species I've observed that our hands are getting weaker. Shake hands with any high school or college student, and you'll notice how weak their grips are. Among men, the messages once subtly encoded in a handshake—strength, dryness, moisture, hand size itself—may no longer be relevant.

The collective loss of hand strength has caught the notice of the fast-moving consumer goods industry, the industry term for low-priced drinks and produce designed to sell quickly, including soft drinks, processed foods and over-the-counter medicines. It's the main reason why bottle manufacturers are loosening the grips of bottle caps, why today's car door handles are easier to open and why our kitchen drawers slide out more easily.

Our digital habits are even affecting how we eat. As a boy growing up in Denmark, on hot days my friends and I ate our ice cream cones in a predictable way. We first licked the ice cream in a circular motion, as if to seal it in the cone. We continued eating our ice cream this way, and once the ice cream was gone, we finished what was left, eating from the bottom up or the top down.

If our culture today can be partly defined by the need for immediate access, it's no surprise that the desire for instant gratification has also migrated to our ice cream cones. As I travel around the world, I've made it a point to watch how children raised in a digital environment eat their ice cream cones. There is less waiting around; the concept of "anticipation" no longer exists. Instead of licking around the sides, most of them bite the ice cream off from the top. Accustomed to websites loading fast, texts and e-mails sent off and delivered in seconds, they want their ice cream *now*.

How will the absence of anticipation affect today's and tomorrow's younger generation? It is easy to romanticize the concept of *waiting* for weeks and sometimes months for something to appear in a store, or in the mail, as people did in the 1970s and '80s. Today we have it at once—and then what? With foreshortened anticipation comes less gratification, and I can't help but wonder whether today's ice cream cones pack as much satisfaction as the ones kids ate three or four decades ago. I call today's young teens and adolescents the Power Plug Generation, or Screenagers, as they're constantly searching for the nearest wall socket. The fear of being without power is like the fear of being consigned to a barren island, marooned from friends, forced, perhaps, to face who you are without a phone in your hand.

It's also worth noting that smartphones are also responsible for the increase in the time it takes to begin and end a meal in a restaurant. By analyzing footage from the early 2000s on, one New York City restaurant owner posting a study anonymously on Craigslist estimated that back in 2004 diners spent an average of 65 minutes at a table, a figure that rose to one hour and 55 minutes in 2014. In 2004, diners came into a restaurant and out of a 45-member sample group, three asked to be seated elsewhere. The sample group spent an average of eight minutes deciding what to order. The appetizers and entrees they ordered showed up within six minutes. Two out of 45 customers sent back food they complained was too cold. The average diner left five minutes after paying the check.

A decade later, things have changed. Today, 18 out of 45 customers entering a restaurant ask whether they can sit somewhere else. From that point on, their digital lives take over. Diners take out their phones and try to connect to the nearest Wi-Fi. They hunt down information or check if anyone "liked" their Facebook post, often forgetting that their menus are waiting there on the table, which is why when the waiter asks them if they're ready to order, most respond that they need more time. Twenty-one minutes later, they're ready to order. Twenty-six of them spend up to three minutes taking photos of their food. Fourteen snap photos of each other eating, and if the photos are blurry or unflattering, they retake them. Approximately one-half of all diners ask if their server would take a group photo and while he's at it, would he mind taking a few more? The second half sends their food back to the kitchen, claiming it's cold (which it is, as they've spent the past ten minutes playing with their phones and not eating). Once they pay their check, they leave the restaurant twenty minutes later, versus five minutes in 2004. As they exit, eight diners are so distracted that they bump into another diner, or a waiter, or a table, or a chair.

An imbalance? Yes, and it's also one especially prevalent right now in the United States. The cultural exaggerations I spend my business life trying to find operate both inside societies and between generations. Societies swing back and forth in more or less predictable ways. Generally speaking, in the United States, a Democratic administration follows a Republican government; in the United Kingdom, Conservatives will cede a follow-up election to Labour. This unconscious reflex to redress "imbalance" affects our wardrobes, too. One generation gravitates toward form-fitting jeans and wide neckties, while the next favors looser-fitting pants and skinny ties. One wave of young men will go through their teens and twenties cleanly shaven, and the next gravitates toward stubble or a scruffy beard. Considering Russia's history since the fall of the Berlin Wall, the issue of imbalance was one I couldn't help thinking about when I took on a complicated assignment in one of the most remote regions of the world.

MY TRIP TO THE EASTERNMOST REGION of Russia began with a phone call I would describe as cinematic, except that the dialogue could only have been invented by a very bad screenwriter. The voice on the other end belonged to a Russian-English interpreter who was calling on behalf of his employer, a Moscow-based businessman. The businessman wanted to launch a new business in Russia with the goal of generating at least a billion dollars a year. When I asked the obvious question—*what was the business?*—I was told it was up to me. A few days later, the businessman and I had worked out an agreement: I would fly to Russia, spend several weeks interviewing Russian consumers, and see if I could uncover one, maybe even more, unaddressed national needs, or desires, with the mission of launching what we both hoped would be a profitable business.

What's the difference between a consumer need and a national need? It depends, but the two are often intertwined. A new business concept generally has its origins in a cultural imbalance or exaggeration—too much of something, or too little of something—which indicates that something is either missing or blocked in the society. By gathering fragments of small data, it's up to me to figure what that need is, and how it might be met.

Identifying the desire that creates these imbalances is a detailed process that can take anywhere from two days to a month to six months. Clue gathering is almost never linear. Some clues lead nowhere. Others are quirky, and potentially interesting, but irrelevant to the project I'm working on, which isn't to say they have no value, since a random observation may someday contribute to the launch of another product in a country thousands of miles away. Another, more pertinent clue may feel significant enough to form the foundation of an entire concept, start to finish. Sometimes I get things completely wrong, or the company I'm working for rejects my idea as too costly or unrealistic, and I have to start all over again. But again, no insight or observation is ever wasted. Everything we see, hear, touch, taste and feel can be recycled, or repurposed, or seen in a new perspective one year, two years, five years later.

Before entering a country I don't know well, I make it a point to ask myself a few questions. To what degree does the population—say, Italians, or Australians, or French people—come together during a crisis? (Alternately, how and in what ways, do various cultures show off their flags? In contrast to Swedes, who almost never display their national colors, Norwegians and Canadians generally sport a flag decal on their backpacks, the latter making sure the rest of the world doesn't mistake them for Americans.) One good way to answer this question is to study a population when they are overseas, and traveling as tourists. When they hear or see a familiar accent or piece of clothing, do Americans or Germans or Canadians move toward or away from one another? The reluctance to align overseas generally derives from two things: the small size of the country of origin (Norwegians, for example, are pressed up against one another enough at home), or the nation's internal socioeconomic divisions. Typically I get to see sides of countries that most tourists don't. How do the less well-off residents behave toward those with more money or privilege? What is the mood around them—fearful or relaxed?

Another thing I do when I arrive at a new airport is handpick a taxi driven by a non-native. Foreign-born residents are likely to tell you the truth about a country and a population that natives can't or won't. A Nigerian taxi driver in Los Angeles once told me that he found it ironic that everyone in the city was rushing around buying Christmas presents for people who in most cases they didn't know. He didn't have to tell me that an unspoken level of guilt, and utility, underlies many American friendships, especially in the film industry. Denmark shows up regularly on magazine and online lists as "the happiest nation on earth," yet every year tens of thousands of business professionals leave the country. In a nation of only 5.6 million people, where one in four Danish women admits to suffering from high degrees of stress, its hard not to believe that some lists can be misleading.

Denmark is also a country where, in household after household, families set out Brio train sets across their living rooms. Brio is the Swedish manufacturer of wooden, nonmotorized trains and tracks, all of the highest possible quality. At first glance it's tempting to believe that Danish families are not only happy, and want to give their children old-fashioned, well-made toys rather than iPads and computer games, but that they also welcome the cheerful disorder that comes along with having kids. Over time, though, I began noticing that none of the Brio trains or tracks in any of these Danish houses showed any evidence of chipping or degradation. No one was playing with them at all. Those train tracks and small, simple, beautiful trains were like props in a stage setting, a surface snapshot of conformity concealing deeper levels of national unease. I might add that Danish kitchen manufacturers often use the term "Conversation Kitchen" to refer to an expensive, well-appointed kitchen that is used less often for cooking than it is as a theatrical backdrop for entertaining guests.

I'VE TRAVELED AND WORKED in Russia many times in my career. There is a lot I like about the country, and about Russians in general, not the least of which is their directness. When you do business in Russia, you always know where you stand. I've had unsettling dinners with Russian CEOs and their colleagues, during which the CEO discusses the people present in the third person, as if they aren't there, while the rest of the table sits there, nodding, never once objecting or showing any emotion. Metaphorically speaking, if you're in the middle of a negotiation, a Russian will remove a knife from a handy drawer, letting you know the blade is near. In the United States, the knife is at rest, and nearby, ready for use days, weeks or months down the line. In England, the British employ what Margaret Thatcher called "the Kitchen Cabinet Approach." They are smiling, charming and polite until it comes time for the real conversation to take place hours later in the rear of the kitchen. In an analysis of over one billion pieces of emoji data across the globe, across numerous categories, it wasn't surprising to find that UK residents had the highest ratio of "winking" emojis, a means, perhaps, of compensating for their usual reserve.[1] (To me, emojis are condensed emotions, and an unbiased reflection of a society's emotional state, imbalance and compensation.)

Russia's biggest downside, for me at least, is its lack of color. Being in Russia is like breathing different oxygen, and I can feel a gray shade pulling down over me the moment I board a plane to fly there. No one is animated. No one smiles, or laughs. Ask most Russians what they like most about visiting other countries and they'll say it's the sight of other people having fun.

Throughout the 1970s and 1980s, Russian women weren't "allowed" to wear cosmetics. It wasn't a law, but more an unspoken protocol. This all changed in the late 1980s when the Berlin Wall fell, and cosmetics companies like Mary Kay and Maybelline entered Russia for the first time alongside nightclubs, discos, restaurants, gaming companies, car dealerships and high-end stores like Versace. Russia was awash with cash. From the airport all the way into Moscow, the billboards and flashing neon plastering the highway made it look like a colorized Russian version of Pottersville in *It's a Wonderful Life*.

It ended abruptly in 2006. Announcing that gambling was no different from alcohol and drug addiction, as well as a magnet for organized crime, Vladimir Putin exiled casinos and slot machine parlors to distant regions, including Armenia, Belarus, Georgia and Crimea. Overnight, Moscow's color went away, as if the capital had woken up from a short, garish dream. Nothing was left but new hues of the old gray. In short order, Russia was more or less back to its old self.

But the disappearance of color had other associations and meanings, as I would find out later.

IN MIDSUMMER, my two assistants and I flew from Zurich to Moscow on a private jet the Russian businessman had chartered for us. We spent a few days interviewing consumers in Moscow. There, a local crew joined our Swiss crew to fly our plane over certain sensitive military areas in Siberia and the Russian Far East. More than 4,000 miles later, we touched down in the town of Krasnoyarsk, where we met up with a Russian translator, a driver and a car. For the next ten days we traveled from one Siberian city and apartment building to another. At night, the car took us back to the airport, and we reboarded the plane. In four or five hours, during which time the three of us analyzed that day's findings, we touched down in yet another withdrawn Russian town. In a week and a half, we passed through eight separate time zones, and at one point were less than a 45-minute flight from Tokyo.

In his 2010 book *Travels in Siberia,* Ian Frazier writes that no political or territorial entity inside Russia bears the actual name "Siberia." The world knows Siberia as a metaphor, Frazier writes, a geographical or social condition that connotes being rejected, or given the cold shoulder. Siberia is the table beside the restaurant's kitchen doors, the seat in the ballpark so far away from the field you're better off watching the game at home on television, the party you throw for yourself where no one shows up. Geographically, Siberia refers to the roughly eight-million-square-mile landmass from the Arctic Ocean to the Kasakhstan mountains to the borders of Mongolia and China. The American composer Irving Berlin was born in Tyumen, Siberia, and lived there until he was five. One of his biographers wrote that as an adult, Berlin had no memories of his childhood except one: in the wake of a pogrom, he remembered lying on a blanket on the side of a road, watching Cossacks burn his house to the ground. It's no surprise that at the turn of the twentieth century, his parents emigrated to the Lower East Side of New York.

Bordering the easternmost chunk of Siberia, and further north, the Arctic, the Russian Far East isn't a place where appearances matter much. Life is difficult, and the weather is extreme. In the winter, temperatures drop to as low as 50 or 60 below zero. The summers are warm and short. The length of a day varies from 21 hours in mid-July to three hours in December. Political correctness doesn't exist. In the winter, fur coats, fur hats and boots made from reindeer are the only things that can insulate bodies against the cold, and the most desirable winter gloves are made out of dog fur. A Russian fashion consultant once told me that fashion stops at the Siberian border, where instead of showing off, the prerogative is survival.

The cities and towns of *Dalniy Vostok Rossii* lack even the dabs of color a visitor might see in Moscow or Saint Petersburg. The skies, streets, sidewalks, footbridges, lakes, shops and buildings all seem drained of life. Whatever trees there are were planted in a hurry a long time ago, and ankle-high pollen covers the streets and sidewalks like snow. In the winter, locals leave their cars on all day knowing that if they don't they won't be able to restart them. Now and then you catch sight of one that gave up, sunken down over flat tires and abandoned, its undersides rusted out.

TRADITIONALLY THE WAY I CONNECT with people is by subverting the rules. If you can't connect with the natives of a country, you won't get very far. As everyone knows, people send out unconscious signals, and, as I am a chameleon by nature, one of the things I do is "become" the person I'm talking to, since we tend to respond to the people who are most similar to us.

This turned out to be harder than usual in Russia, where trust is generally lacking. Most people there don't look you in the eyes, and their gazes have a cloudy, dissociated look. Decades before Julian Assange and Edward Snowden made headlines, Russians knew their phone lines were being tapped. My Moscow-based employer had a dozen or so cell phones on him at all times. The people who mattered most to him had their own dedicated phones, and whenever one rang, he had to sort through his briefcase to find it. When he spoke, his words were hushed, a hand always covering his mouth in case someone could read his lips.

I'm always looking for topics, symbols, actions and behaviors that ground or define a culture and can serve as a footbridge of sorts between a stranger—me—and the local residents. I might show up at a bar or an outdoor farmer's market or spend an hour or two with a local political figure. Knowing I would stick out immediately in a remote Russian city that few non-natives visit, I needed to make myself conspicuously visible. I needed to prove I was safe and worthy if not of friendship, then of being given a chance.

In the main square of Krasnoyarsk, I noticed that elderly men spent most of their afternoons playing long games of chess. There was a nice, obvious sense of community, fellowship and physical interaction, of residents looking out for one another. In my experience, the more physical touching there is among people, the healthier the country is (a point I'll revisit later on).

With my interpreter translating, I challenged one of the old men to a game. Before long a crowd had gathered. As the games went on, I could feel myself becoming, at least from a local perspective, Russian. The expressions of the people in the crowd grew soft, and now and again, their eyes showed patience, or humor. At one point the old man I was playing against grabbed hold of my finger and moved the piece with me; a few minutes later, someone from the crowd sat down beside me.

It was the moment a stranger came over to where I was sitting that I knew I'd passed a test. Nothing was ever said, but everyone understood what had just happened: if I won the game, or even lost while playing honorably, or well, I would be seen as trustworthy, someone who had earned the right to do his job in their city, whatever that job was. Fortunately I've always been good at chess, and when I won a game or two, I knew I'd surrendered my outsider status.

There's an iconic film in Russia wherein the protagonist comes home after work only to find he's in the wrong apartment, and the wrong building, and the wrong city, but since everything in Russia looks the same, he doesn't realize it, and now he has no idea how to get back home. No matter where I went in the Russian Far East—Krasnoyarsk, Samara, Yakutsk (known, unofficially, as the coldest inhabited place on earth) or Siberia's largest city, Novosibirsk—the apartment buildings, where 95 percent of the population live, were the same. Not just similar but exactly the same. Most were built between the First and Second World Wars. They were all 25 stories high. The metal fences surrounding them were all the same height and painted in the same green and yellow colors. The trees around the circumference of every building had been planted in the same places. On the sidewalks and small lawns in front and on the sides of buildings were ashtrays made from rusted soup or stew cans, with butts sticking up out of them. Now and again I caught sight of a line of clothes drying in the heat. Cats prowled the paths and walkways. Inevitably there was a smell of something decomposing in the air, most likely a pet who'd died. The building lobbies were slapdash-looking. But more important than the exteriors and lobbies of apartment buildings, I later realized, was what went on inside them. If Russian apartment dwellers took the time to make their buildings' exteriors neat, or beautiful, they might be seen as vulnerable. Better to appear not to care.

The first thing I noticed were Siberian doors. There may have been multiple locks on the outside, but inside, every door in every apartment I visited was thickly cushioned and upholstered. The effect was to create a soundproof space that deadened all sounds and cut the inhabitants off from the outside world. Inside, the rooms were functional, cramped and plain. Few residents had taken the time to decorate. Most apartments had two chairs and a couch, a television set, a computer maybe, and that was it.

Whenever I enter someone's home, the first thing I focus on is the artwork. Around 90 percent of the people I interview have something hanging there. If a living place can be likened to a city, the art on the wall, or the lack of art, is the first sign you see on a city's outskirts, the one declaring the start of the city limits. The bedroom brings you closer to the city, followed by the kitchen and the bathroom, both of which take you into the "downtown" of someone's living space. After first asking permission, I will generally look through women's handbags, and even their clothes closets. What hangs there so that they can reach it most easily, and what sort of clothing is hanging the farthest away?

In Russia, I later found out, women are in charge of the home. Therefore, you can be assured that the way a man's clothes are displayed in the bedroom, or the closet, reflects her desires, not his. For the next few weeks I met any number of worn-out, worn-down Russian husbands. They seemed indifferent to how they looked. Their pants were dirty, their T-shirts simple, their shoes old. But inside the bedroom, the fanciest men's clothes could be seen hanging in the closets, visible but unworn. It was a hopeful gesture on the part of their wives. Though they never said so, it seemed they had hung the clothes there in an attempt to bring back the romantic potential of the men they'd married.

You can't really talk about Russian women without bringing up Russian men. Across Russia, women have a much longer life expectancy than men, for one simple reason: alcohol. A 2014 study in the *Lancet* tracked 151,000 adults across three Russian cities for over a decade and concluded that up to 25 percent of all Russian men die before the age of 55, with liver disease and alcohol poisoning the main causes of death. Drinking and alcohol-related morbidity are linked to political volatility, too. In 1985, then-General Secretary of the Communist Party of the Soviet Union, Mikhail Gorbachev, cut back on nationwide vodka production and passed a law prohibiting stores from selling liquor before noon. Consumption and overall death rates both dropped. When communism fell, vodka became available again, and rates of consumption and alcohol-related deaths rose accordingly. Russian women aren't teetotalers by any means, but the average life expectancy for Russian men today is around 64, the lowest of any country in the world outside African nations.

Less important than *what* Russians drink is *how* they drink: like first-year fraternity pledges. Russia is a country of bingers. Natives seem to have convinced themselves that this is an unalterable element of what it means to be Russian, that it's effectively baked into the country's genetics. Others blame the alcoholism rates on the difficulty of life. Whatever the reason, almost every person I spoke to had up to a dozen different vodka varieties on hand. In one Yakutsk apartment, a sectional living room couch even had a hidden compartment in its middle that swung open to reveal a doll-sized magic kingdom of vodka and glasses, as well as a stack of Swiss chocolate bars. Based on the date on the package, the Swiss chocolate had expired 15 years earlier, but that didn't matter. The owners had a private cupboard containing not just a pipeline to their dreams, but also to the safety, efficiency, cleanliness and order that Switzerland stands for.

I jotted down this piece of small data in my notebook, not knowing at the time the pivotal role it would play later on.

The issue of alcohol kept coming up, especially when I entered apartments where it was easy to intuit two levels of life—a public one and a second unseen one. One day I was interviewing a Russian woman when she asked if I wanted some water. When I took a sip, I nearly spit it out. It was pure salt and bubbles. It was like swallowing a mouthful of the ocean. At the time I had no idea why water that tasted like that would ever be for sale commercially, or why she would offer such a thing to a guest. (I later discovered that the salt water came from nearby lakes, and Siberians perceived it as clean, bracing and nutritious.) Later that night, back in my hotel, I realized that the salt water was in some respects an everyday substitute for alcohol. Like alcohol, salt is highly addictive, and if they're not actively drinking, alcoholics are often drawn to things—cigarettes, coffee—that give them the same rush, and that also hurt a little going down.

I was picking up a clue here, a clue there: the indifference and lifelessness of the apartment exteriors and lobbies. The soundproof doors. Of course those doors kept out the cold in the winter, but could that be the only reason they were so well insulated? A high alcoholism rate that led to one hostess serving me carbonated salt water. Was salt water the only compensation for alcoholism in Russia, or were there others? If alcoholism masked or concealed a cultural vacuum, then what was it?

Almost every man and woman I spoke to in Russia told me that if given the opportunity, they would live somewhere else. The top destinations they listed off were Italy, France and Switzerland. Why Italy and France? The food. Why Switzerland? Because of its perceived security and safety. Most Russians had never been to these countries and had no idea what life was like there, but it didn't matter. More important was what they symbolized—good food, smiling people, leisure, romance, beauty, flirtation and freedom. If the first clue revolved around desire, and discontent, the second clue had to do with aspiration, which brought up the subject of what it meant to be a Russian female living in a rough, survivalist nation.

Earlier I mentioned I am always seeking the exaggerated elements in a culture, the things that stick out. Almost immediately, two possible business ideas occurred to me. The first was an online medical clinic where doctors saw patients virtually, between certain hours of the day, but I soon found out that the Russian medical infrastructure is so byzantine that an online clinic would be almost impossible to put into place. Second, I'd noticed that almost everyone I'd met owned a dog, a cat or both. Why not launch an online pet store? Then I found out that Russian pet owners rarely spend money on their dogs and cats, and fed them whatever was left over from their own meals. I would have to do some more digging.

The next clue that showed up was more an observation than anything else. In contrast to the featurelessness of the apartments I visited, almost every woman I interviewed had extremely red lips. Why did Russian women wear so much makeup? By painting their lips like that, what were they conveying exactly? Was it the need to be noticed? If so, why? What sort of culture, or environment, makes a woman feel she isn't getting the attention she needs?

It may sound overly dramatic, but men and women tend to rebel against whatever imbalances exist in their countries. They do this consciously and unconsciously. Whenever I visit the United States, for example, one of the first things I notice is that no one ever touches one another, especially the men. In America, touch is perceived as sexual. At the same time, American culture overemphasizes sports, especially football, which is one of the few places where men are given permission to touch, slap, wrestle, tackle and hug one another. France is renowned for the high quality of its food as well as its drawn-out, multicourse meals. Yet France is also ranked number one in the world when it comes to eating premade food, including frozen food, and McDonald's revenues there are the second highest worldwide. Then there's Japan, one of the most polite, controlled nations in the world, a place where if you bring up the topic of sex with a woman, she will literally blush. But Japan is also the country with the highest number of "sex hotels" and female-only train cars to protect women from being groped.

Back in Siberia, it occurred to me that the red lips I kept seeing symbolized the girl inside—the one eager but forbidden to express herself in a visual way. Those red lips were also a feminine way of controlling the home, a manifestation of a Big Mouth who can speak emotionally and without constraint. The combination of the exaggeratedly feminine and the confrontational kept showing up. One Russian woman I interviewed wore a black T-shirt with a front showing a white Persian kitten gripping an MK-47, as if the shirt were telling the world that its owner may have been soft on the inside but she also wouldn't hesitate to kill you. When I asked another Russian woman to draw me a picture, she sketched out a beautiful mural of a school of underwater fish. The fish didn't look like any I'd ever seen before. They were stylized creatures with Betty Boop eyes and—more confirmation, but of what?—red lips like flowers in bloom. A day later, another woman drew me a tiger, again with a huge red open mouth.

Women as cats. Women as tigers. Women as pairs of oversized red lips. At that stage, I wasn't sure what I was even noticing, but I jotted it all down anyway, along with another strange fact: there were no mirrors anywhere. In several homes in the places where mirrors usually hang—over a dresser or the bed, or against a bathroom wall—there were sheets of cardboard similar to the ones you find in amusement parks, where by poking their heads through a hole, children can inhabit the torso of a prince, or a warrior, or a muscleman, making them resemble their—or more likely their parents'—favorite characters.

Elsewhere, it's unusual to see a house without mirrors—in fact, it's almost nonexistent. Most people are in the habit of looking at themselves in the mirror several times a day. (On my own apartment block, workers recently wrapped the mirrored building elevator in plastic in preparation for new people moving in, and I noticed that someone had poked a hole through the plastic so she could check herself out in the elevator mirror before coming home.) But even the bathroom mirrors I saw were dark and somehow gloomy. Some were cracked, or dented. If a mirror serves as a frame for a piece of human art, the mirrors I saw looked and felt like afterthoughts. In many bedrooms I found small, wood-handled mirrors hidden away in drawers. Based on the smooth grain of the wood, they didn't see much use. The absence of mirrors led me to believe that Russian women were deliberately muting themselves in order to fulfill someone else's needs. The bright red lipstick was a call for attention, yet at the same time, these women avoided looking in the mirror. It made no sense. Or did it?

With almost every Russian female I spoke to, I came face to face with the duality between a woman's red lips and the "male" behavior the culture enforced on all its natives. Physically and in conversation, Russian women were practical, determined and no-nonsense. With their husbands working in labor-intensive jobs like mining, oil and forestry, clearly they kept their families and homes together, with one of their primary goals being to make sure their husbands didn't fall prey to alcoholism. More evidence that Russian women ruled the roost kept showing up: in every bathroom I went into, the women had placed their toothbrush in a shared glass with the bristles facing upward. In contrast, men's toothbrushes were placed with the bristles facing down, as if to signal that their heads were buried in the sand.

I couldn't stop thinking about one Russian woman, whom I called the Orange Lady, for the simple reason that the color orange dominated her tiny apartment. Her tablecloth, the wristband she wore, her socks, the magnets on her fridge, even the fish in a tiny, glass-bowl aquarium were all the brightest possible orange. The clue that helped me connect orange with something bigger was a painting I saw hanging on her living room wall. It showed a little girl standing on a drab gray street, dressed head-to-foot in orange. It was, I realized, the woman standing in front of me, but as a young girl.

Realizing this, I asked her about her childhood. She grew up, she told me, in Yakutsk, and never left. When she was a child, she'd pined for a dollhouse but her parents couldn't afford to get her one. When she asked for a doll, she got the same answer. Both the dollhouse and the doll she'd had her heart set on were orange. Orange, then, was the color of the two things she'd wanted most in her life but couldn't get.

Like all the women I spoke to, the Orange Lady seemed starved to express her girlish or feminine side. In Russia, as a rule, creativity is suppressed. Schoolchildren are taught that the answer to almost any question is found in a formula. In a rote, rational society more or less hostile to creativity and emotionality, stepping outside the approved gray palate and into a universe of color and imagination means flirting with the possibility of being "gay"—a huge stigma in Russia. The only exception is ballet, so it's little wonder that the Bolshoi is as popular as it is.

Color. Imagination. Thick doors. Red lips. No mirrors. What role did these things play in Russian culture? But it turned out that the biggest piece of small data of all was staring right at me: the enormous number of magnets on every refrigerator door.

It took me a few visits to notice them. Fridge magnets have a way of mixing in with their surroundings, and then one day it struck me: every refrigerator seemed to have an extravagantly large collection of magnets. They weren't at eye level, either. Most were at waist level, or a little higher. But why? Most people, I know, have at least a couple of magnets on their fridges. A lot of them are goofy, or sentimental, or both—"Life is Too Short to Drink Cheap Wine," "Nothing Says 'I Love You' Like Bacon," and so forth. Others clasp children's drawings, or grocery and to-do lists. Hipsters display sashimi magnets, or bass guitars, or retro cartoon characters like Casper the Friendly Ghost or Bart Simpson. But on the fridges of the Russian Far East, there weren't just a couple of fridge magnets, there were twenty, thirty, even forty or more. Like a metallic mural, they saturated every fridge door in every kitchen I visited where there were children.

From that point forward, I made it a point to ask the family who had put which magnet where. The answer was always the same: The mother placed the first fridge magnet in the center of the fridge. The father was responsible for the next magnet, and he generally placed it to the right of his wife's. Then it was the child's turn to place his or her magnet directly underneath the parents'.

The magnets made a circle around the mother. She was the nexus of the home. It was further confirmation, if I needed any, that at the heart of Russian culture was a woman. From a symbolic standpoint, the magnets I saw were devoted to freedom, to escape, to foreign travel, to exotic foreign cities. They gazed back out at children's eye level. They seemed to say, "There's a future ahead of you. You can do anything."

By now, I was starting to Small Mine the observations I'd gathered in the hope they would take me someplace worthwhile. Desire, I knew, was embedded somehow in those fridge magnets, but I couldn't say how, and even if I could, there was no real proof. How were these fridge magnets different from Pinterest, the website that allows users to post photos and designs and artwork? I knew that in a study of emoticon use across the world by the British technology firm SwiftKey, Russians were revealed as the biggest romantics, "using three times as much romance-themed emoji than the average," especially hearts and flowers, a compensation, as I saw it, for the absence of smiling people, the gray buildings and the overall lack of color.[2] But what did this say about them offline? Humans all need a channel of expression, or what I like to call an oasis. An oasis isn't a point of departure, exactly, but more an exit ramp where we allow ourselves to relax and float away. For Russian men, the oasis centered around fishing with their friends in the summer in boats weighted down with vodka, Russian cognac and beer. Alcoholism, or any kind of addiction, is at its heart a search for transformation and transcendence. It's an escape from both identity and place. Transcendence isn't possible for humans, but we keep at it until we die, go crazy or give up searching.

By showing off the softer, more artistic, more visually expressive, more "feminine" side of their characters, fridge magnets—at least it seemed to me—had become a repository for these women's hopes, fantasies and aspirations. They weren't just the expression of a desire to escape the hardness and maleness of Russian life. They also symbolized the dreams Russian mothers had, that their children might someday live lives less constrained and more refined than theirs. It took a short stroll around the local courtyards the next day to confirm this observation.

Russian playgrounds are as colorless as the apartment buildings nearby. In every Siberian playground I'd visited, the parents sat on benches on one side, talking among themselves as the children played on the other side. One afternoon, in between interviews when there was no one else around, I sat on one of the swings and rocked there for a while. A few minutes later my fingers picked up something: the wear and tear on the swing ropes. Closer to the swing itself, the rope was smooth, but higher up, where the swing fastened to the bar, the rope was discolored and worn. Up high but not below, the rope had seen a lot of use, which told me something: It was the parents, and not the children, who used the swings, which didn't surprise me, as I had noticed that across Siberia the children I'd met didn't seem to be all that active. Even during the short summers, they tended to play indoors. The older kids hung out with their friends or went in a group to bars. No, it was the parents who'd taken a childhood totem—the playground swing—and turned it into their own. If nothing else, this confirmed to me what Russian parents, in particular the mothers, were lacking in their own lives. Freedom. Release. Irresponsibility. Time. In short, many of the qualities we generally ascribe to children.

The flame of Russian culture, which at the same time communicated what the culture lacked, was inside those fridge magnets, and from there I had the beginnings of a concept—one that would have never come to me if, two years earlier, I hadn't traveled to Saudi Arabia to help design a new shopping center.

SAUDI ARABIA IS A NEW and booming market, and given the success of its oil-based economy—with 16 percent of the world's proved oil reserves, the kingdom is the world's largest oil exporter—life there is seldom lived un-extravagantly. In a country that teems with Ferraris and Lamborghinis, where consumption is proud and relentless, a new mall would have to stand out in some way.

But from a clue-gathering perspective, Saudi Arabia is an extremely complex culture, since some of its protocols can be hard for outsiders to come to terms with. As I'm sure you know, Saudi Arabia is a hugely repressive society for women. In 2014 the kingdom was ranked by the World Economic Forum as 130th out of 142 countries for gender equality.[3] It's the only country in the world where women aren't permitted to drive cars. Nor can women travel, work, attend school or submit to certain medical procedures without first getting permission from their male guardians, typically a husband, a father, a brother or a son. In a society like that, it can be hard for a Westerner to determine what's rational and what's not. Still, the mall developers who hired me knew that women are families' chief acquisitors and decision makers, and that any retail innovations had to take their needs into account—a challenge considering that the majority of the people working on the mall project were men.

In a nation dominated by Sharia law, what did Saudi women *actually* want, versus what they were told they should want by the nation's century-old *Mutaween,* or "morality police"? The Mutaween, otherwise known as the Commission for the Promotion of Virtue and the Prevention of Vice, is made up of men who patrol cities and small towns, restaurants and cafés, stores and malls to report back on and redress any and all breaches of morality. They enforce dress codes and make sure that all stores close for half an hour during noon, afternoon, dusk and nighttime prayers. In such an environment, it's nearly impossible to coax a woman to speak honestly about her needs. "I love surprises as long as I know what the surprises are beforehand," one Saudi woman said to me, which struck me as the essence of the Saudi Arabian mentality.

In some key respects, the populations of Russia and Saudi Arabia are very similar. Russia's cold weather can be paralyzing, and in some regions Russians wall themselves off inside their homes for half the year. In Saudi Arabia, the extreme desert heat prompts similar behavior. During my Subtext Research, Russians and Saudis both expressed frustration with the leadership of their countries, and as many Saudis as Russians told me they would happily move someplace else. The difference between the two cultures lay in the fridge magnets. In Saudi Arabia, most displayed obvious international icons: the Eiffel Tower, the Seine, Rome's Coliseum, Big Ben, London Bridge. What, then, was the connection between Russian and Saudi Arabian fridge magnets? The need for escape. For imaginative travel of some kind. Except in the Middle East, that need for escape kept reappearing in the guise of familiar talismans like the Eiffel Tower.

When I began interviewing Saudi Arabian women in their homes, it was the first time any marketer had visited, or interviewed, native women where they lived. I hadn't asked for, or gotten, permission, and what I did was, in theory, against the law. The country's unspoken rules decree that no male is allowed to be alone in a room with a female unless her husband or father is there, even if he is in the next room. Obviously, I needed to tread carefully.

For instance, in every Saudi apartment I visited, thick curtains were drawn across the windows. No one could see in or out. As was the case in Russia, the heavy fabric served as weatherproofing against the extreme outside temperature, but I also wondered whether, along with the Saudi Arabian dress code, the curtains provided an additional layer of subjugation. In Arabic, *hijab* can literally be translated as "screen" or "curtain." The Qur'an, I knew, directs that male Muslims should address the wives of the Prophet Muhammad behind a curtain. Did the curtains have some unconscious religious significance? When I interviewed local religious leaders, I got conflicting answers. I found out that the Mutaween was known for handing out tickets to homeowners whose bare windows overlooked the street; yet when I asked the Saudi men present at my interviews whether the curtains were religiously prescribed, they told me that closing the curtains was a general courtesy. The curtains, it seemed, were nothing more than tradition, a self-invented rule enforced by the morality police.

The next piece of small data I stumbled on had nothing to do with gender.

As I wrote earlier, you can typically identify the first clue about any consumer's identity on his or her walls. It took me three or four visits to notice that the paintings in Saudi homes all had as their subject matter one theme: water. Streams. Lakes. Waterfalls. Oceans. (It's worth noting that Arabic speakers are four times more likely than other speakers to use flower and plant emoticons.)[4] I took note of this as a curiosity, nothing more. After all, lots of paintings have water as their theme, and no doubt the blue pastels were calming, especially in a sandy, landlocked country where there are no rivers, lakes, ponds, streams or much rainfall, only aquifers that process and desalinize the nation's drinking water from the surrounding oceans.

From consulting work I'd done years before with Colgate, I know that around 40 percent of all toothbrushes sold around the world have red handles. But Saudi toothbrushes were anything but that; the figure, in fact, was 2 percent. There were no oranges, either, and barely any yellows. This wasn't normal. What could the absence of red, yellow and orange toothbrushes imply?

Over the next week, I also began noticing how juice glasses were arranged on trays. They were positioned beside one another, instead of stacked, and the same went for the drinking glasses inside nine out of ten Saudi cupboards. Nothing could fall or topple, break or shatter. Control is generally a sign and a consequence of fear, and for the first time, I recognized that fear—but fear of what?—permeated these Saudi households.

I jotted down other small data, too. The clocks in practically every home, as well as most of the watches on women's wrists, were five minutes ahead of time. In Arabic culture, there is no "good luck" number, but there *are* five pillars of Islam, suggesting to me that Saudi natives were compensating for some as-yet-undefined terror by creating a halo effect in their homes—a way of warding off bad luck or misfortune.

At the same time, what could account for so many Eiffel Tower fridge magnets? They were literally everywhere. They sat on window-sills. They served as paperweights and desk ornaments. The reason I didn't pick up on them at first was because the Eiffel Tower is iconic to the point of corniness. But aside from some Saudis visiting France and bringing home souvenirs, why were there so many of them?

My first thought was that the Eiffel Tower is a symbol of desire. "Desire is full of endless distances," the American poet Robert Haas once wrote,[5] and I couldn't help but think again of the theme of water in the paintings on the walls of every Saudi household. There was no difference between what an Eiffel Tower represented and what water symbolized, or was there? Someone once said that blue is the color of longing for the distances that we as humans can never reach. We can get rid of desire by surrendering to it, or we can resist and deny it. But desire can't help but show up somewhere in our lives—whether it's in a drink, or a drug, or the music we listen to that takes us back to the time when we first heard it; and if desire is frustrated, it will burst through somewhere else, in a curio souvenir bought in a Paris airport, or in a painting of a stream, or a creek, or a waterfall.

Throughout my visit I'd also made it a point to watch Saudi children playing. Their behavior, I noticed, was controlled and careful. Instead of playing hide-and-go-seek-type games, their games seemed to center instead around themes of protection and caretaking. Most of the kids' books I pulled down from the shelves reflected these same themes, indicating that whatever fear I was picking up on had been passed down from Saudi mothers to their children. It's always instructive to leaf through a nation's children's books, since they create our earliest expectations, and the Saudi mothers I met were raised on these same books. What surprised me most were their settings and locales. Few took place in any Bedouin kingdom, and if they did, the children's-book version of Saudi Arabia bore no resemblance to the actual country. Instead of vast expanses of heat and sand, the books showed green fields, farms, creeks, water mills, weeping willows, patches of snow visible on the peaks of nearby mountains. Small exotic animals roamed around. It was a storybook Swiss fantasy combined with a dream world of water, purity and innocence.

But the toys favored by Saudi children challenged that innocence. Nearly eight out of ten of them were fire trucks, ambulances or police and safety vehicles. Having visited the bedrooms of hundreds of children in my work for LEGO, this struck me as anything but normal. Was the emphasis on police cars and fire trucks a result of the television shows or movies kids watched? When I took a closer look at Arabic and international programming as well as national toy sales, the answer was yes, to some degree—but not enough to explain why there were so many rescue vehicles. Digging further, I discovered that sales of kids' emergency toys were 49 percent higher in Saudi Arabia than anyplace else in the world.

It goes without saying that the Middle East has a lot of sand (and dirt), and when I visited a nearby store with a Saudi Arabian woman and her driver, at first I thought nothing about the fact the car seats were wrapped in plastic. As my visit went on, I noticed that the television remote controls in most homes were also enclosed in plastic. So were many chairs and the newly bought clothes I found in bedroom drawers. A similar phenomenon is common in Chinese homes, where the fear of bacteria and infection links back to horrific amounts of urban smog, but Saudi Arabia had no obvious pollution problem. Did the plastic wrap have anything to do with the absence of freedom between Saudi men and women? Was it a symbol for the hijab? Did it connect somehow to the thick curtains or even the lack of brightly colored toothbrushes in Saudi bathrooms?

By now, I was convinced that the combination of toy fire trucks, ambulances and safety vehicles mixed with the plastic wrap covering up so many everyday objects was driven by a desire for protection against some unnamed cultural terror. From the first years of a child's life, fear was rooted in Saudi culture, but I didn't know why, and I had no idea what that fear was, either.

When I asked myself what water meant, in conjunction with the safety vehicles in children's bedrooms, the answer was obvious: water put out fires. But what kinds of fires could break out in a desert climate? Still, I knew I was onto something, and when I brought up the subject of fires with Saudi women over the next few days it seemed I'd struck a nerve. No one could tell me why exactly, but they were morbidly afraid of fire, they told me—of flames, of burning to death. Mostly, they were afraid of burning buildings. Burning hotels. Burning skyscrapers. Shopping centers on fire. No mall has ever caught fire in Saudi Arabia, but they were convinced it happened regularly. Maybe it had something to do with a dread of being suffocated, since the hijab Saudi women wore was, at least to Western eyes, claustrophobic, even strangling.

I began analyzing Saudis' favorite buildings and top travel destinations, while poring through interviewees' photo albums and computer disc drives. If nothing else, the mall that I'd been brought in to help design needed to symbolize an escape from day-to-day reality, as well as offer refuge from the cultural fear of fire. I eventually contacted three Saudi female psychologists to help me uncover so-called "reverse" symbols that would help dampen and relieve this national paranoia.

Reverse symbols are common in children's hospitals—the cartoon animal faces on walls, for example, that soothe children when they are about to undergo a medical procedure. Working together, we created large "fear" maps, which we counterbalanced with "dream" and "escapism" paths, all of which would underlie the mall's future construction. I knew this much: whatever the mall ended up looking like, unless we took heed of the cultural fear of fire, we would have no customers.

A few months later, the mall's construction was under way. Most Saudi Arabian malls consist of a long corridor, with cold, marbled stores on either side. Most were designed and built by developers with strong links to the royal family and reflect the latter's power, mystery and remoteness. The overhead light is either dim, or harsh. The corridors echo and the acoustics are poor. Other malls are ornate and pompous, with huge statues and artificial palm trees planted in sand beds, which is ironic in a kingdom whose natives would prefer to surround themselves with totems of the West.

Our mall was different, in that it was focused on bringing in a more human dimension. The design team and I agreed we wouldn't use certain colors, including red, orange and yellow. Revolving around images of water, with large canals flowing through the mall, our design created as strong a visual negation of the possibility of fires, or flame, or burning, as possible. We imported real bird sounds, and the rush of running water. Working alongside architects and designers, the mall became a dreamlike environment teeming with water images, including fountains, streams and even a wintry landscape with Swiss cabins, snowy mountains and ski slopes, to help Saudi Arabian women feel safe, and also to mirror the protection and the warmth that they felt as children growing up. If the cups I'd seen in Saudi households were arranged so they couldn't fall, or topple, as a burning building might, I made sure that even the hills in the landscape were close to the ground. The calmness of the scene evoked a sense of protection against the elements, eliminating the metaphorical need for "plastic wrap," as why would anyone need that level of immunity in such a cool, soothing environment?

WHAT DID ANY OF THIS have to do with the Russian Far East? Well, a few things. As is true in Saudi Arabia, Russian society was closed, with very few options for escape. In Russia, women were seldom given the opportunity to show emotion; in Saudi Arabia, women weren't even permitted to show their faces. In both cultures, public expressions of creativity barely existed, and rulership and religion were dominant. Russia had Vladimir Putin and the KGB's current incarnation, the FSB. Saudi Arabia had Islam and Sharia law. In the Middle East, however, children, and not women, were the center of the family. Since women weren't permitted to reveal their bodies or identities, their children acted out their emotions for them. Saudi children, even young females, were allowed to express what Saudi women couldn't.

In common with Russia, the most popular cuisine in the region was Italian food. Russian fridge magnets were situated low enough to serve as toys for kids, whereas in Saudi Arabia they were beyond reach for most children, serving only decorative purposes. Russia needed toys, and Saudi Arabia didn't.

There is no way I would have picked up on the fridge magnets in the Russian Far East if I hadn't worked in Saudi Arabia, no way I would have been reminded, again, of the unspoken balances between men and women, freedom and restriction, appearance and reality. When a society is out of balance, its natives will always find ways to compensate—or, in this case, escape. Alcohol in Russia is an escape. Cannabis in Holland is an escape. Prescription pills in the United States are an escape. What, then, were Russians escaping from?

Generally speaking, Saudi families could afford to travel with their kids, whereas most Russian families couldn't. Hence, the profusion of fridge magnets in Russian homes, symbolizing the places families wished they could expose their children to but couldn't. I may be paraphrasing Sting circa 1985, but did Russians love their children, too? Yes. Did they wish they could provide for them, pay for long-distance travel, expose them to the world? Yes. But as I said, foreign travel is beyond the average Russian budget. As compensation, and in contrast with Saudi Arabian households, Russian families gathered and hung fridge magnets at a level where their children could see, touch and maybe even draw inspiration from them.

The magnets were an oasis, a charging station for escape. Russian men had alcohol, but my guess was that fridge magnets were oases where Russian women and children went to refuel. By nature, oases belong to the past. As time goes on, they grow in romance, mystery and dimension. If most of us paid a visit to the real-life oases we remember—a summer at Martha's Vineyard, a childhood trip to Europe—chances are we would be disappointed. Our memories can't help making those places larger than life, slightly unreal. Situated in the most visited room in the home, fridge magnets were a pipeline to those imaginary places and experiences. They ensured a stream of energy from Paris, or London, or Tokyo directly into the kitchens of the Russian Far East. They gave Russian women—and Russian children—a ticket to another place and time, transporting and reenergizing them before dropping them back inside everyday life.

In both Saudi Arabia and Russia, life isn't easy, and escape routes, if they exist, are often blocked. Over the years many Russians who travel or live abroad have told me they feel out of place in other cultures. "The place where you are born best suits you," is a well-known Russian saying, and most Russians believe the only possible place where you can find out who you really are is in the country where you were born.

Still, what struck me most about life in the Russian Far East was the sense of community I found in every town I visited. I had a strange feeling I'd caught it on its last legs, too. In a Novosibirsk courtyard, I saw two Russian boys enthusiastically playing catch with a rock, in contrast to the United States and parts of Europe, where a new smartphone app occasions a few moments of excitement at most, followed by boredom. The Internet was gradually making its way into more rural areas of Russian society, even in areas as remote as Siberia, but full penetration was still one or two years away. One man I spoke with told me that since the Russian government had limited any and all personal initiative, or entrepreneurship, "freedom" had no choice but to find its way online. It was the only place Russian citizens could express themselves without the fear of reprisal.

If trust doesn't exist in Russia, the natives certainly don't trust the Internet. The most popular social networking site in Russia, with around 110 million users (compared to Facebook's 10 million), is VKontakte.com, or VK. Online privacy is a very real issue in Russia. In 2014, Vladimir Putin signed a law requiring all Internet operators to store their user data in centers within Russia by 2016. Companies that refused to comply, he said, would be banished from the Web, which means that any data stored on Russian servers is vulnerable to censorship. Additional regulations require blogs with a reader base of over 3,000 daily views to register officially as "media," thereby subjecting

them to governmental monitoring. In the wake of the political up-
heaval in Ukraine in 2013, VK founder Pavel Durov made headlines
when he refused to hand over information on his website pertaining to
Ukrainian protesters to Russian security agencies, or to block the VK
page dedicated to Alexey Navalny, the anticorruption foe and Putin
critic. Durov posted the government's orders instead on his VK home
page. It took only a few months for Durov to be dismissed as VK's
CEO. A longtime proponent of freedom of expression, Durov made it
clear that VK had been taken over by the Russian government.

Even when the government is not involved, e-commerce in Russia
involves ordering a product online, then picking it up at a nearby outlet.
As an analogy, imagine ordering books from Amazon, and going to an
Amazon warehouse around the corner from your house to pick them up.
Order something in Russia, and there's no guarantee that your package
will show up when it's supposed to, or that it will show up at all.

Back in my hotel one night, I placed every fragment of small data I
had on a bulletin board—photos, videos, notes, observations, insights.
I pictured the fridge magnets in every apartment. I thought back to
the Orange Lady, and how the two things she'd wanted most as a girl,
a dollhouse and a doll, were denied her, and of the emotional power
of the things we crave the most when we're young. I thought about
the guilt that Russian parents, especially mothers, carried around with
them, of not being able to give their children more than they themselves had as kids. Then there were the lack of mirrors and the frayed
top ropes of the playground swings. Still, everything came back to the
distilled emotional power inside those fridge magnets, and back to the
imbalances in Russian society: the cold weather, the frustration, the
distrust, what it means to be a Russian parent who wants more for her
children. The preoccupation with children showed up in the worn rope
swings and in the cardboard sheets of princes and warriors crowned
with the heads of sons and daughters. Suddenly, I had my business idea.

Over the next few days and weeks, I set in motion the rollout of
a huge online website devoted to Russian mothers and their children.
We called it Mamagazin, which in Russian means "Mums' Store." Our

mission was to create the most honest, reliable e-commerce site in Russia. To help combat the high levels of distrust in Russia, I knew instinctively who to call upon to help me with the website: Russian mothers. They may have been nominally in charge of their households, but almost no one listened to them or sought out their opinions. Almost every Russian woman I spoke to told me how friendless and isolated she felt. Across Siberia, the strongest communities women have, now and in the future, are online.

Mamagazin, then, was the first-ever online community that respected, and listened to, Russian women. It was built by mothers, for mothers. Yes, it is a company first, but it's also a resource where mothers can tap into advice from other mothers, which is why we asked those very moms for their help in creating it. In Russia, we found out that most mothers buy toys in partnership with other mothers, to save on shipping and handling costs. In response, we created a mechanism that enables them to make one order, splitting the payments and even the products, using a single account. Realizing that grandparents buy around 40 percent of all toys in Russia, we also created a system where grandparents could submit the characteristics of the grandchild in question, their preferred price range, the child's dreams, the topics on which they bonded the most with the children and even a wish list.

Our goal? To let Russian women be heard. To appeal both to their actual children and to the little kids who still lived inside these women. Not least, one of our mission statements—smiles are infectious—was a way of trying to bring a measure of happiness to a country where smiles were rare.

It had never been done before, but to help launch the business, we next recruited a select group of Russian women to serve as our "mom ambassadors." What did the ideal "trustworthy" Russian mother look like? What were her characteristics? We then put the candidates who matched those characteristics through a two-month-long boot camp where they learned social and communication skills, and how to cope with unforeseen crises. Russian women are extremely introverted. They're unaccustomed to small talk, or to letting a conversation build up slowly, or to building up a rapport; most go straight to the point. In effect, we taught them how to create casual conversation with strangers. They then partnered up and traveled across the country in pairs to thirty different cities, to meet with 150 additional mothers daily to discuss any and all issues they face. No selling, no pushing—just conversations in which women with children could talk, and listen. For most, being in the spotlight was a new, and emotional, experience. Every day we collected more than 500 good and great ideas. We implemented many of them, too, crediting the mothers who came up with them on a special honorees' page.

Our next step was to create a series of nationwide family festivals we called Mamafests, devoted to creating an experience for both mothers and children. We invited approximately 250,000 Russian mothers and their families. When they got there, children were given a mock passport, and told they had to accumulate stamps they would receive once they'd completed certain activities, including painting a character's face, icing cookies, playing *Angry Birds* and tic-tac-toe, and racing other kids in cardboard cars. Eventually they could swap their passport stamps for prizes.

Up until the point Mamagazin ran up against 2015's sanctions on imports, and was temporarily "frozen," the website—as well as our Mamafest projects—was the fastest-growing, most user-friendly e-commerce site aimed at parents in all of Russia, with over 500 employees, and Russian moms consistently voting the site as "The most appealing to visit." Never before had thousands of mothers come together to help create a company, and never had a company gone to market by simply listening to what mothers wanted. In contrast to most other businesses, we had made the time to grow our business organically. We spent a year talking to Russian mothers, and another year building the website in line with what they wanted. Our bigger mission was to create a collective experience for Russian mothers, all of whom wanted the same thing for their children—a chance to satisfy desires their lives prevent them from expressing. Whether in the Middle East or the remotest regions of Siberia, it was a need reflected in the radiance and romance of a universally adored Parisian landmark.

CHAPTER 2

SAUSAGE, CHICKEN AND THE PURSUIT OF *REAL* HAPPINESS

TRANSFORMING THE FUTURE OF HOW WE SHOP FOR FOOD

WINSTON-SALEM IS THE FIFTH-LARGEST CITY IN NORTH Carolina, with a population of around 235,000 people. Along with Austin, Texas; Portland, Oregon; and one or two other US cities, Winston, as the locals call it, is a popular retirement destination for northerners who dream of good weather, good manners, an arts scene and enough variation from the American norm—grits on the menu, country music on the radio—to make them feel they are living in the United States, but also visiting. Still, a century after its founding, and despite an active biotech and medical research scene, Winston-Salem is still best known as the headquarters of R.J. Reynolds, which named a pair of popular cigarette brands after the city. Some locals, citing the city's deep involvement with tobacco, call the place "Camel City."

Industry aside, the sidewalks of downtown Winston-Salem empty out by 5 p.m., as in almost every other American city. Most retail takes place in malls and shopping centers accessible via a series of highways and loops. Lowes Foods, a local family-owned grocery chain with supermarkets in North Carolina and South Carolina, is one of the region's biggest retailers, but its revenues had been down since the 2008 recession. Walmart had infiltrated many of its markets, and Lowes couldn't compete with the Internet on either volume or prices. Unless the company turned around its 100 or so supermarkets, it would have to shut down some of its stores. It's not often I take jobs with regional companies, but Lowes was an unpolished gem. I wanted to prove to them, and myself, that with strategy and new ways of thinking, it was possible for a "smaller" organization to compete with the bigger-budgeted, better-known players in the supermarket industry.

Many American strip malls and shopping centers have a derelict feeling about them. Most are similar in appearance. National food and retail chains—Chili's, Applebee's, Staples, Bed Bath & Beyond, Pier 1 Imports—stand alongside local businesses that trim nails, style hair or offer classes in self-defense. If asked, most natives would tell you that if they closed their eyes and shut out any nearby landmarks, or local signage, they could be almost anywhere in the United States. The sameness of everything has a numbing effect, just as it did for the Norwegian writer Karl Ove Knausgaard who, assigned to take a road trip across North America for the *New York Times Magazine* last year, wrote, "Ever since I landed in Cleveland the previous day, the landscape had been the same, a sort of centerless, semi-urban sprawl of highways, subdivisions, shopping malls, warehouses, gas stations and factories."[1] Nothing in the landscape, he wrote, felt surprising or natural. Concluded Knausgaard, "I was supposed to write something about this trip, and not only that, I was supposed to use this trip to grasp something essential about the United States, perceive something with my foreign gaze that Americans couldn't see for themselves. Instead, I saw nothing. I experienced nothing."

The Lowes supermarket anchored a shopping center a few miles from downtown Winston-Salem. Sharing the space were a neighboring arts and crafts store, an optometrist, a veterinarian and two vacant stores with cardboard across their windows and SPACE FOR LEASE signs with phone numbers on them. Inside, the store was cavernous, but its most distinguishing feature was that it looked and felt like any other

American supermarket. A row of gleaming shopping carts up front. Stacks of baskets. Produce stands crowded with fruits and vegetables. Aisles filled with every kind of food or drink, surrounded by a refrigerated ring where orange juice, milk, yogurt and cheese were stocked. Batteries, candy, gum and celebrity magazines clustered around the check-out lanes. The overall color scheme was white, with touches of hunter green. The store was clean, but dated, and the shelves looked like they hadn't been straightened out in a while. The few employees I met in their tan caps and black shirts and aprons were teenagers or college students: friendly, but inexperienced and not all that engaged.

One of the first things I did was blindfold Lowes management in each one of its stores and take them up and down the aisles. The human sense of smell "resets" every seven minutes, meaning that we rarely notice if something smells odd, or old, or stale. Knowing this, I took them outside into the parking lot, and when they reentered the store, they saw the store in a new light (and smell). In some cases they discovered a fragrance in this or that store zone was unpleasant to shoppers, not necessarily because of spoiled food, but simply because of a broken ventilation system.

Trying to turn around a family-owned supermarket like Lowes would be a huge, expensive risk. But with their future in jeopardy, the company had no other choice. The stores' demographic trended toward people in their late forties and older, which wasn't a good sign for future profitability. Lowes also faced very real competition from larger chains like Food Lion and Harris Teeter, as well as from more upscale, hipster-friendly stores like Trader Joe's and Whole Foods. In the end, I told the Lowes management team it wasn't enough to repaint the parking lot lines, or alter the store logo, or increase the store's social media presence. We had to transform *everything*.

As usual, the question lay in Small Mining what was missing in American culture. It lay in figuring out what desires and dreams were going unfulfilled. This wasn't easy in a country famous for manufacturing desires and longings, whether it's Apple iPhones or Hollywood films. In an era dominated by the latest smartphone app, it was hard to put a finger on an unmet desire that a comparatively small bricks-and-mortar southern supermarket chain needed to deliver that America wasn't able to dream up.

But less than a year later, in an industry where an increase of 4 percent is considered impressive, Lowes sales had risen substantially. Tim Lowe, the inspiring, pioneering president of the Lowes Foods, was quoted as saying, "I would say that the results we've been able to achieve—and the overall organizational change we've seen—are quite heroic and have made a significant impact." According to CBC, in just a few months the average basket size and average transaction volume at Lowes were up 7 and 23 percent, respectively, and last year, Lowes was awarded the North Carolina Retail Merchant's Association Retailer of the Year Award, thanks in part to its innovative ways of connecting with customers. Moreover, the chain had launched its own Small Data Department.

Even better, Lowes supermarkets were packed. People were driving in from miles away, bypassing supermarkets closer to where they lived, for the sheer sensory experience of shopping at Lowes. What helped turn around Lowes wasn't a local or regional solution. It didn't come out of a Harvard Business School or Wharton case study. It didn't require teams of consultants. The small data insights that helped transform a local supermarket into a national phenomenon began in the Russian Far East, and drew inspiration from cultures as various as Japan, China, France and Italy.

LIKE MOST PEOPLE who didn't grow up in the United States, I've been exposed to American culture—popular music, television shows, movies and cable news channels—since I was young. Still, spending time in the States is another matter entirely. Like every other country in the world, America has a set of unspoken rules and protocols that have been handed down from one generation to the next, most of them imperceptible to natives but obvious to an outsider's eyes. For example, in most European countries, when you board a crowded elevator and find your space, it's considered good manners to gaze straight ahead of you without speaking as the car goes up or down. In Europe, elevator passengers almost never exchange a nod, or a greeting, with other riders. This isn't considered rude, or unsociable, either. Your silence is simply a sign of respect for other people's privacy.

American elevator etiquette is very different from unspoken European protocols. During my first few visits to the States, I boarded elevators without greeting the other passengers, and at night, as is my habit, I swam laps in hotel pools without saying a word to the other swimmers. I very quickly learned that Americans find this behavior cold, off-putting and even menacing. These days, whenever I'm in the United States, I make it a point to acknowledge the other elevator passengers, even if it's only with a smile. If another passenger is holding a bunch of flowers, for example, I've learned that it's considered impolite not to comment on them, just as if you board an elevator to see a woman in a wedding dress, it's bad manners not to compliment her on her gown, or ask her when her wedding is taking place. In America, you have to say *something*.

Why, though? It's tempting to believe that in a country that is home to numerous nationalities and races, the tacit tradition of making small talk with your neighbors springs from the desire to establish commonality, even if you're talking about something as generic as the weather, or how the local sports team did last night. Small talk also has the secondary effect of defusing conflict or even resentment. A few years ago, I remember flying from New York City to Medellín, Colombia, and, once I landed, climbing inside a taxi to take me to my hotel. At one point, I asked the driver if he knew anything about the upcoming weather forecast. When he didn't answer, I began chattering about the weather in an effort to engage him, and when he still didn't respond—he seemed confused—it finally struck me that the global talking point known as The Weather simply didn't exist in Colombia. I later found out that no one asks or talks about the weather in Medellín, as it never varies, nor are there any television meteorologists. Every day the temperature is in the mid-seventies, with sunlight and an occasional cloud cover. Yet even in Southern California, where the same is true, natives talk about the weather constantly.

As I mentioned earlier, in sharp contrast to Americans' reputation for friendliness is the absence of physicality. In the United States, no one ever touches anyone else and if they do so by accident, most apologize immediately. Physical contact is seen by many as analogous to trespassing on posted land, possibly even the first step to sexual interest. It's instructive to compare how dolls in toy stores are sold in America versus how they're displayed in European toy stores. In Europe, dolls stand side by side on shelves. They're touching, holding hands with, even embracing each other. In America, a doll is displayed and sold as a single unit, inside a sealed plastic container, as if to communicate that she is alone or, if not, would be smart to keep a distance from her peers. It seems that dolls—and people—are expected to go it alone, and without any physical interference, either.

Why, though, apart from shaking hands and the occasional hug among friends, is the idea of physically touching another person perceived as so threatening? Heterosexual American men who make physical contact with one another first have to enter an unambiguous "permission zone," usually athletic. The male taboo against physical contact, or making direct eye contact with another man, is a crucial element of a code American boys pick up when they are young, and extends to the protocol most men follow in public bathrooms. Males entering a rest room only to find one or two others males in front of the urinals generally make their way toward a urinal as geographically distant from the others as possible. Once they're in place, they gaze straight ahead of them, fearing, maybe, that if they look anywhere else other men might misinterpret their gaze as predatory.

From my perspective, there is something amiss in a culture where no one touches. The United States isn't necessarily a sexually prudish country, but it *is* physically very vigilant, in part because, more than other cultures, Americans seem more aware of the signals, messages and implications they are sending out to others. In contrast, South America is probably the healthiest continent for physical touch. I've sat in business meetings in Peru and Colombia where men of all ages sit around a table with their arms draped casually around one another's shoulders. They don't think anything of it.

The presumption of everyday friendliness, combined with the lack of physicality—those were the first two pieces of small data I picked up in the United States. There was a third, too, that could be distilled to one word: *rounded.* In the United States, almost no public rooms or areas are rectangular, or sharply cornered. America is a place where the square and the angular give way to the curvilinear, the circular and the blunted, as if hotel rooms and boardrooms were somehow wrapping occupants in an embrace. It was as if architects and designers were relying on furniture and rooms to provide the illusion of physical touch in a country where it barely exists. As you might imagine, I spend a lot of my time in hotel rooms. Some are rectangular, but the curtains covering the windows, the bowed shower curtain in the bathrooms, and the contours of the furniture convey circularity and security, with an emphasis on the latter.

Security. In every other country across the world, guests staying at a hotel are free to open the windows in their rooms, with the exception of one: the United States. American hotel windows are sealed, or painted shut, or manufactured in such a way that they can't open or close in the first place. (This even extends to the White House. In a 2015 interview with Ellen DeGeneres, First Lady Michelle Obama said about herself and the president, "We can't do little things like open windows. I haven't been in a car with the windows open for about seven years. The windows in our *house* don't open." She added, "We go on the balcony, but that's really the only door we can open."[2]) Once they're inside their rooms, hotel guests are imprisoned, like royalty in a tower. Why? Does management fear that guests staying on the first floor who open their hotel windows are at risk of killing themselves? People fall or leap to their deaths from hotel windows daily across the world, but is the fear of suicide really the underlying issue?

The circularity I kept encountering in the United States had the effect, deliberate or not, of eliminating the possibility of conflict, or dissent. In a country with the world's highest incarceration rate, that spends around $640 billion a year on its military,[3] which is more than the next seven countries combined, and where 37 percent of all Americans say that they, or someone in their household, owns a gun,[4] I couldn't help but find this paradoxical. America is a military superpower whose prevailing design aesthetic does everything it can to muffle, discourage and eradicate any trace of conflict. Most American malls, motels, hotels, big-box stores and fast-food chains are climate-controlled, mood-controlled, secure, antiseptic and completely the same. Sharpness and angularity have been smoothed out. Whether you're entering the lobby of a Holiday Inn or sitting down at a table at Chili's, guests can be assured they are in for no surprises at all.

If the architectural mandate against conflict gave me another clue about what drove American culture, another observation confirmed it: political correctness. Like my experiences in American elevators and swimming pools, it was something I found out about the hard way.

Understand that like most Danes, and Scandinavians in general, I grew up with a nonexistent, and certainly nonauthoritarian, relationship to religion. Fifteen years ago, that suddenly got me in trouble. I was giving a speech in Cincinnati, Ohio, about the differences and similarities among some of the world's best-known brands and the world's best-known religions. In my industry, a brand is a brand, but I didn't realize how sensitive and controversial a subject religion is in the United States, and how treating it as anything short of sacrosanct could get me into trouble. The first slide of my PowerPoint presentation featured a photograph of Pope John Paul II, and the second was of Ronald McDonald. To a Midwestern audience made up of marketers and brand builders, I pointed out that both the Pope and the McDonald's mascot had things in common. Both wore branded, identifiable costumes, and both were leaders of highly successful organizations.

By the end of the third slide, people began walking out of the room. By the end, the conference room was only half full. When my speech was over, I went up to my host. Had something gone wrong? Had I upset one half of the room for some reason? That was when

I found out that treating religion dispassionately was, at least in the United States, off-limits.

No country in the world is as "politically correct" as the United States. Few Americans would ever identify themselves as a "racist," or a "misogynist," or intolerant of the rights of minorities, whether it's homosexuals or Latin Americans, and even Americans who exhibit what seems like baldly racist behavior strenuously deny they are "racists." At social events and parties, the topics of sex, politics and religion are all off-limits. (In fact, a lot of what goes on in America is off-limits—or at least too risky to raise in polite company.) Few Americans are willing to discuss things everyone knows but won't admit—from how tedious it is to stay home all day with a baby, to their true feelings about hip-hop, to how they feel about sex. Most Americans won't even talk about how they feel about political correctness itself.

From country to country, I make it a habit to study the national sense of humor. Is it ironic? Sarcastic? Sly? Direct? Indirect? What's most striking about mainstream American humor is that it focuses on much of the material they won't talk about over dinner. Visit any comedy club, or watch *Bridesmaids, Curb Your Enthusiasm, The Simpsons, South Park, Family Guy* or Louis CK's routines on YouTube, and you'll realize that Americans pay comedians millions of dollars to talk about things most of them have felt, or thought, but never said in public. In 2014 the biggest-selling American game, and the country's most popular Christmas gift, was *Cards Against Humanity,* described on its website as "a party game for horrible people," and "as despicable and awkward as you and your friends."[5] Its topics include "Auschwitz," "Lance Armstrong's Missing Testicle," "Penis Envy," "Not Giving a Shit about the Third World" and almost every other topic a lot of Americans take pains never to discuss around the Christmas tree.

Political correctness doesn't just involve words, it also links back to the rounded American design aesthetic. When gathering together in bars, Americans, like the Chinese, create a large crowd—eight to ten people isn't an anomaly—which forms in a crescent shape. In southern Europe, for example, groups will number no more than three or four people, and the concept of the large "public group" barely exists in northern Europe. In America, entourages are sizable, and everyone is given the chance to face forward, and to talk, and be heard; while in Brazil, everyone tends to speak at once. In common with the curvilinear design of American furniture, the crescent formation, which forms automatically and unconsciously, seems designed not to hurt or exclude others. The desire not to offend has made its way onto restaurant menus, too. The multitude of options American diners face on restaurant menus isn't just a smart business decision. It deliberately avoids offending all tastes, palates and dietary restrictions. Even selecting a salad dressing becomes a labor-intensive task, faced, as no other diners in the world are, with half-a-dozen choices from French to Italian to vinaigrette.

The United States comes by its political correctness honestly. Americans are exposed to other cultures and races in ways natives of other countries simply aren't. Denmark, for example, is as homogenous as a country can be. Ninety-nine percent of Danes are Protestant, and most call themselves agnostic. Without exposure to foreign cultures, or sensitivity to other races' cultures, habits or tastes, the conversation is blunter. Political correctness ultimately derives from two things: fear and tribe. Who wants to risk expulsion from your gender, your community, your town, your state? More often than anywhere else in the world, Americans come of age hearing that they're responsible for their own futures. It's a message both inspiring and pitiless. Children who grow up in the slums of Chicago or Los Angeles can someday become political leaders, successful entertainers, influential businesspeople. But if they don't, or if they fall on hard times, they're left on their own to survive. The American safety net is fragile, and under continuous barrage, making the prospect of rejection by our tribes even more terrifying than it would be elsewhere.

I kept coming back to one word: *fear.* The circularity of American design and architecture. The bolted hotel windows. The political correctness. The sameness of the retail and hospitality landscape. It puzzled me. What were people scared of? Being sued? Being injured?

Firearms? Fear, of course, contradicts everything most people want to believe about everyday life in America. The United States, after all, is synonymous with freedom and social and profession mobility. Which is why the padlocked hotel windows, climate-controlled buildings, paranoia about offending others and emphasis on rules and regulations seemed to counter the official version of the American "brand."

From what I could tell, most Americans were so accustomed to their regulated, rule-bound status they barely noticed the restrictions to their freedom. Whenever I fly into New York, I stay in the same Midtown hotel. One of the amenities provided by the management is a package containing four cotton ear swabs. The instructions on the side seem to be addressed to a not-very-bright three-year-old: *Place the cotton squab in your ear. Do not insert completely. These instructions are for your own safety.* When I showed the package to an American visitor, he gazed at me without comprehension. "What's so interesting about this?" he said. As a native, he couldn't see what I saw as an outsider— that most people who know what a cotton swab is can also be counted on to know how to use one, and what's more, in no other country in the world would you ever see instructions printed out for its correct use.

To me, this was the core of life in the United States: Rules and restrictions, most of which are reframed so that Americans believe they are, in fact, safeguards. Which begs the question: If most of the time they do and feel and think and watch and eat and drink precisely what everyone else does, are Americans really free?

THERE WAS A FINAL PIECE OF SMALL DATA, one obvious to anyone who took a moment to glance up long enough from his or her smartphone: smartphones. Mind you, of the 7 billion people on earth today, 5.1 billion of them own a cell phone. Over half of all Americans own a smartphone, with 29 percent of them owning either a tablet or an e-reader, up from only 2 percent three years ago. In 2014, *CNN Money* reported that for the first time ever, Americans used smartphone and tablet apps more than laptops to get onto the Internet. In terms of sheer numbers, this means that 55 percent of all US Internet usage comes from mobile devices, with apps making up 47 percent and mobile browsers making up the rest.[6]

Their use may be epidemic across the world, and increasing all the time, but nowhere is smartphone use as prevalent as it is in America, with fully fledged adults as preoccupied as younger generations. This makes sense: our phones, and the Internet itself, are often more exciting, more surprising, more new, than our surroundings. They also make natives feel *safe*. In a country whose workers take the fewest number of vacation days of any people in the world, smartphones would seem to compound the pressure Americans feel to look and seem busy. I was once on vacation at a hotel on Italy's Amalfi Coast, and among the other guests in the outdoor swimming pool were four men whom I soon determined from their accents were Americans. They were shirtless, and wearing their bathing suits, but not one of them was looking at the stunning seascape directly behind them. All four were fiddling on their phones.

Anyone who has been in an airport recently will tell you that the twenty-first-century airport has transformed itself into a tech-accessory mall. It seems sometimes as if one out of every two airport stores is in the business of selling earphones, earbuds, battery-juicers and power adapters. One concourse in the Minneapolis–Saint Paul International Airport has taken this concept to ridiculous lengths. In a place devoted to waiting, where almost no one is not gazing down at his or her phone, the Minnesota airport offers a waiting area populated with white plastic tables, each one with its own iPad. These tablets provide weather reports and flight information. They offer drink and food menus from a nearby restaurant. Since there is literally nowhere else to sit but at an iPad-equipped table, travelers can't *not* look at the iPad, leaving them with three options: engage with it, put on headphones, or gaze up at one of the television monitors broadcasting 24-hour cable news. In short, there is no refuge from technology or from the anxiety it engenders.

Life has never been safer in America than it is today. Cited in the *Christian Science Monitor* in 2012, James Alan Fox, a criminologist at Boston's Northeastern University, concluded, "We are indeed a safer nation than 20 years ago," a trend he and other experts credit to factors including increased incarceration and law enforcement technology, and a larger percentage of older Americans. Despite America's relative safety, Fox says, "Citizens overwhelmingly feel crime is going up even though it is not . . . because of the growth of crime shows and the way that TV spotlights the emotional. One case of a random, horrific shooting shown repeatedly on TV has more visceral effect than all the statistics printed in a newspaper."[7] The Internet magnifies bad news, placing it, literally and physically, in our hands, without providing any perspective. It is analogous to the difference between checking the financial markets in real time in contrast to waiting to see how they did over the course of a week or month. Real-time information can be falsely alarmist.

The Internet isn't going anywhere, but I have a second objection to smartphone use. From experience I know that a country's level of "happiness" falls in direct proportion to that country's level of transparency. Before the Internet, young people compared themselves to their peers in school or in their hometown. Today, they contrast themselves, and how they are doing, to peers in every school across the world. Once, when children graduated high school, odds were good they would lose touch with the friends they had growing up. This wasn't always a bad thing, especially for kids with reputations or kids who had been sorted into a role, or social position, that didn't mirror who they felt they really were. With increased transparency comes higher levels of envy and unhappiness, as well as the death of any hiding spaces. How do you reinvent yourself when the original version lives online forever?

From my perspective, smartphones are squeezing creativity out of society, especially among younger generations. The Internet is analogous to junk food. It satisfies your appetite for 30 minutes, but an hour later you are hungry again. Even Apple CEO Steve Jobs once told a *New York Times* reporter that, "We limit how much technology our kids use at home,"[8] an opinion seconded by Chris Anderson, the former editor of *Wired* magazine: "We have seen the dangers of technology firsthand. I've seen it in myself, I don't want to see that happen to my kids."[9]

Consider Russia, or China, where online media is controlled and monitored. The Russians and Chinese have no concept of a "perfect marriage," nor can they easily access the films and television shows responsible for creating impossible expectations of happiness. Are these countries better or worse off? A lot of things are better imagined than seen. We may believe we want and deserve infinite amounts of data, but in truth, we can't handle it, and it merely stirs up our appetites. That said, technology is not the problem: imbalance is.

What, you may wonder, did this jumble of observations and clues about American life have to do with a southern supermarket chain on the ropes, wrestling with local and online competition? A lot, in fact. It bears repeating that America has created a brand around concepts like "freedom" and "individuality." America is a country, but it's also a collection of ideas and aspirations. Yet in my experience, the very last thing the United States actually had was freedom, or even individuality. From the moment I entered the country, I saw sign after sign telling me I had to do this, or that, but that it was "for my own safety." Please remove your shoes, belt and laptop *for your own safety*. The sidewalk is under construction *for your own safety*. Bottles of Purell hand-sanitizing lotions are situated every few feet at the airport *for your own safety*. Americans kept being told that they were free, but were they really? Was there any space in America to be different? With Lowes, I would give it my best shot.

A LOT OF THE WORK I've done in the United States is centered in New York and Los Angeles, places that are hardly mirror images of the rest of America. Did I know, someone asked me later, that I was working not in the faster-paced East Coast, or the trendier, more appearance-oriented West Coast—did I know, in fact, that I was working in the American *South*? No: I knew only that I liked what I saw of North and South Carolina, and I liked the people, too. Without realizing it, when I came up with a set of new concepts for Lowes, I was responding to the fact that North Carolina resembles neither New York nor Los Angeles. I was responding instead to the gated communities, and the look-alike homes.

From my outsider's perspective, many of the neighborhoods and gated residences I saw in North Carolina couldn't help but remind me of Disneyland. The pathways were immaculate. Everything felt manicured. Each tree was planted a certain distance away from the next tree. There were no restaurants or shopping centers nearby. If you wanted to shop, or eat out, you got inside your car, and onto a highway. My Subtext Research revealed that the women I met cared less about the time they spent in their cars than they did about leaving the safety nets they called home. Distance wasn't an issue; leaving the safe space was. In general, their lives as nonworking wives and mothers revolved around routines and rituals, with their cars becoming almost like small houses on wheels.

One of the first things I noticed as I made my way around the American South was the lack of community. There were no town squares. The downtowns were empty. What's more, church attendance was down across the United States, a fact confirmed by numerous recent studies. In 2015, a Pew Survey of 35,000 adults revealed that the number of Americans who identified themselves as "Christian" was at its lowest point in history at 70.6 percent, 7 points lower than its 2007 figure of 78.4 percent, a decline happening all over the United States, including the Bible Belt.[10] According to the *New York Times,* an increasing number of ex-Christians "have joined the rapidly growing ranks of the religiously unaffiliated or 'nones': a broad category including atheists, agnostics and those who adhere to 'nothing in particular.'"[11] Added the *Times,* "There are few signs that the decline in Christian America will slow." The essence of community had dispersed onto highways and into strip malls and shopping centers, or else it had migrated online onto social media. Americans, I knew, would travel miles to get a feeling of belonging and community—the same kinds of community, I might add, that I'd seen in the town squares of Krasnoyarsk, Samara, Yakutsk and Novosibirsk.

What defines a community? The answer I've come up with, which draws from my experiences in countries including Lebanon, New Zealand, Germany, Colombia and Italy, is this: communities come together in the face of conflict and disagreement. When North American tourists come home from a vacation in Europe, often the first story out of their mouth has to do with an incident of antagonism they observed. Parisians, for example, understand that unless they demand a certain cut of meat, or a ripe cheese, they will probably not get what they want. Europeans are comfortable with indignation and making a fuss. If, during a European vacation, Americans observe an altercation or an argument in a French *marche* or an Italian restaurant, they remember it. When other people are arguing, the crowd around them comes together as a community.

Again, Lowes was up against half-a-dozen food retailers, and it couldn't compete with either the Internet or with Walmart and Target on prices. In what ways, then, could it compete? I'd gathered a notebook of clues about American culture, but when it came time to interview consumers inside their homes, a decisive fragment of small data came from the frogs adorning the home of a 52-year-old housewife and mother.

Frog plant holders. Frog door guards. Frog lawn figurines. Frogs half hidden behind bushes in the garden. Inside her house were frog doll holders, even a frog Scotch tape dispenser. Not only frogs, but other animals, too, stone or stuffed, ranging from koala bears to owls. After visiting nearly a dozen homes, it was clear that many of the women I'd interviewed had never quite outgrown their childhoods. They weren't at all embarrassed about setting out a stuffed dog on their couch, or a teddy bear on their mantelpiece. One woman even kept Christmas lights and decorations strung and lit all year round.

After my work in Russia, I'd made it a habit to study refrigerator door magnets. Most American fridges had at least a couple. In contrast to Russian fridges, they served double-duty by pinning photos in place. In most, the photograph of my hostess had been taken a decade earlier, often during the first blush of marriage. Perhaps she and her groom were drinking from a single glass, with two straws. Or they were at Disneyland, with Mickey Mouse or Goofy or Cinderella behind them, or at the Grand Canyon, or in Florida or Los Angeles, relaxing by a hotel pool.

America reminded me of Russia in other ways, too—namely, the uncannily similar neighborhoods. The houses and communities in North Carolina were more upmarket, carefully choreographed versions of the ones I had seen across the Russian Far East. How different, after all, is a look-alike house from a look-alike apartment building? The spacing between the trees, the foliage, the homes and the walkways all followed the same emotional rules. Behind the walls of a gated community, conflict was rare, but so, too, was animation or spontaneity. In common with Russia, American children seldom play outdoors. Russia can use the excuse of cold weather, but in the United States, the daily torrent of bad news from televisions and smartphones leads most parents to believe that murder or abduction lies at the end of their driveways. In both countries, men escape. In Russia, men disappear on fishing boats weighed down with cases of vodka. In American, men go golfing.

In an era of pervasive solipsism, where we hear the continuous refrain that technology has unified the world as never before, community in America was vanishing, eroded by big-box stores, a homogenous landscape and the Internet. The American women I met were kind, generous people, but they seemed as isolated as the women I'd met in Russia. They spent most of their time inside their cars. They traveled in lockstep to malls and shopping centers whose density falsely replicated that of cities. Outside their marital and family lives, they never made physical contact with one another. Many were also preoccupied with their children's food allergies. One mother I met had four children, each one with a different allergy, which meant she had to cook five separate meals every night. Fearing that their children might fall behind socially and academically, the mothers I met devoted so much time driving and coordinating their kids' schedules that they had no time left for themselves, or for much of anything else, in fact.

How did this pertain to Lowes? On the basis of my Subtexting, I knew that many consumers were ambivalent about shopping there. Lowes was too "corporate," some said. More than one woman told me that Lowes didn't feel "local" enough. Many told me that Trader Joe's and Whole Foods had more of a "family" feel. One man praised Lowes

wine and beer selection, before telling me about a supermarket he'd
been to once in Milwaukee that allowed customers to sip beer while
they were shopping. Still, there seemed to be consensus around a single
item. "One of the first things I smell when I go into Lowes is the rotisserie chicken," one woman told me. "They have just come out of the
oven. I buy one almost weekly." Every customer I spoke to, it seemed,
loved Lowes chicken, and not only its taste, either. Lowes time-stamped
its broiled chickens so that shoppers could tell how long they had been
sitting there.

From what I'd observed about the larger culture, Americans were
in need of an escape, or reprieve, from the sameness of their lives. A
current of tedium and familiarity runs through every culture, but the
uniformity of the American shopping landscape had drained away an
element of unexpectedness. As Paulo Coehlo wrote once, "If you think
adventure is dangerous, try routine. It is lethal." No wonder Americans
were so smitten with their smartphones, which gave them a simulacrum
of stimulation that many of their physical environments lacked. Just as
I'd done in Russia, in Lowes I needed to create an oasis, a destination
for dreaming. If possible I would also restore a feeling of community
that most Americans didn't even realize they were missing.

In Mamagazin I'd created an oasis—a concept I would have never
been able to come up with if I hadn't traveled and worked in Saudi Arabia. That said, what did Russia have that many parts of America didn't?
Community. Despite the coldness, and the hardships of daily life, cities like Krasnoyarsk and Samara still had a strong sense of solidarity.
I'd felt it in the courtyard chess matches, in the sights and sounds of
Russian children playing outdoors, captivated by an object as simple as
a rock. Spending time in Russia was, in some ways, like glimpsing an
earlier version of the American small town before the arrival of online
"connectivity."

As the Internet slowly penetrated the more rural areas of Russia, I
knew that the community feeling I'd witnessed was probably on its way
out. The question was, could I somehow bring it back to the American South, a region where community had been splintered by cars,

highways, deserted downtowns and heads bent in seeming prayer over smartphones? Could I help reverse the fortunes of a southeastern supermarket by appropriating a slowly vanishing concept from a communist country where freedom, at least as Americans understood and defined the term, was restricted?

BEFORE I DID ANYTHING ELSE, I first had to create within Lowes what I call a Permission Zone. This is a term I use to refer to a moment, or an environment, that allows consumers to "enter" an alternate emotional state. A Permission Zone can be literal, like a zoo, a ferry ride or a movie theater, or even a fast-food restaurant where we eat the foods we generally avoid. (Little wonder that fast-food companies have had no success selling salads or fruit, as the impulse to eat fast food is all about entering a Permission Zone where we permit ourselves to gorge on greasy, un-nutritious food.) Five Guys, for example, is a highly successful hamburger chain with 1,000 locations that showcase bags of potatoes leading from the entrance up to the counter—giving customers "permission" to eat French fries, even though fries are packed with carbohydrates, and the frozen potatoes for sale at the supermarket are about as unhealthy as any food on the market.

A Permission Zone can be linguistic, too. If you've ever sat in a meeting, or had a conversation with someone you don't know well, you probably remember the first time one of you swears. Without even realizing it, you've just granted the other people in the room permission to use profanity. You can almost feel the unbuckling of formality in the room, and from that point on, everyone at the table will begin swearing.

The Permission Zone I needed to create in Lowes came as a direct result of the clues I'd picked up about American culture. After all, I kept coming back to that one word, *fear.* Americans believed they lived in the freest nation on earth, but did they? When was the last time most Americans felt genuinely free? The answer: when they were children.

The Somatic Marker Hypothesis is a term coined by neuroscientist and author Antonio Damasio in his 1994 book *Descartes' Error:*

Emotion, Reason and the Human Brain. In it, Damasio describes in this hypothesis a mechanism wherein our brains modify and bias our emotional responses to decision making. If you've ever placed your hand on a hot stove and got burned, your brain remembers that moment. But rather than putting your hand on the same stove every night from that point on, and hoping that the outcome will be somehow different, we become cautious around ovens and burners. Credit this behavior to the somatic marker in our brains that permanently marks our experience, using an equation that goes like this: hot oven = the probability of pain. Some somatic markers are conscious, others unconscious, but most are forged from long-buried past experiences. I tell audiences, for example, that the World Trade Center attacks of September 11, 2001, comprise a negative somatic marker. We all remember where we were when it happened and who we were with. But do we remember what we had for dinner on our birthdays last year? That's the difference between a somatic marker and a typical memory.

Damasio's Somatic Marker Hypothesis has always intrigued me in the process of brand building, considering that our brains typically "flag" the intersection of two dissonant images. Out of the thousands of hours of television commercials we are exposed to every year, why do we recall at most only two or three? Why, for example, do we remember the Geico lizard? The answer? Because a lizard and life insurance have nothing in common. The same is true for a cymbal-playing bunny and an Energizer battery. If someone brings up *The Godfather,* what is your first association? Most people will say "horse's head," in reference to a scene in the book and the movie where a Hollywood film producer who has angered the mob boss, Don Corleone, awakens to a blood-soaked bed and the head of his favorite stallion under his sheets.

To that end, and as a response to the absence of conflict in American life, I created my first somatic marker: I insisted that rectangles, not circles, dominate the new Lowes. Squares, after all, are edgy and, to Americans, unfamiliar. From now on, I told management, Lowes supermarkets would sell only square cakes inside square containers. My goal wasn't just to overturn the tacit national predilection for circularity; it was to wake shoppers up by forcing them to operate by someone else's rules. To accompany the square cake concept, we hired a singer to sing a song whose melody was deliberately wavy and circular. A square cake. A circular song. A somatic marker. Another reason why I introduced the square cake concept was because it subverts the rules—with rare exceptions, cakes are supposed to be round—thereby giving shoppers "permission" to break the rules (of their diet). Even though they are made of mostly natural ingredients, and with real butter and whipped cream in the frosting, I needed Lowes cakes to make a dramatic statement in order to stand out from all the other "chemical" cakes typically on display.

Manufacturing square cakes was only the first step. The second was to create a sense of storewide community. Based on my experience that people come together in the presence of disagreement, I set myself the task of igniting in-store conflict. As I wrote earlier, based on my Subtext Research, there was a consensus that the best thing at Lowes was its rotisserie chicken. Even rival supermarket executives had nice things to say about Lowes' chickens. The problem was, at first I had nothing to build on but the promise, the anticipation and the taste of the chicken. Not least, in a digital era where the concept of anticipation is disappearing, I wanted to reintroduce the concept of craving, as studies show that the more anticipation a brand, or an event, can create, the more people enjoy it when it finally shows up.

Most Americans who came of age in the 1970s remember the *Back to the Future* film franchise. Michael J. Fox played an adolescent boy who, with the help of a mad scientist, is transported back in time, where he has to play matchmaker for the high-school couple who will eventually marry and become his parents, thereby assuring his own existence. *Back to the Future* inspired my next idea. Why that film, and not another? I chose a movie it was safe to assume most adults had seen in their own teens or early twenties. Three decades later, I wanted to give them permission to feel like a child again, this time inside a Lowes supermarket.

A few months later, Lowes Chicken Kitchen was up and running. Imagine a stand-alone counter selling chickens and only chickens, manned by an employee wearing a specially tailored Chicken Hat. He's engaged in perpetual disagreement with his rival, who stands behind a second kiosk, the SausageWorks, and is dressed as *Back to the Future*'s Doc Brown. With the help of Lowes management, I created scripts for both characters, and asked them to remain in character and spend all day bickering and hollering at each other.

Again, when people witness disagreement—in this case, orchestrated, cartoonish conflict—they not only feel more alive, but the "community" feeling that conflict generates ripples through every department and aisle of the store. In no time at all, huge crowds had formed around the Chicken Kitchen and the SausageWorks. At first, shoppers looked concerned. Then, when they realized it was a game, they came together as a single tribe. Today, as a result of the Mad Professor at the sausage counter "fighting" with the proprietor of the Chicken Kitchen, Lowes not only sells more chickens and sausages, it sells more of *everything*.

What's more, every time a chicken comes out of the oven, Lowes' proprietary "Chicken Dance" song plays over the store's loudspeakers. Overseen by a stage manager, every member of Lowes staff participates in the dance and the song, creating exactly what the local community craved: a sense of belonging. No matter where they were in the store, customers stopped what they were doing and began dancing. It sounds ridiculous, and it was, but it was ridiculous in an un-self-conscious, liberating way. For a few minutes, shoppers felt free to behave like children again. Today, Lowes follows an internal rule: everyone from senior management to hourly wage employees should be prepared to participate in the Chicken Dance. If they don't feel like it, well, they simply do not fit into the organization.

It's worth taking a short detour to say a few words about the visual representation of animals across the world. In 2014, the Copenhagen Zoo sparked international outrage by euthanizing a healthy, year-and-a-half-old giraffe, which was then dismembered before an audience and fed to the zoo's lions and tigers. European zoos have a narrow gene pool, and zoo administrators, defending their decision, told reporters they were concerned about the risk of inbreeding. "The emotional debate over animal euthanasia also reflects a cultural divide between the United States and Europe, which is relatively more open to euthanizing animals in the name of conservation and ensuring genetic diversity," the *New York Times* noted. Which is another way of saying that across Europe, a certain hardheaded common sense trumps sentimentality.

The smiling chicken logo atop the Lowes Chicken Kitchen was, of course, a deliberate attempt to de-couple the animals themselves from the products on sale. This is a rule of thumb in the United States, but nothing you would ever see in Europe. Europeans have known extensive food shortages, and rationing, and Americans, fortunately, never have. When US tourists visit a *marche* or *charcuterie* in France, many are startled and even repulsed by the displays of meat and fowl and fish. A dead rabbit unmistakably resembles a dead rabbit; a turkey still wears its comb and claws. Contrast this presentation to the meat and chicken for sale in the United States, which arrives precut in a white or black Styrofoam container, as severed from the actual animal and the way it met its death as possible.

My belief? The American perspective on animals, and the death of animals, can be traced back to the books and films they read and watched as children, whether it was *Bambi, Dumbo, Lady and the Tramp* or E. B. White's *Charlotte's Web* and *Stuart Little.* Snow White and Cinderella, after all, are surrounded by talking birds and animals, and the idea of animals as protective, and near-human, stretches as far back as the popular mythology of cows and donkeys guarding Jesus in his manger.

IT WAS ONE THING to create a sense of theater and community inside Lowes, but I was convinced that two additional techniques would ensure that Lowes customers remained loyal to the supermarket. The first requires some context. In most parts of the world, at least in the West, men and women exchange business cards reflexively and thoughtlessly. The gesture is automatic, and even indifferent. Businesspeople will tell you that almost all of the business cards they receive end up in a stack of other look-alike cards, or placed inside a Rolodex, never to be looked at again.

But in Japan, the exchange of business cards is formal and ceremonial. A Japanese businessman hands you his business card using two hands, and at chest level, as if communicating he is giving you his card from his heart. In stores throughout China and Japan, employees also take enormous pains wrapping and boxing objects. In some Tokyo stores, clerks spend up to 45 minutes carefully packaging a customer's purchase. When a Japanese butcher hands a customer a steak, he doesn't merely slap it on the counter. He intricately folds the butcher paper around the beef. Next, he comes out from behind the counter, and places the folded beef in the consumer's hands. The effect is twofold. First, shoppers leave the store feeling that the employees who work there care about them as individuals. Second, by using both hands to place the package in the customer's hands, an employee is indirectly "holding" a stranger's hands, drawing him or her into a kind of intimacy, which as humans we can't help but reciprocate.

Not only that, but when we use both hands to give something to someone else, they automatically receive it with two hands. I instructed the hosts of both the Chicken Kitchen and the Sausage Works to wrap and present their wares to shoppers using just this method. By doing so, both convey to consumers that what they have just received is special, and even exceptional, and that the person giving it and the person receiving it are just as exceptional. As I wrote earlier, one of the measures of a country's happiness is its natives' capacity to physically touch one another, and in some small way, I wanted to restore an aspect of tactility that most Americans didn't know was missing.

This new "rule," I hoped, might even create a sense of employee pride. Lowes employed approximately 100 employees per store. Most showed up for work in the early morning or midafternoon, changed into their tan caps and black aprons, worked six- or eight-hour shifts, changed back into their clothes and went home, only to return the next day. Most were understandably unskilled college students, or high-school kids looking to make extra money. Still, I couldn't help but think back on the days where cities and small towns had butchers or fishmongers proud of both their profession and expertise. Today, with butchers and seafood shops a vanishing species, the pride that came along with that identity has also disappeared.

Within the French and Italian hospitality industries, food service employees take pleasure in being the best at what they do. They may be the finest oyster shucker, the most knowledgeable vintner, an expert cheese purveyor. Toiling in an American supermarket is widely presumed to be a stopgap job, seldom a vocation. My hope was that by retraining Lowes employees and teaching them a new way to interact with customers, and wrap and hand over their cuts of meat with care, some employees would begin to feel, for the first time in some cases, proud of what they did.

THERE WAS ONE MORE SECTION of the store to tackle, and that was the produce section. In response to consumers letting me know they would be more likely to buy local produce grown by area farmers, Lowes rolled out a new initiative to ensure that its fruits and vegetables were as fresh as possible, and also locally sourced. Along the way I helped management redesign the store's fruit and produce section by using a wide variety of symbols intended to make shoppers feel "close to the earth," including wicker handle baskets and chalkboards on which the current market prices were scrawled in chalk. We renamed this new section "Pick and Prep."

By evoking farms and fresh produce, this new Pick and Prep section subconsciously evokes the ideas "Made in the U.S.A." and "Healthy" and "Community" and "Mom" and "Table" and "Kitchen." Lowes teamed up with farmers to create a "community table," helping shoppers connect with the local farming community. Lowes Pick and Prep staffers also took special courses where they not only learned how to cut fruit efficiently, but also how to create fruit sculptures, which attracted the attention of children. (If fruit is "fun," children will eat it.)

By positioning Pick and Prep in a part of the store geographically detached from the rest of the aisles, Lowes communicates to shoppers that fruits and vegetables are essential to a healthy life, and shouldn't have to share physical space with mass-produced, chemical-laden factory foods. In turn, if fruits and vegetables are kept separate, most consumers will pay a premium price for them.

What I tried to do at Lowes is, in fact, just the beginning of what bricks-and-mortar stores can do to wage battle against larger Internet retailers. Why not revolutionize what the inside of a supermarket looks like? What if a supermarket could create fresh yogurt on the spot, or even fresh baby food? In my work across the globe, any number of mothers have told me that their babies dislike the taste of homemade food. New mothers are preoccupied with freshness, but few have any interest in buying a squash or a sweet potato, grinding it into single-serve portions, and throwing away what's left. (But we'll come back to that later.)

Amazon, and even Walmart, can't begin to compete against freshness delivered literally a minute or two after a shopper has placed an order. Nor, it seemed, at least in North and South Carolina, were any local supermarkets equipped to compete with the new Lowes, where sausage sales rose several thousand percent in only two months, and chicken sales increased 120 percent. Inside the store, the environment had been transformed. It now felt casual, welcoming, playful, the layout one of structured chaos, creating an illusion of improvisation and even wildness while bounded by pathways, trees and roadways. Like the courtyards in eastern Siberia, the new Lowes was built around solid values and community and the concept of "local." Also in the works was a Beer Den—a place where, if they wanted, men could relax and kick back a beer as their wives did the shopping. Victoria's Secret has a "parking lot" for men in many of its outlets—a seating area with high walls on each side where males can bide their time as their wives, girlfriends or daughters shop. The Beer Den was Lowes' version of this parking lot, helping to increase the amount of time both female and male customers spent in the supermarket, with no one exerting pressure to hurry up or wrap up.

But if you asked me to convey in a single sentence what the management team working collaboratively brought to Lowes, it was this: we gave shoppers, most of them middle-aged and older, the freedom to be themselves, and to be children again. "'Big data' never told us to build a SausageWorks," a member of Lowes' executive team told me later. "In fact, the opposite is true." The largest untapped desire in America is to be truly liberated. By freedom, of course, I don't mean the kind advertised in slogans, or trumpeted by political leaders, or used to package and sell wars fought thousands of miles away. I mean the freedom that comes from lack of worry, responsibility and self-consciousness, the luxurious liberty, that is to say, that comes from being a kid again.

Which is why, in every single Lowes, we hired a store manager whose only task was to determine whether or not shoppers were happy. They did, too. When people shopped at Lowes, they told me afterward, they felt "at home." Not one of them could tell me why.

CHAPTER 3
THE UNITED COLORS
OF INDIA
SELLING BREAKFAST CEREAL TO TWO
GENERATIONS OF WARRING WOMEN

FOR A LONG TIME I'VE BEEN STRUCK BY HOW EVERY COUN-
try in the world "skims" other cultures, appropriating the best of what
foreign cultures offer, and leaving behind the rest. Across France, for
example, you can find any number of "American diners" that serve
cheeseburgers, hot dogs and French fries to a musical soundtrack of
rock and rockabilly from the late 1950s and 1960s. In the United Kingdom, natives visit nightclubs with names like Malibu, and the Planet
Hollywood chain stretches from the United States to France. Japanese
consumers can visit a Japanese-owned chain known as the Andersen
Bakery, inspired by Hans Christian Andersen, which, ironically, only recently opened its first bakery in Andersen's birthplace, Denmark. Across
the world, diners can eat at a Chinese, Mexican or Italian restaurant,
or at an Outback Steakhouse, the Australian-themed restaurant that
has literally nothing to do with Australia (it was created in 1988 by
four Florida businessmen). But perhaps the all-time clearest example of
skimming from the top of a culture is yoga as it's practiced in the West.

To a melodious soundtrack of low-pitched ragas, students per-
form anywhere from two to three dozen asanas, most of which are

introduced in Sanskrit. Some studios jack up the temperature to over 100 degrees, the goal being to replicate the weather conditions in which Indian men practiced in caves 6,000 years ago. From its beginnings as a meditative, spiritual and philosophical practice, yoga has evolved, at least across the West, into a controlled sport saved from its very strenuousness by an emphasis on breathing and awareness. With yoga, you can appropriate the best of Hindu and Buddhist traditions without ever paying a visit to India.

All these thoughts filled my mind when I traveled to Mumbai and New Delhi on behalf of a global cereal manufacturer. Along with most other forms of packaging, cereal boxes sold in Indian mom-and-pop stores had long been distinguished by eye-catching colors strategically designed to arrest the attention of new mothers. The packaging had worked well for decades, but in 2013, the company couldn't figure out why its most popular breakfast cereal had been steadily losing market share among younger female buyers. Could I help them hatch some ideas about new packaging that would appeal to the brand's demographic?

I wrongly assumed it would be a simple assignment. I had no idea I would soon be running up against an issue that crosses all castes and classes across India: the combustible relationship between Indian mothers-in-law and their daughters-in-law.

THE BRICS NATIONS—a widely used acronym referring to the developing countries of Brazil, Russia, India, China and South Africa—are often treated as indistinguishable, but nothing could be further from reality. Having run workshops in both China and India, in my experience, China places an emphasis on structure and operations, and creativity is all but nonexistent. India, by comparison, is all about creativity and chaos, with almost no attention paid to structure and operations. (If the two countries merged, they would become a serious threat to Western business.) With a population of 1.3 billion, India is a country of dramatic and sometimes shocking contrasts. The poverty is real and immediate, beggars are everywhere, and the pollution is among the worst in the world. Indian children are more likely to be malnourished than children from Zimbabwe, Somalia and the Democratic Republic of Congo, Africa's three poorest countries,[1] and in Delhi, nearly 5 million school-aged children have irreversible lung damage from that city's air quality, which is twice as bad as Beijing's.[2] The sanitation is poor—one *New York Times* estimate reports that more than 620 million people in India defecate outdoors, with Hindu devotees regularly bathing in the Ganges River, the end-destination of any number of sewage pipes.[3] The infrastructure in even the most modern Indian cities is inadequate for the millions of people who live there, and electrical blackouts take place several times a day.

Yet alongside the literally breathtaking levels of pollution, and the whiskey-brown dust that enshrouds everything from cars to buildings to sidewalks, and the everyday presence of stray mutts, monkeys and cattle, as well as the fumes from nearby trash fires, a visitor can also catch vestiges of tea-caddy British colonialism, as well as dreamlike glimpses of hallucinogenic beauty.

Traveling in India, I was reminded again and again of its extreme contrasts: rich and poor, clean and unclean, modern and traditional. Exit your hotel into the steamy afternoon air, and you'll find that traffic has come to a halt to permit a slow-moving cow to cross the road. (I once led a workshop attended by more than a hundred CEOs on behalf of a large Indian conglomerate. After spending two hours addressing every conceivable local political issue, I made the mistake of saying, "I think it's fair to say that there are no sacred cows left—we've killed them all," when my host sternly reminded me of the expression's very origins.) Some streets, in cities like Mumbai and Delhi, can't even be called streets as the word is traditionally defined. They are more like very large pathways, made up of mud and puddles, and lined by markets selling fruit and vegetables, or meat or fish that has been left hanging too long, or that is squirming with insects, or that has fallen into a puddle, only to be briskly swept off by the store owner and rehung.

Turn another corner, and underneath the glowing emblems of marketing and industry—Coca-Cola, Pepsi, Vodafone—you may catch sight of a proud, exquisitely costumed Indian family on the third day of a four-day wedding ceremony. Or a couple riding a vintage motorbike, a twist of black tailpipe smoke filling the air behind them. The young man wears the classic business outfit—white shirt and black pants—and holding his waist tightly as they race over ruts and potholes is his girlfriend, garbed in a bright cyan-blue dress, both legs swung over to one side of the bike and gingerly suspended only inches from the wheel. The scooter shudders over puddles, splashing other pedestrians, as dogs bark and chickens chatter and cars honk and pedestrians converse in multiple dialects amid the odors of shit, sweat, animals, smoke and mud.

With a population density ten times higher than in the United States, there is nowhere in India anyone can be truly alone, no sidewalk where you are the only pedestrian, no vistas that do not encompass other human bodies. Up, down, sideways: no matter where you look, men, women and children of all ages are hanging from windows, shouting and gesticulating, and on a nearby rooftop you will suddenly catch sight of two naked people in full carnal embrace.

Literally and metaphorically, India has always been a nation blazing with colors, which is why my first night in Mumbai, the question I kept asking myself was, What do colors mean generally—and specifically, in India? I would find out the complex answer when I carried out Subtext Research inside the homes of Indian consumers, only to come face-to-face with the voluble intragenerational waltz that has long existed between Indian mothers and the women, some as young as 15 years old, who have married their sons.

AS ANYONE WHO'S BEEN to the movies or watched television knows, the mother-in-law is the classic butt of any number of stale jokes. She criticizes. She dominates. She butts in. She believes she knows best. In the United States, with families more and more geographically isolated, and the concept of multiple generations living together under one roof a relic of the past, the humor around mothers-in-law feels increasingly dated, like watching a comedy show from the early 1960s.

This isn't true in India, where families are interconnected in ways most Westerners might find hard to fathom. Every year, around 8 million mostly teenaged Indian brides marry young men chosen by their parents. Many don't have the privilege of meeting their new husbands until their wedding day. The *New York Times* reports that if these young women balk at the arranged marriage, "Refusals can be met with violence and, sometimes, murder," adding that in one case in 2014, "a 21-year-old New Delhi college student was strangled by her parents for marrying against their wishes."[4] Once the marriage has taken place, the bride and groom move in with the latter's family, where they remain until their own sons and daughters come of age, at which time the situation repeats itself.

Having moved in with strangers, a new daughter-in-law is expected to cook, clean and, naturally, provide grandchildren, all under the oversight of her mother-in-law. An Indian mother-in-law sheriffs the household, exerting quality-control regulations over every aspect of domestic life. She knows what foods to buy, and the best recipes and cooking techniques. She knows the right way to hold newborn infants and to coax them to sleep. In some extreme cases, a new bride is forbidden to touch, or even speak in front of, their older relatives. The concept of dowry—where a bride's family hands over money or jewelry or other assets to the groom's family as a precondition of marriage—may be formally against the law, but it's still common in more rural areas of the country.

The relationship between Indian daughters-in-law and mothers-in-law, or *mummyji,* the Hindi word for "honored mother," is neither exaggerated nor anecdotal. It is such an issue across India that it has given rise to approximately 50 Hindi-language soap operas known as *saas-bahu,* which can be translated roughly as "mother-in-law, daughter-in-law." The immense popularity of these television shows across Nepal, Pakistan and Bangladesh indicates that saas-bahu isn't a problem restricted to India. Quoted in one newspaper article, Delhi-based journalist Veena Venugopal, author of a 2014 book, *The Mother-in-Law,* says that saas-bahu "is the one relationship that has gone contrary

to the rest of India; it has regressed."[5] Among the most frequent con-
flicts are how the younger woman dresses (provocative attire is unwel-
come), whether or not she works (ideally, she doesn't), her looks (the
bride's beauty reflects on the mother-in-law, as well as on her son), and
whether or not she observes the rules and religious rites of the household (mandatory). Venugopal asserts that saas-bahu disputes have actually worsened over the past two decades. She blames the relationship
for social problems ranging from increased domestic violence to the
attrition rate of women in the workplace. Saas-bahu can even lead to
violence. In 2013, the *Economist* reported that "of the 12,000 prisoners
at Delhi's sprawling Tihar jail, a portion of female inmates are kept in
a dedicated, barracks-like 'mother-in-law wing.'"[6] Most are mummyji,
who assaulted their daughters-in-law "in a fit of anger."[7]

Some speculate that the mummyji's oversized power across India is
simply a reenactment of the older women carrying out what was done to
them when they were young brides, as well as a stark example of what
little power females have in Indian culture. Whatever the case, I had no
idea that when I flew into Mumbai, I was walking into a war zone.

THE SHANTYTOWNS OF MUMBAI have been written about at length,
but as we will see later, they differ from Brazilian favelas. Corruption
in Brazilian favelas is mostly unchecked, with drugs and drug deal-
ers controlling sections of the neighborhoods, and regular police raids
replete with machine-gun fire, after which life returns to normal. In
contrast to the favelas of Rio de Janeiro or São Paulo, Indian slums are
not gunfire zones, nor do they inhabit prime urban real estate. They are
crooked, disjointed, improvised settlements, typically slapped together
from a mix of plywood, plastic, corrugated strips of metal and cardboard. The walls are thin, the roofs tin, and with some shantytowns
boasting a population of a million people per square mile, it can seem
as if the homes serve as rooms in one huge, chaotic, snakelike house.
The social connection among neighbors is strong, as is the ubiquity of
Hinduism, which is less a religion—there is no word in Sanskrit for
"religion"—than it is a way of life. It goes without saying that there are

no street numbers, which is why having a local Indian guide is a necessity, though even veteran guides occasionally have to rely on a penciled map drawn by a neighbor.

The daughter-in-law is invariably the person who opens the door and greets a visitor. Her mother-in-law waits inside, as she is, literally and symbolically, the proprietor and ruler of the home.

Across India, the mummyji I met shared a similar, even classic appearance. Most were physically small, in their 50s and 60s, though they looked much older. Almost all of them wore oversized, not entirely clean eyeglasses with thick lenses. Still it wasn't the women's size I first noticed, it was their colorful clothing: dark blues, pale ambers, powdery greens, ocean-blues. From previous work I had done in India, I knew that the concepts of "luxury," "rich" and "aspirational" are linked to the widespread use of colors, largely because most of India's milestones, ceremonies and rituals—from births to weddings to deaths—are defined and even dominated by colorful cloths. Color matters in India, and it begins early on in life.

A case in point is the soap brand Lifebuoy, which came to market in England at the turn of the nineteenth century. No longer available in the United States or England, Lifebuoy is still the most popular brand of antibacterial soap in India. The bars themselves are larger than most hand soaps—they are as big as an adult human hand—but far more compelling than its size is Lifebuoy's signature dark-red color. It's safe to say that every single Indian child is born and raised with a bright-red bar of Lifebuoy soap, a habit, and a color preference, that is passed along to the next generation. Lifebuoy's red color contrasts deeply with nature—nothing about the soap could be said to look or feel remotely "natural"—yet one of the strongest national symbols of health in India is that of Switzerland, and the Red Cross, an image used in any number of Indian pharmacies and medical clinics, which may help explain Lifebuoy's popularity across India. Unilever, which owns Lifebuoy, has tried to release the soap in neighboring markets without even a fraction of the popularity the soap enjoys in India, largely because of India's singular relationship with color. Lifebuoy's success soon spread to the packaged goods world. Manufacturers rolled out a rainbow of colors on every pack, the better to attract an entirely new generation of consumers.

It may be hard to believe, but our color preferences often form based on the colors of our bedroom walls as children. A few years ago, a European multinational asked me to help them align the nearly half-a-dozen companies in its portfolio under a single color. It wasn't simply a question of deciding on red, or yellow, or orange, or green. Every man and woman in the business meeting had their own ideas, or preferences, meaning that I not only had to find the right color but also bring together a dozen senior executives, all of whom believed their color choice was the correct one.

The first thing I did was convince them that our choices, preferences and tastes have their origins in childhood. Over the next week, I asked each board member to write down the colors of the walls of their childhood bedrooms. If they could bring in a photograph, even better. A week later, when we met again, I tacked the colors and photographs onto a PowerPoint presentation. For the next hour, we flipped through the childhood bedrooms belonging to the members of the executive team. In the end, there was a roughly 80 percent correlation between the color each person had chosen to represent the "family" of companies, and the color on the walls of his or her childhood bedroom. Not surprisingly, it turned out to be color that helped me understand why cereal sales were flagging in India.

ONCE A VISITOR IS INSIDE an Indian home, a few things become immediately apparent. The daughter-in-law may have been the one to greet you at the door, but once you take a seat, she sits there quietly, saying nothing, unless she is called upon to speak, at which point she shyly volunteers a few words. (Even in homes where the saas-bahu relationship was apparently serene, I'd say almost all could best be described as "love-hate.")

The larger point is that conversation starts and stops with the mother-in-law. Early on I understood that unless I was able to establish a rapport with her, the chances were good that I would never hear the truth about anything. Which is why I came into the house armed with two fail-safe conversation points: tea and Bollywood movies.

Tea, of course, is a given. A host always offers a cup of tea to a visitor who, in turn, is expected to compliment its taste or flavor, though figuring out what Indians mean when they shake their heads—the motions range from up and down, side to side, quick and vigorous, tilted to the right, tilted to the left, one nod, two nods—can be a science by itself. In some cases, praising the tea I was offered brought me nowhere—the mothers-in-law, stingy with their smiles, nodded at the compliment. That's when I rolled out my second strategy, this one inspired by my work in North Carolina for Lowes, where I'd borrowed a character from the *Back to the Future* movie franchise.

Before arriving in India, I'd watched anywhere from between 70 to 80 Bollywood movies. The term *Bollywood* refers to the Mumbai-based Hindi language film industry and the films under its umbrella, which are shot using an assortment of dialects from mixed Hindi to Urdu. Some Bollywood films are mythical and romantic—*Mughal-e-Azam,* for example, chronicles the love between a prince and a courtesan—while others, like *Lagaan,* which chronicles the efforts of a small Indian village banding together against colonialist rule to play cricket, are fiercely nationalistic. Speaking generally, most Bollywood films are lighthearted and tend to illustrate a serious cultural theme in a lightly comedic fashion.

India is a film-obsessed country, and Bollywood films serve as crucial reference points for the population. And not just a small or even a majority demographic, either, but literally 100 percent of all Indians. The work I do depends on establishing trust as soon as possible, and I knew that if I could come up with a well-known fragment of dialogue from a Bollywood movie that a mother-in-law was bound to have seen when she was a teenager, I stood a better chance of creating cordiality.

I was relieved to find that, thanks to the Bollywood films, the mothers-in-law gradually softened to my presence in their homes. It was now time to ask permission—because I'd been informed that a visitor must *always* ask formal permission—to engage with the daughter-in-law. It was only when I managed to physically separate the two women that the truths underlying their relationship became clear.

As the mother-in-law took me into the kitchen, telling me what techniques she used to make her tea taste as flavorful as it did, my assistant remained in the sitting area with the daughter-in-law. As I continued conversing with the older woman, my assistant began politely interrogating the younger woman. I was now free to ask the mother-in-law what her true feelings were about her daughter-in-law, while in the next room my assistant did the same, but in reverse. By interviewing the two women, 20 years apart in age, I was able to engage in an intimate investigation of the world as two generations of Indian women perceived it.

I eventually steered the subject to food, and food preparation. *Who does the cooking in your household?* was the question that I asked most often. It wasn't a trivial question, either, considering that the answers I received would determine whether the breakfast cereal should target the mothers-in-law or the daughters-in-law.

Unfortunately, this proved to be a contentious issue. Both the daughters-in-law and the mothers-in-law claimed that they were in charge of the kitchen.

Even for someone who tries to make his living from his powers of observation, there are some obvious things I fail to pick up when I visit consumers' homes. Remember I usually find myself in an unfamiliar country, where I'm forced to take stock of new faces, new climates, new rulerships, new complexions, new ways of dressing, new customs of behavior. In the Russian Far East, after all, it had taken me a few visits to even notice the refrigerator magnets and the role they played in consumers' lives. In India, I found myself bypassing a piece of small data so commonplace in Indian kitchens it was easy to overlook.

In close proximity to the stove inside every Indian kitchen I visited sat a spice box. In most cases, it was an enclosed, airtight round metal container, similar to a Western cookie tin. It opened to reveal half-a-dozen smaller containers of the most common Indian seeds and powders used for flavoring both sweet and savory dishes. The seeds include cumin, black mustard and fenugreek, while the powders are coriander, turmeric, red chili pepper and garam masala, which is a blend of cinnamon, cardamom, cloves and pepper. The colors are so vivid and otherworldly, the yellows so dramatically yellow, the greens so profoundly verdant, that they can't help but capture a visitor's attention.

It was a small data, but at the time it made little sense to me. The mothers-in-law seemed proprietary about the stove and the oven. Many described the signature dishes they liked to make—the same dishes, it turned out, they had cooked for their own children when they were young. Ten or twenty feet away in the living room, my assistant was getting another story entirely. To hear Indian daughters-in-law tell it, *they* were the ones in charge of all the household cooking, as well as the ones who went shopping, and decided what to buy for their infants.

Everywhere in the world, cooks lay out the spices they use most often within reach of the stove, in the same way casual eaters position the foods and drinks they prefer front and center in their refrigerators. A week into my visit to Mumbai, I started making it a point to ask the Indian mothers-in-law if they would mind showing me the spices inside their spice boxes. The first time one agreed, the spices were positioned in a sequence with no apparent order. Another home, another kitchen, another spice box, and again, the exact same half-a-dozen spices positioned in precisely the same order. The ones nearest the stove and oven were the most colorful ones in the tins—sooty-yellow cardamom, fire-red chili powder—while the more drably colored seeds sat farther away from the stove. Why? One afternoon, as I raced from one home to the next, it hit me.

The powders nearest the stove mimicked the same colors of the clothing worn by most if not all Indian mothers-in-law. Not only that, but they were the same colors highlighted in framed photographs around the house, depicting family ceremonial occasions such as weddings and births. That's when I realized that the spices were trying to tell me something. Contradicting what almost every single daughter-in-law had told my assistant, in fact it was the mothers-in-law who did most of the cooking in Indian households, and the colors of the spices confirmed it.

Still, a single piece of small data is never enough to create a working hypothesis, or a foundation for a business strategy as critical as the overall look and feel of packaging. Around this same time, I asked both the daughters-in-law and the mothers-in-law if I could possibly take a look inside their bedrooms. In most of the daughters-in-law's bedrooms, which they shared with their husbands and more often than not their children, the walls were pale, cream or sand-colored. This wasn't the case with the bedrooms of the mothers-in-law. Their bedroom walls were as colorful as the attire they wore, and the spices with which they cooked. Then I noticed something that would have a strong effect on the colors we eventually placed on our cereal packaging.

In general, we hang things—paintings, posters, mirrors—at the height where we best appreciate them. A painting is always slightly higher than the direct approach. We hang mirrors in such a way that we take in our faces, hair, neck and shoulders. Now and again we position something depending on how it looks from the perspective of a bed, or a couch, or from a place where we're in the habit of sitting. But as I made my way through one bedroom after another, I saw the artwork on the walls was positioned at almost the exact eye level of its owners. Not higher. Not lower. Level. Straight ahead. I filed this fact away in my notebook.

BEFORE GOING ANY FURTHER, here is an experiment for the natives of the Western world. Imagine that you have just removed a load of warm, clean laundry from the dryer. As you transfer the clothes to a basket, a light floral fragrance or the aroma of fresh oranges or lemons envelops you. You may be washing and drying your clothes in the middle of winter, but once you take them out of the dryer, they impart the essence of fruit, and flowers, and spring. Most Americans and Europeans aren't aware of the degree to which advertisers and scent specialists have trained them to believe that the concept of fresh is linked to seasonal flowers, or to citric fragrances, especially in the United States, where fragrance additives tend to be heavy, resonant and unsubtle, with a faint chemical tang.

It's a different story in eastern Europe and in most developing nations. Years ago, when I helped create a laundry detergent brand with a floral scent in Russia, I discovered that what people perceive as "fresh" varies dramatically around the world. As a concept, fresh often bears no relationship to whether a product is actually "fresh" or not. Fresh, I knew from my global studies, had nothing to do with a product's expiration date. In France, for example, "fresh" is routinely used to describe foods or drinks with a limited life span, to impress on consumers the need to cook and eat them quickly. Thanks to the popularity of Picard, the frozen food emporium in France, "frozen" is often seen by consumers as "fresh," as is a screw-top with an unbreakable seal. Conversely, products with a longer shelf life are generally perceived to be "less fresh." Across the world, I often ask consumers to empty the contents of their fridges and then replace every product based on what they perceive to be its freshness. The freshest go on top, while the least fresh items go on the lower shelves. In the United States, I'm often very surprised to find that among the products most consumers consider even fresher than a just-tossed salad are Heinz Tomato Ketchup and Hellman's Mayonnaise.

In the process of figuring out why the new laundry detergent was initially doing so poorly, I learned that Russian consumers there perceived "fresh" differently than Westerners do. In Russia, after it's been washed, clothing is generally hung outdoors on backyard lines. So how do babushkas assess whether or not their clothing has passed the "fresh" test? They hold the piece of clothing close to their noses and inhale a mixture of fabric, wind, soil, damp and the stiffening that comes from textures hanging outdoors in minus-degree temperatures. This aroma is by far the most popular fragrance among the Russian consumers I interviewed, and it explained the slow sales of a flowery-smelling laundry detergent. Floral scents not only had no emotional relevance to Russians, they made Russian men feel self-conscious. Ultimately, I convinced the laundry detergent manufacturer to get rid of the smell entirely. We then rebuilt the fragrance to duplicate the scent of cold air, soil and the outdoors, and the detergent began selling again.

My experience in Russia came to mind once my Subtexting with mothers-in-law and daughters-in-law was done, and I began spending time with young Indian women at local universities, as well as in tea and coffee shops (in India, coffee is sweet and milk-based, and bears no resemblance to the coffee that Westerners drink). My mission was simple: I wanted to understand young Indian women *before* they officially became daughters-in-law. Spending time in their dorm rooms, and scouring their Facebook pages, it became clear to me the extent to which Western imagery dominated their lives. There were photos of Western pop stars, and they had "liked" any number of Western and Korean brands, from Apple to Samsung. Seeking the answer to the question of whether it was the mother-in-law or the daughter-in-law who ran most Indian households, I had become convinced that the daughters-in-law had virtually no place in the Indian kitchen. The colors of the spices had convinced me, and so did the bright colors on the mothers-in-law's bedroom walls.

I had been ignoring something else entirely—something essential, and ultimately game-changing. It was a scent. It was light. It smelled like roses. In short, mixed in with the fragrances of Indian spices and powders was the faint vestige of a floral dishwashing detergent. It was an extremely Western fragrance, one I knew that Indian mothers-in-law, schooled as Russian babushkas were on the natural, outdoorsy concept of "fresh," would never use. What, then, was this very Western scent of scattered daffodils and roses doing in a traditional Indian home?

Something was off. Something was wrong. How had floral scents made their way into India, a country where I knew that "natural" scents of rain and mud had much more emotional resonance to traditional generations? The answer, I realized, was that twenty-first-century Indian daughters-in-law increasingly saw themselves as "modern," and "contemporary," an identity that could be credited to the Internet and to the lower-cost smartphones, known as "feature phones," most of them owned. All of a sudden, the floral scents I'd smelled during my visits to local Mumbai and Delhi colleges made sense. The young women were using floral fragrances because they were living away from home for the first time.

Along with China, as I mentioned earlier, India is one of the most polluted countries on earth. Most young mothers are rightfully concerned about the effects pollution will have on their young children's growth and health. They are aware of India's sanitation problems, and the country's high levels of bacteria, and perhaps even that India is the host to half of the globe's 20 most polluted cities.[8] In contrast to the Western world, where people have arguments over natural versus organic, *natural* is a relatively new trend in India, especially as it relates to babies. What, then, from the perspective of young Indian mothers, was the color most associated with "natural"?

So I carried out an experiment. I asked the mothers-in-law and the daughters-in-law to rank a range of colors from the "freshest" to the "least fresh." A week later, I tallied up the results and was baffled to find that the two groups had radically different, even opposing definitions of what constituted "fresh"—that they literally perceived the world using separate senses. To Indian mothers-in-law, "natural" referred to the colors of their cooking spices. The more florid and flamboyant the colors, the fresher they perceived those spices to be. Deep purples, limpid oranges, fluorescent yellows: these were the freshest colors an older generation could imagine, a preference that trickled down to the clothing they wore. Older Indian women would dress themselves using the same colors of the spices they used, in order to look, and feel, at their "freshest." Younger Indian women, on the other hand, increasingly schooled on Western imagery and perceptions, unanimously preferred green.

It was a tie, just as it was frequently a "tie" between mothers-in-law and daughters-in-law for dominance and control within Indian households. Ultimately, though, neither group was in complete control of the domestic front. Both, and neither, were in charge of the home. But generally speaking, Indian mothers-in-law were in charge of cooking, while their daughters-in-law were in charge of tidying up and dishwashing.

What to do? The conclusion I came to was both obvious and, from my perspective at least, a big challenge. The cereal manufacturer was dealing with two radically differently demographics that not only shared a home but also shared "emotional custody" of the family. Whatever new packaging we came up with had to satisfy two warring decision makers. Indian mothers-in-law were enticed by vivid, colorful packaging designs, made up of colors that daughters-in-law saw as unnatural, unorganic and artificial.

I had to figure out a packaging strategy to entice two generations simultaneously. To ensure I did it right, I had to perceive the world from the perspective of a much older person, a strategy I'd been using for many years, and one that began in the United Kingdom.

IN 1981, A COLLECTION of elderly New England men disembarked from a van and made their way inside a former New Hampshire monastery that had been retrofitted for the experiment that was about to take place—what its creator, Harvard psychology professor Ellen Langer, called the "Counterclockwise Test." All of them were males in their 70s and early 80s, with many suffering from the physical indignities endemic to that age. But once they passed through the doors, a radically different scene, and even year, greeted them. It was 1959 all over again. Nat King Cole and Perry Como serenaded them from a vintage radio. A black-and-white TV screened variety shows and even commercials from 1959. There were no mirrors. The men had been given explicit instructions: They were not only encouraged to exchange reminiscences about this era, but as much as possible, to become the same age they were nearly two decades earlier. They were urged to refer to events that took place in 1959 in the present tense.

A week later, a second group of males the same age were asked to duplicate this same experiment. This second group was asked only to think and speak nostalgically about the experience, as opposed to literally impersonating their younger selves. Before entering the monastery, both sample groups agreed to have their vital signs, including vision, hearing, memory and flexibility, assessed by a medical team.

This "psychological intervention," as the *New York Times* called it,[9] was conjured by Langer who, over the course of a brilliant academic career, believed that in order to improve their health, older people needed a jolt, or a trigger, that would fool their own minds and bodies into healing themselves.

Five days later, both groups of men had their vital signs retested. In every case, their posture and gaits showed signs of improvement. Their eyesight and hearing were both better. Physically, both groups were more agile and flexible. They even scored higher on IQ tests. But the men who had been asked to pretend they were the same age they'd been in 1959 showed markedly more improvement than the group who'd been asked to simply swap reminiscences. As Langer told the *New York Times,* the men had "'put their mind in an earlier time,' and their bodies went along for the ride."[10]

Langer's study was very much on my mind when I began working in England in the early 2000s on a project for Saga, the English equivalent of America's AARP, an organization aimed at men and women over 50. Saga had asked me if I could help them identify and understand its elder demographic, with the goal of helping to design a cruise ship, the *Saga Sapphire,* that would make the passengers feel at home. Intuitively, I knew I wanted to fill the cabin suites with the same furniture, music, appliances, colors and games these men and women had grown up with in the 1950s and 1960s, the goal being to cement the strongest possible bond between passengers and the era in which they came of age.

A bigger challenge was to ensure that Saga management understood the importance of perceiving the world through the senses of an elder demographic. Most Saga employees were in their 30s and 40s. I asked them to consider the design of the ship by pretending, for 24 hours, what it might feel like to be 75, 80 or even older. I asked them to imagine putting on an outfit similar to those worn by firefighters, to imagine adding aluminum weight to their shoes to detract from their agility, to imagine wearing glasses that blurred their distance vision, earplugs that compromised their hearing, and thick gloves so that when they pressed the elevator buttons, they would know what it felt like to have limited dexterity in their fingers. We proceeded to design the *Saga Sapphire* with these perceptions and experiences in mind. The *Sapphire* proved to be a big success, and it also taught me the importance of putting yourself, literally if possible, in another person's shoes, which I was about to do in India.

THE HABIT OF NOTICING, like letter writing, is a vanishing art, in part because today our cell phones give us an automatic out whenever we are alone with ourselves, away from the usual distractions that keep us from focusing on our surroundings. Even if we weren't seduced by the digital sirens in our hands, it's fair to say that most of us aren't in the habit of stringing together clues as evidentiary; moreover, what if a single clue causes all the others to unravel?

The truth is that sometimes you have to entertain a symphony of insights or observations that at first make no sense, and follow them to wherever they take you. You may in fact end up Small Mining a bunch of clues that lead nowhere. But you may also notice that a narrative has begun forming, that threads connect the figurine on the windowsill with the old, half-tied shoe with the mayonnaise inside the refrigerator—or in this case, that a thread links together the placement of kitchen spices with a generational color preference that's ubiquitous across India.

Understand that even in huge, relatively modern cities like Mumbai, Delhi and Hyderabad—and notwithstanding Walmart, which owns and operates twenty Best Price Modern Wholesale stores in eight Indian states—no organized retail really exists in India. Instead, *Kirana,* or local retail, made up of a congeries of mom-and-pop stores, is the dominant form of buying and selling. Inside these stores, almost every food is sold in a single-serve portion, an essential concept in India, Thailand and the Philippines, where natives lack the space, and the money, to do a single weekly shopping trip.

For the next few days, I stood on the sidewalk and observed the mummyji going in and out of stores. The temperature was close to 100 degrees, but I stayed where I was and tried to see what they saw through their own eyes. I even trailed some mummyji inside, maintaining a discreet distance behind them. Did they glance to their right, or to their left? Did they hesitate? What made them pause? When they reached out for an item, was it at eye level, or below or above eye level?

Similar to how I had asked Saga employees to see the world through the senses of an elder demographic, I was trying to put myself in the shoes of a 50-something Indian female. I went through store after store in an effort to perceive the world from her height. It didn't take me long to notice colors and patterns that people in their 50s weren't able to see. The aging eye is the same all over the world, and most people over the age of 40 are vulnerable to presbyopia, the medical term for the natural hardening of our eyes' natural "zoom" lens. I went so far as to visit an Indian optometrist, who told me that the eyesight of a glasses-wearing population in their 50s and 60s is two or three times worse than the average eyesight of a 40-year-old man or woman. Once I could see for myself the differences between what Indian daughters-in-law perceived versus the mothers-in-law, I had, I believed, the beginning of a solution.

A day later, I had found glasses that duplicated the mothers-in-law's weakening vision. I returned to the stores, this time walking around with my shoulders hunched. I never put on a wig, or makeup, but I came close. By the end of my experiment, I returned to my hotel surprised to learn how unfamiliar the universe was from the perspective of an older Indian female.

But I kept returning to the concept of vision. From an Indian mother-in-law's perspective, almost everything had blurred edges and lines. The only thing she could really make out were colors. The problem was, those she was least able to discern were the same ones— "natural" browns and "fresh" greens—that the daughter-in-law preferred. There were other considerations, as well. From what altitude, or angle, or perspective was the mother-in-law gazing at the breakfast cereal on the store shelf? To understand this question, it's important to grasp a physical phenomenon about supermarkets, and shelving, and the critical role that both darkness and light play.

In supermarket lingo, the "shadow line" refers to the darkness that falls over the top of a package when a supermarket shelf is too deep, or when the overhead light lands at a wrong angle. The mixture of light, and how it strikes a product, tends to leave a lot of products in darkness. This same shadow line had a marked effect on what an Indian mother-in-law saw when she gazed at cereal packaging. At the same time, from her height and perspective, what she saw was, in fact, ideal. There were colors she liked and appreciated the most, the vibrant, vivid, rich-hued ones that conveyed to her that the product in front of her was "fresh."

It was time for me to switch roles and impersonate a straight-shouldered, younger, clear-eyed 20-something Indian daughter-in-law. From her perspective, the world was entirely different. She didn't see the bottom of packages; her glance began at the top of the package and swept downward. Gazing at the cereal packages from a daughter-in-law's perspective, I discovered that the cereal container, flush with bright spice-like colors favored by an older generation, looked no different than a candy box, packed with chemicals and about as far from "fresh" or "natural" as it could be. In contrast, thanks to the shadow line, the mothers-in-law would be able to make out the vivid colors on the bottom, but not the top two inches of the package.

I would have to use two separate—and completely uncomplementary—color codes, and a few weeks later, the cereal manufacturer approved my template for a new package design.

Historically, when a mother-in-law went out shopping with her daughter-in-law, the two of them would disagree, squabble and often leave the store with two different varieties or brands of cereal. From now on, if the two women shopped together, they would both be enticed by the colors of the same package. My solution was to appeal first to the mothers-in-law by decorating two-thirds of the package (the bottom) with rich, bright, spice-inspired colors. I would also add a tactile dimension to one side of the package, to appeal to an older generation's desire to handle products. The top third of the package, which the taller daughter-in-law would see, would be adorned with "natural" browns and greens, as well as a description of the cereal's natural ingredients.

But the package couldn't simply be made up of competing colors; it also needed people on it! In Mexico I first became aware that the experience of bonding between mothers and children is made up of a handful of isolated flashes, or pivot points. Of course, our lives in general are nothing more than moments linked together, but this structure is especially true for first-time mothers and their newborns.

Despite humans' fraught relationship with weight and calories, infants are generally given latitude about how much they eat. A new mother wants her newborn to gain weight. It means the child is healthy and a healthy baby, in turn, tells an inexperienced mother that she is doing something right. In short, a direct correlation exists between a baby's appetite and a new mother's peace of mind. If infants or babies finish their bottles, or clean their plates, mothers gain points, not just in their own eyes, but in the eyes of their husbands or partners, and the culture itself. All around the world, babies are fussy about what they eat and drink, but in Mexico, if a baby rejects a meal his mother has prepared, it is the mother, and not the baby, who receives the blame from her husband. In response, mothers serve their babies even more food. The babies put on weight. If they eventually develop baby chins, all the better. Mothers win, and more to the point, the Mexican culture looks on approvingly.

Each "moment" between infants and mothers lasts around 45 seconds. Among the most potent moments is the one when infants begin to doze in their mothers' arms (and every respondent told me he or she somehow "feels" the baby is getting heavier), followed by the moment when a baby closes his or her eyes to sleep. Other moments include the baby splashing around in the bath, and new fathers engaging or interacting with the baby, though in general dads are rarely central characters, as mothers prefer to be seen as the parent in charge of an infant. In Brazil, and across the developing world, the most popular moment, I knew, was when new mothers realize that their babies are learning new things. Needless to say, these moments are highly emotional in nature, and when I asked Mexican mothers to tell me what they were feeling, they used words like "comfort," "harmony," "trust" and "bond."

From a marketing standpoint, the question was clear: Was there a way to incorporate these moments between mothers and their newborn babies into a product or even a television commercial? Could the cereal manufacturer "own" a universal moment, in the same way that Kodak used to "own" taking photographs, and America Online "owned" You've Got Mail, and Apple today "owns" the left-to-right "Slide to Unlock" finger-swipe, and Volvo "owns" Safety, and Google "owns" Search, and Marlboro "owns" Cowboy? I hired a creative team to help the company understand the essence, and the weight, of every single moment between mothers and their babies. Pictorially speaking, could a photo somehow convey the "heaviness" of the instant that a baby's eyes are beginning to close?

Most cereal packaging around the world depicts a child, but India has the strictest rules against advertising in the world, and prohibits any human representation on package designs. The Indian government doesn't want to encourage young children and mothers to eat breakfast food that is unhealthy or perceived as unhealthy, and they also believe that if products show babies on the packaging, manufacturers might mislead consumers into believing they might someday become as beautiful as the models on the pack.

When we finally rolled out the new packaging design in India, the new graphics showed a baby-sized spoon holding a spoonful of cereal. It was, in short, a Moment. In a populous country, the package emphasized whiteness, sparseness and simplicity. If you look carefully, you will also see something else: two separate sets of colors. One is designed for women anywhere between the ages of 50 and 70, while the other appeals to younger women in their late teens and early 20s. It is the exact same breakfast cereal, the exact same packaging—but unless you were wearing glasses, you would never know the difference.

CHAPTER 4
GETTING A BEAD ON WEIGHT LOSS
(WITH HELP FROM FAST FOOD, A MIDDLE EASTERN MOVIE THEATER AND A HOTEL LAP POOL)

AT OUR CORE, WE'RE ALL MEMBERS OF A TRIBE, OR A SE-ries of tribes, starting with our nationalities and families, and extending to the towns or cities where we live. Our tribal membership and loyalties include where we went to school; the clubs, if any, of which we're members; our neighborhoods; and the region of a country we call home. Gender is tribal. Profession is tribal. Political affiliation is tribal. Religious belief is tribal. Our friend groups are tribal, as is our age and even our appearance.

Friendship may be tribal, but it works the other way around, too. The *bodies* of our friends can affect our own physical appearance. A nearly ten-year-old study in the *New England Journal of Medicine* found that "obesity can spread from person to person, much like a virus . . . When one person gains weight, close friends tend to gain weight too."[1] Explains Harvard professor Nicholas Christakis, a principal investigator in the new study, "One explanation is that friends affect each others' perception of fatness. When a close friend becomes obese, obesity may not look so bad." In short, the *New York Times* article on the study concludes that we alter our concept of what an acceptable body type is on the basis of the people surrounding us.[2]

As everybody knows, the obesity epidemic is increasing worldwide. A decade ago, according to statistics published by the Centers for Disease Control and Prevention, the average American woman weighed 166.2 pounds, which is only slightly less than the average American man weighed in the 1960s. During this same period from 1960 to 2002, the average American male put on 30 pounds on his own.[3] Popular reasons include that Americans are exercising less, and also consuming more cheap, higher-calorie foods; often a single meal contains as many calories as most of us need in a day. Still, in spite of widespread media attention around childhood obesity, a recent *New York Times* article about overweight children noted that, in the United States at least, "Parents increasingly seem to be turning a blind eye as their children put on pounds," adding that around 70 percent of parents of obese daughters "described their children as 'about the right weight,'" a phenomenon that Dr. David Katz, the director of Yale University's Prevention Research Center, dubbed "oblivobesity."[4]

Americans spend more than $100 billion annually on fast food, and fast-food chains have become a big part of everyday life in Europe and the Far East. On my frequent visits to Japan, I've begun seeing a striking number of overweight children, which would have been unheard of 20 years ago. The popularity of McDonald's in Japan, where it has over 3,000 franchises, is likely its affordable "100-yen menu"—US$0.81 at current exchange rates. Such an irresistible bargain has even chipped away at the nation's historic predilection for seafood over meat.

That said, probably the two most overweight regions of the world are Saudi Arabia and Mexico. The tacit cultural connection between a baby's weight and his or her health and happiness is one reason why obesity levels are as high as they are across Mexico and, for that matter, across all of Latin America. In 2013, Mexico overtook the United States as the "most obese country" in the world, with approximately 70 percent of the Mexican adult population considered overweight, including 30 percent of all schoolchildren, and one-sixth of the adult population, or around 10 million people, diagnosed with diabetes. These figures proved to be so alarming that Mexican president Enrique Peña Nieto introduced a nationwide soda tax in 2013 to discourage consumers from bingeing on empty calories.[5]

In Saudi Arabia, no such measures exist. Earlier, I mentioned that the Mutaween, or religious police, enforce the country's nationwide dress code. In public, Saudi women are required to wear an *abaya* that covers everything but their face and their hands, and a *niqab,* or face veil. Saudi males of all ages wear a white *thobe,* and often a cloak, as well as a headdress. These not only satisfy the standards of the Mutaween, but also serve a secondary effect of camouflaging people's shapes, which, in turn, detach them not just from their own bodies but from the everyday judgment of others. In cultures that require people to live their lives costumed in loose-fitting clothing, there is little social pressure to keep healthy or fit.

Along with Mexico, the Middle East has one of the globe's highest rates of adult-onset diabetes, with nearly half the overall population expected to be diagnosed before 2030. Middle Eastern culture is sedentary, and the local diet is mostly sugar-based, made up of blended sweet foods, minced meats, breads and hummus. Restricted by the year-round hot climate, which discourages exercise or most outdoor activities—the heat is so relentless I typically pack two pairs of shoes in my suitcase, knowing that at some point the soles of one pair will melt—the Middle East also claims the world's highest consumption of computer and screen-based games. Moreover, Saudi women have been traditionally dissuaded from exercising, in contrast to Saudi men, who are "allowed" to appear in public and even jog. In 2015, Saudi women and girls were granted their own exercise and sports programs at school, but not without controversy. According to National Public Radio, some religious conservatives believed that exercising for girls "is a Western-izing influence . . . that could lead to adultery and prostitution."[6]

The weight problem has trickled down to the younger genera-tion. According to *The Wall Street Journal,* an estimated 9.3 percent of school-age Saudi Arabian children meet the World Health Organiza-tion's body-mass-index criteria for obesity."[7] Most Saudi schools lack physical fitness programs for children, leaving kids with nothing else to do but sit at home or in the backseat of cars or play at their computer consoles.

America and Europe, on the other hand, have a notoriously fraught relationship with weight. The Western diet book industry is huge and, along with the beauty industry, is predicated on a recurring cycle of hope and discouragement. Westerners will attempt a new dietary regime—or facial moisturizer, or lipstick—for, on average, three weeks to a month. When it doesn't "work"—i.e., deliver instant results, or even transform identity—they move along briskly to the next diet, or brand. The South Beach Diet, the Paleo Diet, the Atkins Diet, the Hormone Reset Diet, the Belly Burn Plan, the Gluten-Free Diet, the No More Excuses Diet—how different are these from applying a Clarins facial moisturizer, fol-lowed by creams made by Shiseido, Clinique, La Mer, Jurlique and La Prairie? Another issue, across America at least, is that overweight people often eat sparingly in public, but at home, feeling hungry and deprived, they'll reward themselves with a second calorie-laden meal.

Whenever I visit consumers' homes, I always make it a point to scope out the insides of refrigerators, knowing the owners have pre-pared for my arrival and that I'm in the presence of a choreographed scene. The interiors of most consumer fridges—including my own—are beautifully and carefully arranged. Objects sparkle and sweat. There are bowls of celery, carrots, radishes or cherry tomatoes. But by their very nature, shame and secrecy are private, a perspective that be-comes clear when I get down on my knees in a consumer's kitchen and look at what sits on a refrigerator's bottom shelves.

The lower shelves are where the "bad stuff" resides—the cheese, the cold cuts, the breads, the alcohol, the chocolate bars. By keeping unhealthy food out of sight, consumers can convince themselves they eat more healthily than they actually do. Over the years, I've found six-packs of soda buried among shoes, potato chips concealed in storage rooms and, in one case, a huge stock of chocolate and Gummi Bears hidden underneath someone's bedroom floorboards. Consumers often justify the presence of a case of Pepsi or a dozen bags of corn chips by reminding me that it is more cost-effective to buy in bulk, which is true. At the same time, studies show that the more soda and snacks we buy, the more likely we are to consume them.

Along with studying the insides of refrigerators and the food caches hidden in cabinets, sometimes I'll go so far as to ask whether I can go through someone's garbage. One aspect of my job that I especially enjoy is talking with local garbage collectors. No matter where they live in the world, they get to see, and smell, privileged information. When most of us toss something in the garbage and tie it up, we seldom think about it again. The evidence of our recent history, and our habits, good or bad, is rendered neutral and harmless once we toss it away, or at least this is what we want to believe. One garbage collector in Sweden told me he could tell a lot about people from the way they sealed their garbage bags. His more self-confident customers never placed separate plastic ties around their bags; they simply maneuvered the plastic into a knot. The more insecure the person, he said, the more knots or ties there tended to be.

What's inside garbage cans—"the blend," as another garbage collector I interviewed called it—can also communicate a lot about their owners. If someone crushes a tube of toothpaste and tosses it away capless, experience tells me they are prudent about saving money, though at the end of the day they will spend money on themselves, as if to compensate for their earlier inattention. Consumers who discard a toothpaste tube with its cap screwed down tightly seldom allow themselves to relax, and are reluctant to expose who they really are, or to indulge themselves with a luxury. Consumers who throw away a half-full toothpaste tube are, in general, less secure than people who wait until the tube is depleted. All this and more . . . from a simple garbage bin.

A FEW YEARS AGO, I got a close-up perspective on obesity and fast food when McDonald's Europe asked me to help them create a new, healthier Happy Meal. The job began in France, spread across the European Union and migrated to the United States—where, I might add, the concept I came up with was roundly rejected. The idea later bounced back to Europe, where Germany and a handful of other countries eventually implemented it.

First, some context. As the world's largest food chain, McDonald's has 35,000 franchises in 118 countries and territories, and serves 68 million customers every day. But a decade or so ago, McDonald's was facing a public relations firestorm. In 2001, journalist Eric Schlosser published *Fast Food Nation: The Dark Side of the All-American Meal,* a best-selling expose of the fast-food industry, which revealed many unsavory details its main players would have liked to keep undercover. Three years later, filmmaker Morgan Spurlock released the documentary *Super Size Me,* chronicling his decision to consume only McDonald's food three times a day for an entire month, and the consequences of a fast-food diet on both his physical and psychological well-being. By the end of his experiment, Spurlock had gained 25 pounds and was depressed and lethargic. His cholesterol had skyrocketed, and he had heart palpitations. When studies were published around that same time showing that obesity levels across Europe had more than doubled over the past two decades, McDonald's found itself on the defensive about the ways in which its menu contributed to the epidemic, and poor eating habits overall. It was at this perilous moment that the chief marketing officer of McDonald's Europe asked whether I might be able to come up with some ideas to reinvent the concept of the Happy Meal.

McDonald's biggest markets in Europe are Germany, England and France—and it was there I launched my Subtext Research. In France, McDonald's bears little resemblance to its American counterpart. French McDonald's are more elegant, the chairs more comfortable, the tables less flimsy, the décor more subtly upscale, with the brash yellows and reds Americans are accustomed to exchanged for darker, muted forest-greens. The French are renowned for loving *"McDo,"* and with its 1,200 French locations, France is McDonald's most profitable country outside the United States. Of course, in a nation with high taxes, inflation and unemployment, and an expensive capital city, Paris, whose outskirts are home to some of the poorest people in the world, McDonald's is also a comparative bargain.

Some observers attribute McDonald's success in France to its embrace of French eating habits and locally sourced ingredients, including cheese, potatoes and grass-fed beef, a product line augmented by baguettes, pastries and macaroons, and even a separate Halal menu for the country's large Islamic population. I agree, but also believe that the chain's success in France is in part a rebellion against the national tradition of multihour, multicourse meals, with no one permitted to leave the table until everyone else is done eating. A similar rebellion can be seen in the phenomenal success of Picard, France's frozen-food chain and the largest chain of its kind in the world. Every one of Picard's 500 boutique-like stores is noticeably sterile, almost hospital-like, in appearance, with Picard's private-label meat, shellfish, potatoes, vegetables and desserts for sale stacked in waist-high freezers. With a majority of French women working outside the home, frozen food in France has been such a popular trend that even some Michelin-starred restaurants have taken to using frozen ingredients.

McDo's may differ aesthetically from McDonald's in the United States, but both markets adhere to the company's core principles, foremost among which is that McDonald's isn't a place for children, or adolescents, to just hang out, but for families to visit together. And across France, families *were* flocking to McDonald's. After traveling around the country paying visits to franchises in small towns and cities, I found myself facing a uniquely French imbalance. The presence of French families in its restaurants may have been good news for McDonald's bottom line, but it also suggested that the opportunities for French parents to connect with their children were diminishing. When I began interviewing French parents, two things stood out: both parents worked outside the home, and neither believed they were spending enough time with their kids.

Across the world, the Happy Meal, which was launched in the late 1970s, appears under different aliases, from *Joyeux Festin* in Canada to *Cajita Feliz,* or "Happy Little Meal in a Box," in Latin America. Then, as now, a Happy Meal consists of the choice of a hamburger, cheeseburger or Chicken McNuggets; a small order of French fries; and a soda. As everyone knows, the Happy Meal also includes a toy that connects to a popular family-oriented television show, movie or preexisting toy line.

My position was that McDonald's needed to show the world it could achieve anything—and that included proving that healthy food could be "fun," a feat, I might add, that no company had ever accomplished. I went to work—or, more precisely, I went for a swim in a public Olympic-sized swimming pool in a waterfront suburb of Sydney, Australia, known as Milson's Point.

The reason I prefer to stay in hotels equipped with swimming pools is that pools are where good ideas come to me. I'm not alone. Lots of people are inspired by the presence of water, whether they're strolling along a beach, taking a shower or even listening to water running or to a soundtrack of waves hitting the shore. The Greek mathematician, physicist and engineer Archimedes was said to have discovered the principles around density and buoyancy as he drew a bath, and songwriter Pharrell Williams begins each morning the same way: "I shower, and that's where a lot of my concepts come from," Pharrell told *Fast Company.* He even composes songs under a nozzle. "If you don't interrupt (your subconscious) with the ego, or are like, *No it's gotta be like this,* then a lot of ideas will come. Once you start judging it and editing it, then you're no longer tapped in . . . so I spend a lot of that time just standing there in the water with a blank stare."[8]

Why good ideas tend to materialize in pools, lakes, ponds, oceans, showers and tubs is harder to figure out. A popular explanation is that, while we may not realize it, most of us are rarely inside the present moment. We spend a disproportionate amount of time plotting the future or revisiting past events. But when we swim, or shower, or take a bath, we have little choice but to position ourselves in the present, giving our thoughts room to float and wander (though more and more young people tell me they take their phones into the shower with them and, keeping them at arms' distance, send and answer texts). When we actively pursue answers or solutions to a problem, they almost never materialize, but when we engage in routine, relaxing activities that require little active thought, they do. Shelley H. Carson, a Harvard University researcher and psychologist, said once that if we're troubled by a problem, any interruption in focus provides "an incubation period . . . In other words, a distraction may provide the break you need to disengage from a fixation on the ineffective solution."[9]

At the same time, a certain *kind* of activity is better than others at encouraging new or good ideas. Ideally, that activity is both routinized and inventive, like running, bicycling or gardening. All three involve implicit, automatic motions that are also improvisational, allowing disparate ideas to come together. Over the course of my own career, I've taken to calling these revelations "Water Moments," and the one I had about McDonald's Happy Meal clicked for me that day at Milson's Point.

It was late afternoon, and I was doing laps, swimming alone in the center lane. At one point I became aware of a nearby café selling the usual summertime stuff—hot dogs, hamburgers, French fries and onion rings. Children were playing around the shallow end of the pool, and one, I saw, was munching on a carrot stick. *Probably some Australian quirk,* I remember thinking, and then I noticed the children were speaking in German. Halfway through my hour-long swim, a few things had become clearer.

The biggest problem with the Happy Meal, as I saw it, was how prosaic it was. It was exactly as advertised, and not much more than that. It didn't inspire imaginative play, nor was there much fantasy or magic connected to it. As soon as they opened their Happy Meals, children grabbed the enclosed toy, ate their meal, and that was that. There was no story line, no space for them to imagine, or dream.

The new Happy Meal—Happy Meal 2.0, as it eventually came to be called—was inspired by the pool's three swimming lanes. Each lane, I thought, could reflect an ingredient of McDonald's new children's meal. One lane represented tomatoes; another carrots; a third broccoli. The only question was finding a concept, and a story line, that combined all three vegetables.

With the help of a creative team in Denmark, the idea quickly evolved from there. By themselves, vegetables—a bowl of peas, a side of broccoli—aren't all that compelling. But string them onto a necklace, or emboss a carrot in the form of a monster and suddenly vegetables become fun. Over the next few weeks, the team and I came up with a short list of concepts, including a prototype for a new, environmentally friendlier Happy Meal 2.0 container. We realized as well that if the goal was to convince children to eat cucumbers, or tomatoes, or broccoli, McDonald's had to continue its longtime relationship with toys linked to companies like Disney, DreamWorks and Pixar.

We began with the idea that children would find it more interesting to assemble their own hamburgers. Our first Happy Meal 2.0 concept featured a small dragon holding a hamburger bun, with a bare hamburger patty resting nearby. Navigating past a tomato slice, and over "stairs" made out of cucumber strips and carrot bars, children could then uncover a miniature Shrek or Princess Fiona. Our second prototype, "Space," was based on the Space Shuttle. A tomato rested in the cockpit, while carrot sticks manned the back doors, alongside a small bag of melon balls, which children could spear with a small plastic wand. Once kids had managed to find three special numbers hidden on the cockpit floor, they could crack the Space Shuttle's "code" to uncover their hamburgers or chicken nuggets. Happy Meal 2.0 had several others advantages, too. Parents could observe the unfamiliar phenomenon of their children actually enjoying vegetables, mothers could take comfort in the fact they weren't feeding their kids junk and fathers could take their children to McDonald's without risking criticism from their wives.

When I presented my ideas to the senior management of McDonald's Europe, they were enthusiastic. So why, you might be wondering, isn't the veggie-based Happy Meal 2.0 a staple of McDonald's fast-food restaurants across the globe? Unfortunately, the concept fell victim to operational obstacles and went nowhere. When a company as large and complex as McDonald's has been manufacturing Happy Meals for 30 years, and operating multiple factories that focus exclusively on food container and toy manufacturing—McDonald's is the largest distributor of toys in the world—it is just too difficult, and too expensive, to change course. What's more, the company schedules new additions to their menu up to 18 months before they come to market. There were other obstacles, too, including the need to invest in new machinery, find new licensees and educate and retrain thousands of McDonald's employees, and the shelf life of vegetables themselves. Carrots, cucumbers and tomatoes can't be frozen without turning soggy, or losing their taste or shape. In hindsight, Project Happy Meal 2.0 is an initiative I believe I could carry off today with my greater experience with people and politics, but a decade ago it was just too daunting.

Cut to a few years ago when Jenny Craig, the weight loss and nutrition company, contacted me, hoping I could come up with a new marketing innovation to ensure consumer loyalty and make the Jenny Craig brand more "sticky" among dieters.

Founded in Melbourne, Australia, in 1983 by two American expatriates, Jenny and Sidney Craig, Jenny Craig's philosophy is that losing weight is as simple as reducing calories, portion size and fat content. When dieters walk into one of Jenny Craig's weight-loss centers—there are 450 across the United States—they pay an enrollment fee, sign up for weekly one-on-one sessions with a Jenny Craig counselor, many of whom are former Jenny Craig members themselves, and choose from one of several set menus of Jenny Craig frozen foods. The diet ranges from 1,200 to 2,300 calories daily, with the average Jenny Craig client spending around $100 a week on breakfast, lunch, dinner and snacks, and remaining on the program for around 12 weeks. By contrast, Jenny Craig's chief rival, Weight Watchers, allocates points to thousands of foods and drinks, which members are told not to exceed. Weight Watchers dieters attend weekly meetings, and can also access advice and support from online forums. In short, if the mission of Weight Watchers is to equip dieters with awareness about what they're eating, Jenny Craig, with its frozen-food lines, does a lot of the work for them.

When Jenny Craig hired me, the company was a colossus, a corporate machine with approximately 700 diet centers in Canada, the United States, France, Puerto Rico, Australia and New Zealand. Since 2002, it had survived the usual corporate turmoil that takes place once a founder leaves a company, and it was on its third owner. Jenny Craig had both the advantages and disadvantages of a global business that could almost run itself. It was an organized machine, but it had lost some of the personality and intimacy that had led to its success. It also wasn't cheap, and the dropout rates were higher than they should have been. Could I come up with a new initiative to increase the odds that new dieters would stick with Jenny Craig, recommend it to their friends and, ideally, serve as brand ambassadors?

AFTER NEARLY TWO MONTHS of conducting Subtext Research across Southern California and elsewhere, I'd developed a profile of the average Jenny Craig dieter. Let's call her Caroline. (Jenny Craig offers a customized program for men, as well as teens, diabetics and elderly people, but the majority of Jenny Craig clients are female.) Caroline was a woman anywhere between the age of 30 and 45, married, with children. She enjoyed watching television game shows, and kept the television on in the background as she carried out her chores and family responsibilities. She was also noticeably superstitious. She didn't let a day go by without glancing at her horoscope in the newspaper. She also visited eBay more often than the average woman, and bought more lottery and scratch tickets than most.

What explained Caroline's ritualized—and to me, unusually superstitious—behavior? In principle, the answer was simple. When we gamble, our brains release dopamine, a neurotransmitter that floods our senses whenever we anticipate anything rewarding, from food to alcohol to sex. Reading a horoscope, it seemed to me, was largely about the attempt to control a world that seemed chaotic, and superstitious behavior links back to control itself, an issue in the lives of many dieters. But what reward might a Jenny Craig dieter be anticipating? There really wasn't one. Both Jenny Craig and Weight Watchers promise clients that if they stay on the program, they'll lose one or two pounds a week, but in this case, losing a pound didn't seem to be enough.

The question was: What was Caroline, and each Jenny Craig dieter I interviewed, compensating for? When they checked their daily horoscope, or bought lottery tickets, or bid on clothing and appliances on eBay, what were they getting or, rather, what were they *not* getting?

My concept of a new way to approach this question took place during an interview with a 52-year-old housewife and mother in her carpeted, suburban home in Carlsbad, California. Her name was Jan. Her 26-year-old daughter lived in a nearby suburb, but when I asked about the young man I kept seeing in photos wearing a military uniform, Jan told me her son had died in battle overseas. As her eyes filled with tears, her fingers grasped the charm bracelet she was wearing around her wrist. Gently, I asked her if there was any connection between the loss of her son and the bracelet around her wrist. There was. The airplane charm on her bracelet couldn't help but remind her of her son, an Air Force pilot in love with planes and flying ever since he was a boy. When I asked what would happen if she ever lost the bracelet, Jan shook her head. She didn't want to think about it.

WHY DO WOMEN—and men for that matter—wear jewelry in the first place? A few years before I began working for Jenny Craig, it was a question I asked consumers around the world on behalf of a Danish jewelry brand known as Trollbeads. Among the responses I got were as follows: "Jewelry enhances the way I look—and it makes me look pretty." "People notice you, and you want to feel noticed, especially when you become a mother." "It's a very important fashion accessory. When I put on a necklace, or wear a certain bracelet, it changes my whole outfit and my whole attitude, too." "Jewelry is timeless—it never goes out of style." "Jewelry is just something other people are drawn to automatically." Above all else, it seemed, jewelry was an essential talking point when two women were trying to establish an emotional connection.

Despite its un-euphonious name, Trollbeads is an extremely successful jewelry company with a presence in 35 countries, including Holland, Italy, Switzerland and China. Trollbeads' handmade bracelets, rings and necklaces vary in size and are made from Murano glass, freshwater pearls, gemstones, leather, glass and Swarovski crystal. Still, when I began consulting for the company, I wasn't quite prepared for the fanaticism of Trollbeads' core customers. Most were middle-aged, with a competent, slightly tough manner about them. None, overall, were especially trusting, and a few expressed unease about having an interviewer come into their house and ask them questions. Many told me they'd felt excluded as children, or as high school or college students. On the surface, they may have been hardworking and accomplished, but inside they were superstitious, compulsive, vulnerable and adept at hiding high levels of stress. Trollbeads, it seemed, gave many of them the chance to reveal a creative, interesting, highly visual person they'd never been able to express comfortably in other social situations, and also helped them forge a powerful sense of belonging with other Trollbeads fans across the world.

Trollbeads, I realized, were far more than random pieces of silver, gold or glass. Trollbeads were fun. Trollbeads were personal. Trollbeads were whimsical. Trollbeads were almost human. One Dutch Trollbeads fan told me she devoted anywhere from eight to ten hours a week to international conference calls with other Trollbeads fans as far away as South Africa and Asia. Another woman likened Trollbeads' passionate following to her own family growing up. "From the time I was young, my family and I all had a secret language—eye movements, hand gestures, facial expressions," she said. "I have that today with my own children and my husband, and I have it with other Trollbeads fans." What's more, each colored bead that Trollbeads put out signified something that "only I, and the other person, know about." The biggest revelation: each and every Trollbead women collected served as a badge of honor, or a memento, that signified a cherished time or event in their lives.

The question remained: What was behind this particular obsession? How did it begin, and why? Most of the women I spoke to were mothers, and I soon realized that their obsession with Trollbeads began when their teenage children began closing the doors to their bedrooms, thereby shutting their mothers out of their lives. Most of the women I spoke to described this moment as shattering, akin almost to a death. After all, they'd spent the past decade and a half attending to their children's needs and desires. They were cooks, chauffeurs and confidantes. In many cases, becoming a mother had given many of them visibility, influence and power for the first time in their lives. Now, without warning, psychologically at least, they'd been, temporarily, closed out of their children's lives.

The vacuum, or imbalance, that I kept seeing? Many of these women no longer had someone who relied on them, or sought them out. They'd become invisible, and for women who admitted feeling left out or socially excluded during their lives, this was especially difficult.

In the marketing world, an "entry point" refers to those times in our lives—among them marriage, pregnancy, first parenthood, buying a home, the empty nest—when identity is either challenged or transformed. During these periods, consumers are especially vulnerable to new perspectives, as well as new brands; for Trollbeads users, the entry point appeared when their adolescent children closed their bedroom doors.

I couldn't help but think of my experience with Trollbeads fans when Jan, the Jenny Craig dieter in Carlsbad, California, touched the airplane charm on her bracelet when discussing her late son. Like Jenny Craig dieters, Trollbeads fans were also dependent on their daily horoscopes, and many also knocked on wood for good luck. Every time a Trollbeads customer bought a new bead, it took on an emotional meaning and weight. One woman, for example, showed me a Trollbead she said was a gift from her late grandmother. Another woman displayed a Murano glass bead she'd bought to commemorate her daughter's middle-school graduation.

Trollbeads, then, symbolized many things. Via Trollbeads, women could tell the world that despite their age or appearance, they were still interesting and creative. Wearing a Trollbeads necklace was also a socially acceptable way to showcase in public a private obsession. Nothing illustrated this better than a German woman who, during our interview, held up what she called her "Ocean Bead." A lifetime fan of water and the seaside, she told me a story about a trip to the beach she'd taken years earlier with her father, her husband and her children. "It was the best beach day I have ever had in my life. I can still see my dad holding my kids' hands as they picked up seashells and sea glass." She passed me her Trollbeads bracelet. "Every single color of that day—all the ocean colors of green and blue—is in that bead."

In short, like many leading brands, Trollbeads functioned on both a rational and a highly emotional level. Intriguingly, this was a duality that also interested the British film director Alfred Hitchcock, of all people. Most remember Hitchcock as a skilled storyteller, but what few know is that the director shot his movies using two separate scripts. The first, known as "the Blue Script," was entirely functional. In it were all the tangible onscreen components, including dialogue, props, camera angles and set descriptions. The second script, which Hitchcock referred to as "the Green Script," chronicled in fine detail the emotional arc, or "beats," of the film he was shooting. Hitchcock relied on both scripts, but the Green Script reminded him how he wanted moviegoers to *feel,* and at what point, as they watched *Suspicion,* or *Shadow of a Doubt,* or *North By Northwest.*

Some of the most powerful brands in the world make unconscious use of a Blue Script and Green Script. Disney Chairman and CEO Bob Iger and Apple CEO Steve Jobs once had a conversation about retail, during which Jobs told Iger that retailers should always ask themselves one question: *If a store could talk, what would it say to the people entering it?* Disney Stores may have a functional layout, but from an emotional perspective, Disney's Green Script intent is to create the 30 happiest minutes in a child's life. Enter an Apple Store and its architecture, simple wood and sparse, jewel-like product selection intentionally evoke the layout of a contemporary art museum. What does Whole Foods "say" to customers? Whether it's the fresh flowers on display as you enter the store, or the products on shaved ice (most of which have no need for refrigeration), or the hand-scrawled signs describing a product's provenance, Whole Foods conveys freshness, purity and localness, while tacitly congratulating its customers for their discernment and even education level. It helped inspire a strategy I'd used at Lowes, too, creating an emotion-based story line by inviting in local farmers to discuss their fresh produce and chefs to provide customers with the latest recipes.

MY WORK WITH TROLLBEADS gave me a part of a solution that might strengthen brand loyalty among Jenny Craig dieters. Another missing piece came from work I'd done in Dubai, Oman, Beirut and Bahrain that confirmed my observations about the importance of beads, or "palpables," as they're referred to in the industry. My employer was VOX, one of the Middle East's largest theater chains, and I'd been asked to help redesign their movie theaters.

Middle Easterners go to the movies as regularly as Indians do, which is to say up to three or four times a week. Typically, the entire family goes as a unit and orders large amounts of junk food—at theaters worldwide, you will find the exact same snacks, including hot dogs, hamburgers, French fries and, in the Middle East, five different flavors of popcorn—before commandeering half a dozen or more seats. (Filmgoers are offered three different tiers of seat, at escalating costs.) Middle Eastern theaters, in fact, closely resemble airplanes, which reminded me that native moviegoers go to the movies not just to watch a new film, but to escape their real lives and identities for a while. Nor can the climate be underestimated. Along with shopping malls, the movies provide one of the few means of relief from the daily 100-degree-plus temperatures.

Westerners who've never traveled abroad don't realize the extent to which American movies and actors, and Hollywood imagery, dominate overseas cinemas and markets. In an attempt to instill an elegant, glamorous feeling in the theater decor, and to escort moviegoers on a "dream" journey, I impressed on management the necessity for heavy velvet ropes and heavy crimson curtains. From my Subtexting, I knew that Middle Eastern moviegoers wanted to feel special, as most inhabit oil-rich countries where they are constantly faced with flamboyant emblems of wealth. Many regular cinema-goers are Indians, Pakistanis and Filipinos, who compose the region's emigrant workforce and whose long working days couldn't be further removed from such opulence.

I was so preoccupied with the design of the theaters—*How thick should the velvet ropes be? Should they be plum or crimson? Should a silhouette cutout of Sean Connery or Cary Grant or Bette Davis be situated here or there?*—that it took me awhile to notice that seven out of ten moviegoers were holding a clasp of beads. The clasps held anywhere from 10 to 15 beads on them, and as families trooped in and out of the cinemas, both the men and the women used their fingers to rub and flick them. The fiddling was constant, but it accelerated when moviegoers came into the theater lobby to buy food or drinks.

What did the beads mean? Were they symbolic of the region's aggregate nervous system, a regional anxiety expressed via their palpables, or did they mean something else? For the next two weeks, I studied what happened when filmgoers across the Middle East bought sodas, snacks and other unhealthy concessions. There seemed to be an almost direct correlation between bead-flicking and the consumption of popcorn, hot dogs, hamburgers and candy. The worse the food was nutritionally, or calorically, the more rubbing and flicking there was. When moviegoers ordered or ate or drank healthier things, like water, or fruit, the flicking didn't stop, but it slowed down. Beads, at least across the Middle East, seemed to be a repository for self-censure, a symbol not of memory, as was the case with Trollbeads, but of gentle reprimand.

What if you could bring together these two ideas as one, on behalf of Jenny Craig?

OVER MY YEARS AS a branding guy, I've come to realize that both men and women have two ages: a chronological age, and an emotional age they feel inside. (I'll explore this subject in more detail in a later chapter.) Men typically conceal evidence of their younger selves in drawers, or buried inside online folders, whereas women are less embarrassed about publicly showcasing their younger selves, and express it openly through jewelry, stuffed animals and collections. The female body has more visible real estate, and more opportunities, and permission, for display than the male body does. The last few square inches of unused real estate of a woman reside in the underside of her footwear, which is one reason I've long been intrigued by Christian Louboutin shoes, with their signature patch of red between the sole and the heel. Louboutin heels are not only a display of sexiness, sauciness, rebellion and economic status (or all of the above), they also serve as a kiss and a wink to other Louboutin tribe members.

If my mission was to retain Jenny Craig dieters, and enlist them to serve as unofficial brand dignitaries, then it wasn't enough to coin a new slogan, or hand out free fitness trackers. Americans, I'd learned, walked less than any other industrialized nation on earth, with the average US native taking 5,117 steps daily compared to 9,695 in Australia, 7,168 in Japan and 9,650 in Switzerland.[10] In a car-dependent culture, encouraging walking wasn't enough. I needed to come up with something visible and tactile, and the solution I came up with was a Jenny Craig bead.

The global community of Trollbeads fans taught me something important: beads gave many women an identity they had recently lost, and also served to prove membership in a tribe or community. As a company, Jenny Craig had become so large and cumbrous it risked losing its sense of community and belonging—that is to say, its Green Script.

The concept was this: What if Jenny Craig's trained counselors gave dieters their own free charm bracelet? The bracelet wouldn't be expensive, but nor should it be cheap or flimsy. Each bead on our new Jenny Craig charm bracelet would serve as a symbol of experience, success, hope and, in some cases, setbacks. From Small Mining, I knew that many Jenny Craig dieters who had gained a pound or two were reluctant to call the company's consultants, and knowing this I invented what I called a "Get-Out-of-Jail" bead. If a Jenny Craig dieter gained weight, her counselor was now instructed to give her a Get-Out-of-Jail bead, as if to say *No harm done, slipups happen.* The bead was a badge, a promise and a commitment to stay on the program. What's more, it had the potential to make dieters cry.

A weight-loss specialist working at Yale told me once one of her goals was to make people burst into tears. This is not an altogether bad thing. When people cry, it creates a "bookmark" in their brains—it is a moment, or experience, they are unlikely to forget. She pointed out that tears also precede the process of transformation. With our phones and laptops eternally on, the concept of *transformation*—of finding ourselves in an emotional state distinct from our everyday emotional lives—is vanishing. Transformation is critical when men and women conceive of losing weight, which is why when the specialist makes her clients cry, they are more likely to complete their dietary programs. It can happen as a result of dieters' frustrations around losing weight, or during a "seat belt" moment. (Many prospective dieters sign up for a weight-loss program on the day they experience the negative somatic marker of being unable to secure their car seat belts.)

Earlier, I wrote that while I consulted with Lowes, I imported the Asian custom of handing over an item of worth to customers. With Jenny Craig, I recycled this technique once again. When a consultant handed out a charm bracelet to a dieter, the new company-wide rule was that they would hand it over using two hands. Again, the idea behind handing someone something with two hands conveys the feeling that the gift comes from a person's heart and soul, that it represents a pact, or exchange, between two people. My intent was to create the strongest possible psychological and emotional connection with Jenny Craig, with each bead reflecting not just losses and gains, setbacks and successes, but memories as well.

Over the next few months, pilot tests—as well as smaller, subsequent rollouts across the United States—showed a dramatic increase in customer retention at Jenny Craig. The charm bracelet concept literally halved Jenny Craig's attrition rate, or as one American executive told me, "It was almost like doubling the number of customers signing up for the program in the first place." Trailing Weight Watchers in market share,[11] and competing with upstarts like Nutrisystem and the Zone, only three years after Jenny Craig rolled out its new bead program, an independent group of doctors and government officials voted Jenny Craig America's number one diet program. If nothing else, it was a jewel in the company's crown—or maybe I should I say wrist.

CHAPTER 5
HOW HORSES, SHIRT COLLARS AND RELIGIOUS BELIEF HELPED RECARBONATE A STRUGGLING BRAZILIAN BEER

ONCE, WHILE WORKING FOR A LOCAL TELECOMMUNICA-tions company in Medellín, Colombia, I learned that one of the city's poorest neighborhoods, Comuna Trece, was home to the largest escalator in the world, one as tall as a twelve-story building. The escalator was opened to the public in 2011 as part of an initiative to connect neighborhoods on Medellín's outskirts to the downtown. Despite the amount of traveling I do, I almost never have time to visit tourist attractions—I collect insights from people, not monuments—but the Medellín escalator sounded too good to pass up, and the telecommunications executive agreed to come with me.

Twenty minutes later, we were in the backseat of a cab, heading to Comuna Trece when, without warning, the driver pulled over. Afraid for his own safety—Comuna Trece had a reputation for petty crime and gang violence—he had changed his mind. The executive and I hailed another cab. This driver, too, had no interest in taking us to Comuna Trece. We must have gotten in and out of half-a-dozen taxis before we finally reached our destination.

Bisecting a sprawling shantytown, Medellín's escalator was modern, stylish and immaculate, with a serpentine red roof covering its 357 stairs, stories and landings. A team of red-shirted neighborhood residents milled around the bottom, answering questions and making sure no one stole the "magical" stairs that seemed to vanish into the earth, as escalator stairs can appear to do. The executive and I were there for a half hour before catching a cab back to downtown Medellín. Later, she told me, that to her colleagues' surprise, she was considering buying a home in the area.

People have asked me over the years if I ever feel unsafe visiting unfamiliar countries. My response is always the same: the day I let myself feel fear is the day I stop working. When you surrender to apprehension, or worry, or nerves, you effectively place a filter over your senses and are no longer able to see what's right in front of you. Yet why wouldn't I follow the lead of nearly half-a-dozen experienced taxi drivers who, it's safe to assume, know their city neighborhoods better than I do? My response is that very often, a "fear halo" surrounds a city or country, the result of events that took place years earlier—in this case, the 1980s, when Medellín was synonymous with drug cartels and violence—and this fear halo affects residents, too. I had a very similar experience years earlier when I was preparing to visit Nigeria. People warned me about random terrorism threats, power outages, widespread corruption and more. I encountered none of these things, and, in fact, Nigeria is still one of my favorite places to visit.

Which isn't to say that over the years I haven't had one or two close calls. Once I was nearly kidnapped in Venezuela. I'd just finished giving a keynote address in Caracas, and my taxi had just pulled up in front of the airport when two men greeted me by name. They were there, one told me, to make sure I reached my gate in a timely manner. Not for a second did I believe them, and I also had a nagging feeling something wasn't right. Thinking quickly, I told them that I had changed flights, and obviously no one had alerted them to the last-minute switch. Would they mind watching over my suitcase while I paid a quick visit to the bathroom?

Who leaves his bag behind with strangers if he doesn't plan on coming back for it? Gripping my smaller computer bag—it had my toothbrush in it, I told the two men—I made my way toward the men's bathroom and, once inside, looked behind me. The men looked fretful and anxious. By now convinced something was wrong, I left the bathroom a few seconds later via a back door. Having lost sight of me, the men were now craning their necks. They looked panicked. For the next fifteen minutes I did whatever I could to avoid being seen. I ducked through a series of waiting areas. I crouched down behind kiosks. At one point I caught a glimpse of a black car driving away. I never saw either of the men, or for that matter, my suitcase, ever again.

Fear often shadows tourists paying their first visit to Brazil. Most websites and guidebooks issue the same warnings: Don't bring anything to the beach. Avoid wearing jewelry or expensive watches. Make sure you leave your cell phone and wallet in your hotel room, preferably in a locked safe. A friend told me that when he told friends he was planning his first trip to Brazil, two of them told him—jokingly, or maybe not—that Brazil is famous for its organ trafficking industry, and he could find countless stories online about tourists blacking out and awakening to find a kidney missing. Like many stories about Brazil, this one is an urban legend.

Still, I found that Brazil's fear halo had affected some of my Brazilian colleagues. During a visit to Salvador, in northern Brazil, where I was doing interviews on behalf of Brasil Kirin, my host not only provided a translator but a local driver. And, in some areas of Salvador, even the driver was reluctant to go inside the favelas. Another day, when we pulled up in front of a crowded Brazilian elementary school during a soaking rain, I saw that my assistant was literally shaking. I suggested that the two of us take a short walk, and he could show me what "fear symbols" he was picking up on in the neighborhood. We did just that. No bars covered any of the windows; there were no padlocks on any of the doors. Residents sat outside, smiling and talking and fanning themselves. My assistant finally admitted he could find nothing obviously, overtly fear-inducing about the neighborhood, and from that point on he came with me everywhere.

Kirin is a Japanese-owned beverage conglomerate, known for its beers and soft drinks. Brasil Kirin, the national affiliate, has a wide portfolio of local brands, including Devassa, which means "libertine," or "naughty," a tropical lager founded by locals in 2001 in Leblon, the wealthiest, most cosmopolitan and desirable neighborhood in Rio de Janeiro. Then and now, Devassa's logo is a kneeling, scantily clad, alabaster-white female posed with both arms behind her neck.

The problem? Somewhere along the line, Devassa had lost its identity. At one time a premium ale, the beer was now just another supermarket brand, indistinguishable from the others. My mission: to restore Devassa to its upmarket status by creating an "aspirational" brand, meaning a higher-priced beer that consumers associate with a desirable, even elusive lifestyle. In a country like Brazil, with its rigid class divisions and strong commitment to façade, this was a complex problem that would require, in the end, a complex solution.

OF ALL THE COUNTRIES I'VE VISITED, Brazil is the one whose image and veneer are most radically at odds with its everyday life. Brazil, it is said, is home to the world's most beautiful women, the best-looking men, the most seductive music, the most sinuous dancers and the most libidinous nightlife. But with the exception of parts of Rio de Janeiro, during the next two months in Brazil I found few glimpses of ease, or glamour. Brazil is a soulful, warmhearted, hospitable nation unlucky enough to be saddled with high levels of government corruption, an overburdened infrastructure, a poorly funded education system and stark discrepancies between rich and poor. At the same time, compared to the efficient, highly developed countries of northern Europe, Brazil is also raw, emotional and direct. A well-known musician who grew up in Rio before moving to Los Angeles summed up to me his experience living in both America and Brazil. "The US is a great place to live," he said, "but I feel terrible whenever I'm there." He paused. "Brazil is a terrible place to live, but I feel great whenever I'm there."

Brazil boasts a population of around 200 million people—a sprawl of races, cultures and ethnicities spread across 5 regions and 26 states. In some parts of Brazil, residents are digesting print media for the first time; in others, residents have just bought their first television sets; in cities like Rio and São Paulo, younger generations are as sophisticated and plugged-in as their contemporaries anywhere else in the world. More relevant to the job I was carrying out for Brasil Kirin, the country is divided into five government-issued class segments, each one based exclusively on a household's gross monthly income. These are class A (Wealthy), B (Fairly Wealthy), C (Average), D (Lower Middle Class) and E, which is synonymous with poverty and illiteracy.

Brazilian natives are born into a class and, barring any surprises, the governmental machinery ensures they will stay in that class for the foreseeable future. Once Brazilians are tagged with a C or a D, it is almost impossible for them to improve their economic future or social standing. A stamp of C or D also signifies the degree of education a person has attained. Members of classes A and B, for example, have usually completed some form of higher education, whereas members of class D haven't finished high school and class E is essentially unschooled. A Brazilian's economic class also determines where a person's children will go to school, and the kind of work he will end up doing. Class A is generally made up of business owners, bankers and highly skilled workers, whereas class C, which includes teachers, nurses and mechanics, generally comprises those who provide services to classes A and B. Less formally, a Brazilian's class designation also dictates the sorts of food and beverages he eats and drinks, where he shops and the kinds of bars and restaurants he frequents. In short, each Brazilian social class brings with it an unspoken suite of "allowable" tastes and desires, from clothing to music to food.

"Being told that there are no social classes in the place where the interviewee lives is an old experience for sociologists," the author Leonard Reissman wrote in his 1965 book *Class in American Society.* "'We don't have classes in our town' almost invariably is the first remark recorded by the investigator . . . Once that has been uttered and is out of the way, the class divisions in the town can be recorded with what seems to be an amazing degree of agreement among the good citizens of the community."[1] Brazil is no exception to this ethnographic truth. Most Brazilians will deny they notice any class distinctions, but after a few beers, most will tell you they can assess the social class of other Brazilians on the basis of teeth, clothing, shoes and—not least, especially for woman—their hair and facial features.

The average Brazilian woman is short and slightly heavy, with a dark complexion and curly or frizzy hair, not at all helped by the country's high levels of humidity. She may or may not have African ancestry, considering that outside Nigeria, Brazil today is home to the largest percentage of people of African descent (during the slave trade era, Brazil was the destination for nearly 5 million enslaved Africans).[2] The straighter a Brazilian woman's hair, the higher her perceived social class, which explains the immense popularity of hair straighteners in Brazil. (An executive at Procter & Gamble told me once that throughout South America, girls and young women spend up to 15 minutes de-tangling their hair.) It may also explain why, alongside Colombia and Venezuela, Brazil has overtaken the United States as the plastic surgery capital of the world. As the *Guardian* reported in 2014, "With less than 3 percent of the world's population, Brazil accounted for 12.9 percent of the cosmetic operations performed [in 2013]. This included 515,776 breasts reshaped, 380,155 faces tweaked, 129,601 tummies tucked, 13,683 vaginas reconstructed, 219 penises enlarged and 63,925 buttocks augmented."[3] As a rule, Brazilians have no qualms about undergoing plastic surgery; plastic surgery signals to the world that they care about their appearance.

I soon grew to understand the intricacies of the national social hierarchy. Brazil's national identity revolves around three things: football (i.e., soccer), beer and the beach. Football is a passion in many countries, especially England, but at some point most English boys give up their childhood dream of becoming world-class athletes. When I asked teenage Brazilian boys about their dreams about the future, nine times out of ten they told me that their fantasy was to become a football player. For them, the images of the country's greatest stars—Pelé, Garrincha, Ronaldhino, Kaká, Zico, Socrates and others—were vivid and enduring. Yet in a country the size of Brazil, the chances of succeeding in sports are small, which is why, at some point, reality is replaced with the harshness and hardship of everyday life.

One contributing factor is Brazil's exhausted educational system. There are so many children to educate that in lower and elementary schools, one-half of the school-age population attends school in the mornings, and the other half shows up for classes in the afternoon. For anyone other than the top economic classes, there is no organized way to get ahead in Brazil—no after-school or mentorship programs or clubs. Compare this to the United States, for example, where many parents are so afraid their children won't get into the right college that they schedule lessons, hire SAT tutors and set up music, karate, dance and language lessons. Few hours in the day of a middle-class American child are unscheduled, whereas for many Brazilian children, life itself is an ongoing improvisation.

Also in contrast to the United States or England, few Brazilians would consider "jumping class" by returning to school, studying for an advanced degree or applying for a better job. In Brazil, class migration is based exclusively on consumption, appearance and brands, which has the unfortunate effect of exhausting people's bank accounts without a plan to replenish them. Even indigent Brazilians spend their money on status symbols. As a 2015 *New York Times* op-ed noted about Brazil, "Many homes have flat-screen TVs, but are not hooked up to public sewers. Many say these 40 million whose living standards have been raised are not a new middle class but are just 'poor people with money.'"[4] Brazil is the only country on earth where entire product ranges exist to help consumers blend into the class just above them.

While Devassa wanted to target all classes, the B class was clearly the brand's favored demographic. To celebrate the brand's origins, I also wanted to relaunch Devassa in Rio de Janeiro, the coastal city where trends and fashions generally take root across Brazil. But to what should Brazilians aspire? The question was familiar, and one that over the years had taken me from Hong Kong to Italy . . . and back to Brazil.

BEFORE EXPLORING ASPIRATION, let's ask ourselves whether it's possible to determine the taste differences among half-a-dozen beers or, for that matter, water. Globally, there are thousands of bottled water brands—one Los Angeles restaurant even has a water sommelier on staff[5]—but if I blindfolded you, could you really describe the taste of one bottled water over another, and mean it? An equivalent number of beer brands swells the shelves of most supermarkets and liquor stores. Whenever I've done blind taste tests with consumers, most say they can detect subtle taste differences among beer brands. But the fact of the matter is that 99 percent of the time, what they claim is the taste of Heineken, or Molson, or Corona is, in fact, another brand entirely. So what lies behind our preference for one beer over another?

More than most beverages, beer and emotion cannot be teased apart in Brazil. Almost every time Brazilians interact with friends or family, beer serves as the centerpiece of the gathering. Ironically, all across the world—including Brazil—a large majority of consumers dislikes the taste of beer. Many have told me that when they had their first taste of the stuff, usually when they were young, their distaste was outweighed by the symbolic meaning of beer as an emblem of adulthood. In this way, beer is like coffee. Most of us like the smell of coffee beans and freshly brewed coffee—but do any of us enjoy the actual *taste* of coffee? With both beverages, it seems, we embed in our memories the moment when we first tasted them, as well as the symbolic transformation we experienced as we made the internal shift from child to adult. The memory of this moment lasts throughout our lives, overriding the taste of both beer and coffee and tricking us into believing that what we're drinking tastes good even when it doesn't.

Considering that I was in Brazil to help transform Devassa, I started to spend my evenings in bars, observing the various local rituals around beer drinking. After a few days, it became clear how Brazilian beer drinkers conveyed discreet class signals based on how they positioned their bottles on the table. If they were drinking a premium beer, drinkers set them down with the label visible to the rest of the room. If the beer was less expensive, the label faced inward. I knew that for many Brazilians, one core aspiration around beer drinking was to order enough of the "right" beer—for example, Heineken. A 22-year-old Brazilian man even told me, "Me and my friends would save money to buy a Heineken bucket at the bar. It makes us feel like kings—until we catch the bus home."

Another phenomenon I noticed was the Brazilian preoccupation with temperature. Inside bars or corner stores, each fridge featured a display showing the current temperature inside the unit. Most were extremely low—24 degrees Fahrenheit was common—meaning that the beers inside the fridge were practically frozen. As is true in many parts of the world, including America, Brazilians prefer their beer impossibly cold. Ice-cold temperatures typically kill whatever minimal flavor beer has to begin with, which in the case of both Brazil and the United States, indicates that residents in both countries are averse to strong bitter flavors.

Beer, of course, was also an incomparable bonding tool. People drank it almost exclusively in social settings, surrounded by large groups of friends. Like any alcohol, beer served as a device of transformation, dissolving emotional boundaries. But what about class boundaries?

On the basis of my Subtexting, I knew that if a Brazilian woman wanted to "jump class," almost always the first thing she did was to go online to study and research her chosen class on both an emotional and materialistic level. On the basis of her research, she might begin to talk differently. She might make plans to straighten her hair, or listen to new music, and in some cases persuade herself to embrace a new style, or fashion, that she knows the upper classes favor. I'd caught any number of Brazilian women flicking through websites, as if through a museum of dreams, fantasizing about the lifestyles, and the brands, of A or B class people. These brands, in turn, become tickets, membership passes almost, to the next social rung.

EARLIER I WROTE THAT OUR perception of the world is almost always local, focusing almost exclusively around ourselves and our neighborhoods and our traditions and our beliefs. But who influences us to buy a certain product, helps us form an opinion or exposes us to a brand we later use ourselves—a wristwatch, a musical genre, a facial moisturizer, a wine label? It's not something we often think about, but when I ask this question to people online and offline, the answer is invariably *celebrities*.

It's fascinating to trace how the concept of celebrity has evolved since the 1960s, when Giorgio Armani first had the idea of giving away free clothing to celebrities, thereby linking clothing with aspiration and glamour. A decade earlier, in the 1950s, there were maybe a dozen or more "real" celebrities, but by the 1990s this list had grown to hundreds of people, including celebrity CEOs, chefs, hairdressers, party planners and interviewers. Today the list includes "subcelebrity" categories, including reality show stars and YouTube personalities. In a 2015 survey of 1,500 respondents ages 13 to 18 conducted for *Variety* by celebrity brand strategist Jeetendr Sehdev found that YouTube stars "scored significantly higher than traditional celebrities across a range of characteristics considered to have the highest correlation to influencing purchases among teens . . . YouTubers were judged to be more engaging, extraordinary and relatable than mainstream stars."[6]

Notwithstanding celebrities, who influences us within the context of our own lives? Every culture, it should be remembered, has its own default topics of conversation, a default script of subjects, ranging from the weather to sports to food. When two people meet for the first time, generally speaking, what do they talk about? What is the first thing out of a waiter's mouth in Russia, in England, in America, in France, in Montenegro? How do taxi drivers greet passengers across the world, and what do they discuss during the ride? What do neighbors say when they meet in the lobby or the sidewalk, or mothers when they meet other mothers in the park?

As I've sat in homes across the world, I've noticed we tend to "read from" a conversational script that seldom varies week after week. Depending on the country I'm in, this script has its local nuances, but it generally goes like this: Two people greet each other. They say something about the weather. They offer each other something to drink or eat. They exchange compliments about each other's clothing. But when we deviate from this script, what causes us to stray? The answer, I found out while conducting an informal, monthlong experiment, is the objects surrounding us.

Once, when I was consulting for Nescafé's instant coffee division, the executive team and I realized that many contemporary kitchens had become so sleek and minimalist there was no longer any physical space for Nescafé's signature glass coffee jars. This meant that Nescafé as a topic of conversation was also gone—which in turn had led to declining revenues at the company. My mission was to bring Nescafé coffee jars back inside the kitchen, and back into the conversation. I tried this same strategy out in Brazil. To see whether I could influence people's conversations, I brought along small decorative objects, which I placed in people's kitchens or living rooms. A coffee mug. A glass jar. A yellow teapot. In more than three-quarters of the cases, the object, or the brand, dominated the conversation for an average of seven minutes. It seemed that by introducing an object into the room, I could alter the direction of a conversation and "change the script."

This insight had strong ramifications for the rebranding of Devassa. What consumers say about a brand can be controlled and in some cases reduced to a preprepared sales pitch. For a brand, this is critical. Imagine: ten words that represent the heart, soul and essence of a brand, no longer controlled by print ads or television commercials, but by consumers themselves. As the popularity of hair straighteners and plastic surgery across Brazil attested, more than most countries Brazil was strongly affected by "influencers" and by "aspiration." I tucked this observation away for later.

Doesn't the desire to "change the conversation" explain why some of us wear glasses with colorful frames, or boldly colored necklaces and earrings, or wildly decorated handbags, or even rubber bracelets? These small touches and additions serve as both calls for attention as well as talking points. Generally speaking, there is a story attached to the lizard pin we wear, or the black rubber strap we wear around our wrist. They position us in the center of the story. When we become the star, the focal point, the narrator or the subject of attention, our brains release dopamine. Any celebrity will tell you that fame and attention are addictive, which may partly explain why most social media users stream a steady barrage of news, food photos and landscapes and receive in return a cannonade of compliments (*"Wow," "Amazing," "Love it"*). Via Facebook, Instagram and Twitter, we have all become celebrities in our own lives.

Up until a few years ago, whenever I gave speeches I asked audience members if anyone was wearing a yellow LiveStrong bracelet. (Over the years I've seen businessmen in Armani suits and expensive Swiss watches wearing the LiveStrong band which, I might add, is manufactured in China.) Invariably two dozen or so audience members would raise their hands. *Why do you wear it,* I asked? Most told me they wore the LiveStrong bracelet to show their support for the fight against cancer. Today, in the wake of Lance Armstrong's doping controversy, almost no one would want to be seen wearing a LiveStrong bracelet. Still, when I asked audience members why they stopped wearing the bracelet—did this mean they no longer believed in fighting cancer?—most admitted they began wearing the bracelet to stand out, to inspire a conversation and even to show their superior moral status.

Across the globe, aspiration exists at every level of society, from the lowest to the highest. But how does aspiration begin? How old are we when we first become aware of desiring what we don't have? More to the point, to what, or to whom, did most Brazilians aspire?

As I traveled across the country, one word kept popping up: *Cariocas.*

Carioca is a demonym used to refer to the residents of Rio de Janeiro. The term originated as a mild insult to refer to the descendants of immigrants, but has evolved today to refer to any Rio native, and to membership in a distinct, coveted, moneyed lifestyle. "To be Carioca, you have to enjoy the beach and be casual in life," one Brazilian told me. Another Rio resident defined Carioca this way: "You are social and friendly with everybody you meet." Among the other definitions of a Carioca: Free-spirited. Not worrying too much about life. Letting things happen. Every Brazilian I interviewed was convinced that the Carioca way of life was exclusive to Rio, and also exclusive to Brazil.

But it wasn't. The attributes of the Carioca lifestyle are, in fact, characteristic of any number of "water-facing" cultures around the world. The coast of Sydney, Australia, has its own version of Cariocas, and so does Southern California, the North Shore of Hawaii and Miami's South Beach. Taking shape around a beach, or shoreline, each one of these regions is nearly indistinguishable from its overseas counterparts. Each places a strong emphasis on physical attributes, and the natives' popularity is connected to their social ranking. Cariocas across the globe are influential in introducing fashions and brands to the rest of the world. My mission was to try and understand the psychology of the Carioca—the mind-set, that is, of anyone who lives on a fashionable coast—and bottle and sell it.

The Carioca sensibility, then, was simply a local Brazilian version of a suite of emotions and desires that exists all over the world, one that originates in, of all places, the Mediterranean. This was something I'd learned a few years earlier while working for one of the world's oldest, most prestigious clubs in Hong Kong.

As one of Hong Kong's largest community benefactors, the Hong Kong Jockey Club has long been perceived as the aspirational essence of Hong Kong: a gilded, privileged circle that everyone wanted to join but few people could. Yet despite its historical legacy, one issue loomed in the club's future, namely, the brand of the "horse."

Since 1884, the year of the club's founding, the horse had been the Hong Kong Jockey Club's most recognizable icon, and a key asset in distinguishing the club from competing gaming providers. The problem was that worldwide, from 2005 to 2013, Google searches for *horse* had dropped 28 percent. In Hong Kong, *horse* searches were down by as much as 42 percent. Even more significantly, since 2005, Google searches for *horse racing* in Hong Kong had declined 61 percent, and there was also a dramatic decline in sales of local children's toys centered around horses, whether it was toy stables, toy farms, or miniature horses.

These statistics were later confirmed in what I saw, or rather didn't see, in children's bedrooms across Hong Kong. There were no horses. The few times I caught sight of one, it seemed merely decorative. Primed by their own childhood memories of *Black Beauty, The Black Stallion* and Hollywood Westerns, Hong Kong parents had grown up revering the concept of the horse—from the 1930s to the 1960s, the film industry's most popular genre was the Western—but they hadn't passed that interest along to their children. Horses no longer played a starring, or heroic, role in the books parents read to children, or in children's books in general. With some exceptions, Hollywood no longer even made Westerns. Was there any hope for the future of the horse?

Around the world, whether they're engaged in jumping, riding, fox hunting, rodeos or ranch work, the horse symbolizes freedom, beauty, grandeur and power. In order to reestablish the horse "brand," I spent the next few weeks reaching out to local toy companies, and also to Hollywood. Unfortunately, the "rebranding" of the horse never resulted in a full-blown campaign, but along the way it dovetailed with another observation that linked to freedom, aspiration and power.

As I spent day after day observing the races at the Hong Kong Jockey Club, I noticed how the members of the crowd paid greater attention to the men and women they aspired to than they did to the people they didn't. Aspiration is difficult to pick up when you're in an audience setting, easier to observe from a height. Looking down from a balcony, for example, you can see that humans tend to form a circle around the people we admire, or wish to emulate, in the same way we do when in the presence of a politician or celebrity.

People with money in Hong Kong like to show it off. Over a period of several weeks, it became apparent to me that people were ordering foods and drinks based on what a wealthier demographic was ordering. Their own friends, in turn, ordered these same goods and drinks, creating, in the end, an unbroken chain of aspiration. As I mingled with the crowds, I couldn't help but notice a second dimension linked to aspiration: superstition. Over the course of an average day, I saw any number of Hong Kong residents knocking on wood, spitting three times or placing their chopsticks beside their teacups for good luck. Superstition, I knew, had already trickled over into local design schemes. In 2005, while constructing the entrance to Hong Kong Disneyland, executives had decided to adjust the angle of the front gate by 12 degrees, and also placed a subtle bend in the walkway from the train station to the gate to ensure the flow of positive energy, or chi.[7]

To whom did Hong Kong's ultrarich aspire—and what was the connection, if any, between aspiration and superstition? If you glanced at the lapels of the coats of nearly every Hong Kong businessman, or strolled through Hong Kong's malls, you came face-to-face with the same three words: *Made in Italy*. Hong Kong's most popular and renowned restaurants had one theme in common: Italy and Italian food. Hong Kong's highest quality cafés were Italian, and the highest-level deals and meetings all took place in Italian restaurants. Not for the first time, I was reminded how the Mediterranean lifestyle influences humans on a subconscious level. In China, according to the *New York Times,* you can find an Italian-themed retailer called Christdien Deny, whose font is eerily similar to that of Christian Dior, as well as a clothing brand known as Frognie Zila, whose website features photos of Venetian canals and other well-known Italian landmarks.[8] Relatedly, the most aspirational cafés in Japan all have French names (some of which don't make sense in any language, including the "Monna Lisa," "Pierre Herme Paris" and "Quand L'Appetit Va Tout Va"), and roughly 80 percent of all Japanese girls fantasize about marrying in Paris—which no doubt contributes to the record-breaking sales of Louis Vuitton across Japan, as well as to a contemporary psychiatric condition informally known as "Paris Syndrome."[9] According to the BBC, "Paris Syndrome" affects roughly a dozen Japanese tourists every year, who arrive in Paris

bearing romantic expectations of the French capital, but end up hospi-
talized "when they discover that Parisians can be rude, or the city does
not meet their expectations," adding, "The experience can apparently
be too stressful for some and they suffer a psychiatric breakdown."[10]

These parallels—between a country and a foreign culture whose
values compensate for elements or emotions missing in that culture—
are common across the world. The Brazilian flag may feature a blue
globe against a yellow rhombus, yet just as visible across Brazil is the
Swiss flag, whose white cross on a red field shows up on any number of
health-related organizations, pharmacies and physicians' offices in an
attempt to communicate trustworthiness and orderliness in a mostly
chaotic country.

More even than France, why is Italy the repository of so much
global aspiration? One short answer is the car industry, whose brands
include Lamborghini, Ferrari, Bugatti and Maserati, but the Italian
fashion industry provides another answer. What aspirational clues do
Italian brands convey so powerfully that even Hong Kong businessmen
line up to emulate them—and could it possibly provide me with a clue
that could help me turn around Devassa?

Years before I worked for the Hong Kong Jockey Club, I found the
epicenter of aspiration in Tiene, Italy, a small city outside Venice, while
helping a company, Cristiano di Thiene—which owns the licensing
rights to a brand called Aeronautica Militare—figure out who made up
its core audience.

With lines for men, women and children, Aeronautica Militare's
clothing is characterized by patches, symbols and "good luck" icons
borrowed from the military and connected to real-life stories. In conversation with the brand's design team, I found that more than any
other fashion demographic, and like Trollbeads fans and Jenny Craig
customers, Aeronautica's core audience was both intensely loyal and
more superstitious than average.

The fashion industry is akin to a highway with three different
lanes and speeds. Colors, cuts and fashions vary from season to season,
but larger trends, like patches, graphics and logos, endure for decades.

In the wake of the 2008 global recession, many consumers were reluctant to wear high-end logos in public, but recession or no recession, Aeronautica fans continued to wear their clothing proudly and boldly. Ignoring changes and variations in cut and color, Aeronautica fans seemed determined to travel in the fashion world's slowest lane.

As I interviewed Aeronautica fans across both northern and southern Italy, in many residences I stumbled across a symbol or a memento of dreams—a plastic fighter jet, a pilot's uniform, a piece of military insignia hidden in a closet or packed away in a box stuffed underneath a bed. When I asked them about it, many told me about a childhood dream they'd had once that never came to pass. They wanted to be a pilot. They wanted to be powerful, or in charge. They wanted things to run on schedule. With its patches and military iconography, Aeronautica Militare, it seemed, had become a compensation for childhood dreams of freedom. (Many of the brand's fans told me that their fantasies growing up centered around flying.)

Fashion, I was reminded again, gives consumers a shortcut to becoming a perceived member of an aspirational tribe. I've also noticed a direct and unsurprising correlation between people's levels of self-esteem and their display of patches, brand names and logos. Like Ralph Lauren, Aeronautica has two variations of its logo. One is overt, the other subtle. The more discreet logo was favored by Aeronautica fans whose childhood fantasies hadn't come true, whereas fans who were still pursuing their dreams tended to wear the more conspicuous logos.

One Aeronautica fan was a student pilot who'd been in a plane crash at age 24 and lapsed into a coma for nearly three months, never realizing his fantasies of turning professional. When he saw his first Aeronautica shirt, he told me, he fell in love. Another 25-year-old male Aeronautica fan I met favored multiple patches and the brand logo embossed across his coats and shirts. Among his proudest moments, he told me, were when army forces entered the café where he went most mornings and asked if he'd served in the military.

Aeronautica Militare, it seemed, had more in common with an addiction than it did a fashion label. It seemed like its fans could never buy enough of the brand. They also considered it their duty to recruit other fans to Aeronautica—and did so by seeking out individuals who matched the values that the brand represented, visible on both its text-based and non-text-based shirts. To explain, among Aeronautica's several lines is one where the shirt collars lift to reveal authentic Air Force–related codes, jargon and terminology that only military insiders might understand, and another that is missing these details. This distinction, as I later found out, was more important than it might first appear.

The critical clue I gathered about the brand came about by accident as I watched consumers through one of the store's CCTV systems. Nothing unusual stood out until I noticed that a small group of customers engaged in a bizarre reflex: when they picked up an Aeronautica shirt, they flipped the collar up and down. It took one or two seconds at most, and was easy to miss. Were they trying to determine where the shirts were manufactured? If not, what were they looking for?

That night, I found myself in the empty store, doing what I'd seen consumers doing: flipping Aeronautica shirt collars up and down. For the first time, I observed the letters and text-based symbols embroidered on the underside of the collars of certain Aeronautica shirts. Returning upstairs, I reviewed the CCTV tape and sure enough, the shirt collars with the text hidden underneath the flaps were the store's top sellers. I noticed another thing, too. Many of the customers wore their new shirts out the door—an unusual behavior that I couldn't help flagging. As I replayed the CCTV recordings, it became clear that in contrast to the other customers, this same distinct group—15 percent of all the shoppers perhaps—flipped their collars up when exiting the store, displaying the symbols underneath for all the world to see.

A week later, I'd arranged to meet a group of Aeronautica fans at a Milanese nightclub. As we stood around chatting, I began noticing the differences between the Aeronautica fans who wore their collars up and the fans who wore their collars down. It was exclusivity. The ones with the raised collars clustered together in small, tight groups. Those with their collars down were scattered all across the room. While talking to members of the collars-up group, it soon became clear they were from the south of Italy, while the collars-down group was from northern Italy.

We all send out clues that convey our membership in a tribe. It could be the brand of watch we wear, or a pair of shoes. It could be layered clothing, or an absence of socks, or the presence or absence of a logo. If you find a bar of soap in your shower, it's doubtful you are in northern Europe, or, for that matter, New Zealand, whose residents seldom use bar soaps either, and whose culture is oddly similar to Scandinavia. Beyond how we adorn ourselves physically, the clue could reside on the rear end of a car. In Zurich, Switzerland, for example, residents with four-digit license plates are perceived to be wealthier and better connected than those with a six-number plate, a subtle distinction among the residents of one of the world's richest cities. In honor of my experience working with Aeronautica, I call this phenomenon "The Flipping Theory." In the case of Aeronautica shirts and collars, I could only guess that among southern Italians, a raised collar made it easier to pick up women.

Still, a crucial ingredient of Italian behavior, one I would later bring into my work for Devassa in Brazil, didn't take place until the following day.

Sitting down for lunch in a café outside Bologna, I noticed that my waiter and, for that matter, *every* Italian waiter, had a habit of pouring soda, water or beer into my glass from a high vertical angle. In almost every other country, waiters pour liquids while keeping the bottle at a subtle horizontal tilt. But in Italy, waiters raised the bottle high, as if wanting to drain it more quickly and accurately. Following their scene-setting, attention-getting leads, Italian customers topped off their own drinks in the same way.

Where had I seen this behavior before? The answer: Brazil. Whether in Rio, Salvador or São Paulo, Brazilian waiters and consumers pouring drinks turned the bottle over until it was nearly upside down, allowing the liquid to drain as quickly as possible. This small habit, shared by Italians and Brazilians, gave me a link that would help me connect the dots between two different, but similar, cultures.

The two countries also shared a love of football, or what Americans call "soccer." I knew that in their work on behalf of Chevrolet, the US automaker, the marketing group Jack Morton Worldwide found a way to turn football into a unique platform. Knowing that football provides a strong, emotional connection with fans of all ages, company executives immersed themselves in the sport and its singular relationship with fans across the globe. The agency ultimately created a partnership with the One World Play Project, a start-up organization whose mission is to bring virtually indestructible balls to children in war zones, refugee camps, disaster areas and other disadvantaged communities around the world.

Which made me wonder: Could a similar alliance take place between Brasil Kirin—which manufactures soft drinks as well as beer—and Brazilian soccer? When I began interviewing soccer coaches in Salvador and São Paulo, it soon became clear there was a dramatic need for mentoring and sponsorship programs in Brazil, but that the expense and the country's infrastructure would make them too difficult to implement. That's when I turned my attention elsewhere.

FOR YEARS, I'VE BEEN INTRIGUED by the similarities between the world's most influential brands and the world's best-known religions. I once went so far as to interview 14 leaders from religions including Protestantism, Catholicism, Buddhism and Islam in an attempt to figure out the ten characteristics their faiths had in common. In order of importance, I found that they were: A sense of belonging; storytelling; rituals; symbols; a clear vision; sensory appeal; power from enemies; evangelism; mystery; and grandeur. When you think about the world's most powerful brands—among them Apple, Nike, Harley-Davidson, Coca-Cola, LEGO—you realize they all make use of some if not all of these pillars. Apple, for example, shrouds its product releases in mystery. Apple fans are among the most ardent brand evangelists in the world, and Apple also offers its users a strong sense of "belonging." Not least, is it any coincidence that the Apple logo hangs from an unseen thread in many Apple Stores like a Bethlehem star?

Among the most elusive of these ten precepts is the sense of community and belonging. In an information age, most of us feel unanchored. The mobile economy has allowed many people to live anywhere they want, and the more "community"—that feeling of localness and belonging—makes its way online, the more it has dropped away in real life.

No less essential to a religion—or a brand—are rituals. Whether you drink a Corona beer alongside a lime, or order a Caffè Misto at Starbucks, the rituals of a shared language, and a shared way of doing things, bond consumers together. Rituals serve as an entry ticket to an exclusive universe consumers want to join, and the more often they repeat a ritual, the more of a hardcore fan they become. This subject seemed worth exploring, especially since religion was declining across Brazil.

Brazil is the world's largest Catholic country, with 60 percent of Brazilians identifying themselves as Catholics, a decline from a Catholic majority of 92 percent in 1970. Studies estimate that the decline in practicing Catholics in Brazil will continue and that "by 2030 Catholics will represent less than 50 percent of Brazilian churchgoers."[11] Expecting high levels of religious enthusiasm across the country, I was surprised to hear from Brazilians how little a role religion played in their lives. Even if they hadn't said anything, the trend was visible in many residences. Fasting and abstinence are common to the Catholic Church's Advent, Ember Days and Rogation Days, but most Brazilians told me they paid them no attention. Two decades earlier, when I first visited Brazil, every room would have had at least one of its corners devoted to the Virgin Mary, or at the very least a religious urn holding a spray of flowers, but in contemporary Brazil, most people's "collections" consisted of branded beer cans or bottles holding flowers or pens. Most Brazilians told me that if they were remotely attracted to religion, it wasn't to traditional Catholicism, but to newer evangelist and spiritualist teachings.

I knew, too, from my own studies that there was a direct correlation between commercial characters from movies, television shows and games in homes (including Homer Simpson, Snoopy and Hello Kitty) and lower rates of churchgoing. In one Salvador favela, I remembered a teenaged boy showing me a figurine common across Brazil: a small white glass horse and a rider. It was St. George, a Roman soldier and Christian martyr famous for battling a dragon with a sword. St. George was a symbol for victory, but not, it seemed, religious victory. Every week, the boy told me, he and his friends would ritualistically fill a small glass with beer and set it in front of St. George and his horse, ensuring that their favorite local football team, Todo Poderoso Timao, won that week's game. More than religion, it seemed, a local Brazilian football team was fulfilling the desire for belonging, and a beer brand was now connected with good luck, belonging and camaraderie.

In the northern city of Salvador, I also couldn't help but notice the colorful local bracelets for sale. These were known as Bahia bands, or wish bracelets, whose origins are said to correspond and intertwine both with African gods and Catholic credo. In Brazil, wearing one or another color is said to bring out the color's innate characteristics. Orange signifies joy and enthusiasm; green is said to impart money and growth; and hot pink represents friendship. Equally as important as what color you wear is how you tie a Bahia band, making a wish on each of the three knots you tie—no more, no less—and keeping the Bahia band on your wrist until it falls off naturally.

If religion was declining in Brazil, what was taking the place of the human desire for belonging, and unity, and mystery, and ritual? What made Brazilians feel like they belonged to something greater than themselves?

The answer, as prevalent in Hong Kong as it was in Italy and Brazil, was superstition and ritual. Keeping in mind the north-versus-south cultural divisions in Italy, and the west-versus-east rivalry in Brazil, I knew I'd found the start of a solution to reinventing Devassa for the twenty-first century. What stood out most about Brazil? Aspiration. The need to show off, to assert membership in a tribe. A countrywide decline in religion and churchgoing. Taking inspiration from the world's religions, I would give Devassa three attributes borrowed from the world's best-known religions: evangelism, sensory appeal and rituals.

ONCE I'VE DEVELOPED THE BEGINNINGS of a hypothesis—in this case, that Brazil and Italy were, at core, similar cultures—I generally begin searching for additional small data that can either support or overturn my premise. For example, how do women wear their hair, and if they color their hair, what is the most popular shade? In Italy, women favor blond hair dye. (Flip through the stations on Italian television, and it sometimes seems that every second woman has hair so blond it's almost white. In addition to getting rid of curls, blond hair dye is equally popular across Brazil, as blond hair is synonymous with wealth and popularity.)

If Brazil had more aspirational consumers than almost any other country in the world, then quite possibly Italy, and Italian culture, could help me decode what Brazilians really wanted. In addition to how waiters and consumers held their bottles, and women colored their hair, there were other parallels between Italy and Brazil, including climate, high levels of governmental corruption and the influence of the Catholic Church. Italy and Brazil were even geographically divided in a similar fashion, with the south symbolizing "pleasure" and "easy living" and the north representing business, and efficiency, and order.

To create a sense of belonging, the first thing I needed to do was link Devassa to the Carioca sensibility. I knew that the authenticity, casualness and freedom of the Cariocas was seductive to Brazilians living outside Rio. Along with its beers, Devassa also owns and operates stand-alone bar-restaurants in choice locations along the coast that offer Brazilian cuisine, free Wi-Fi and, of course, Devassa beer. Devassa's bars were, in fact, my secret weapon. I would use them as "temples," or places of worship, where members of the Devassa "brand congregation" could congregate.

South America is known as a "high contact" culture, meaning that residents stand closer to one another, touch one another more and are accustomed to more sensory stimulation than residents in, say, northern Europe, with Australians and North Americans believed to be more moderate in their cultural contact level. In Brazil and elsewhere across Latin America, music matters, which is why it was important to create a tactile, sensory impression with the Devassa beer glass. My own research shows that if we "record" an experience using multiple senses, we remember it 200 percent more than we would if only a single track were involved. Add a social element, or a sense of belonging, and our memories engage even more powerfully with the experience.

Just as French and Austrian glass makers have evolved the production of glass to a fine art by matching a specific wine to a specific glass—resulting in literally thousands of different wineglasses on the market—the new Devassa-branded beer bottle would enhance and soften Devassa's taste. By emphasizing Devassa's fragrance (60 percent of the taste of any beverage derives from its fragrance), the Devassa-branded bottle would become the new, exclusive way to drink Devassa beer.

As a group, wine drinkers indirectly signal how much they know about the wine in front of them. They swirl the wine around in the glass. They air the wine out. They take a sip, and hold the liquid in one cheek. They talk about the aroma, the astringency, the body and the taste left on the palate, or the "finish." It is almost as though they are persuading themselves that the more they know about the wine they are drinking, the more money they're willing to spend. The rituals of airing wine, and swirling it in the wineglass, had become so synonymous with expertise that over the years I've caught people unconsciously swirling water and ginger ale in cafés and restaurants.

The next step was to create a signature Devassa ritual.

Broadly speaking, a ritual can be defined as a fixed sequence of behaviors or words that transport us from one emotional, social or physical state to another. Most rituals operate on two levels. The first is tangible, and sensory, while the second is symbolic and emotional. Ideally, like the lime in a Corona beer or Amazon's one-click "Add to Cart" button, the ritual should be simple, memorable, easy to execute and anchored in reality.

At heart, our new Devassa ritual—which will soon be rolled out across Devassa bars nationwide—is all about experimentation and "finding your own flavor." Here's how it works: Entering one of Devassa's branded seaside bars, a customer orders a draft. The waiter or bartender is instructed to ask, "Would you like an extra flavor with that?" The staffer then produces a tasting tray on which rest four shot glasses whose rims are dusted with differently flavored powders, from salty to lemony to chocolate-infused, giving the glasses a frosted edge similar to the salt that hugs margarita glasses. (Our waiters are also expert at placing the exact amount of powder on the rims.) Customers test out the flavors, eventually ordering a pint of beer alongside their flavor of choice. So far, the new Devassa ritual has been performing very well, and I'm optimistic about how it will continue to do in the future. Most impressive is how much the new ritual stands out, and attracts attention, creating the best possible synergy with the beer itself, engaging consumers while also bringing in nonbeer drinkers, too.

There was a second important dimension I also wanted to instill: transformation. Across the world, almost everyone fantasizes about sitting by the ocean, especially on hot summer days. Locally, though, access to Rio's most popular beaches is reserved mostly for tourists or members of the upper classes, in the same way the skyboxes at the Hong Kong Jockey Club are for those who can afford them. Yet Jockey Club customers at every price level can catch a glimpse of what it's like to perceive a horse race, and the world, through a skybox. To this end, we redesigned our Devassa bars to ensure the possibility of transformation. My goal was to whisk customers away from their everyday problems and complaints and into a parallel world where "life is but a dream." I might add that Devassa bars have their own set of rules. In each is a pen, a notebook and a black box. Customers memorialize and deposit all their work problems into the box before abandoning themselves to beer drinking and camaraderie.

Transformation. Consumers wanted to escape the crowds, dirt, dust, poverty and relentless church of Rio. How could we help transform them into becoming freer, happier, sexier fantasies of themselves?

To this end, we created a gigantic floating island—in effect, a Devassa-branded bar floating 200 feet off the shore of Copacabana, complete with deejays, surfboard-shaped tables and cameras live-streaming all the festivities to the mainland. The mission? To make the dream of lounging ocean-side "almost real"—but also tantalizingly out-of-reach. In the future, our Devassa island float will make appearances at the Rio Carnival, where Devassa will sell beer not available anywhere else, and at various street parties from Rio to São Paulo.

Having addressed the national need for superstition and ritual, I was left with the topic of aspiration. Here, I couldn't help but think back to what a marketing colleague told me once about working for Sabra, the hummus manufacturers. The hardest part of working at Sabra, she told me, was creating a transformation in the American diet from processed, unhealthy snacks to more wholesome, vegetable-based fresh foods. Her mission, as she saw it, was literally to alter consumer behavior. The fantasy she had of every American man, woman and child snacking on chickpea-based hummus seemed possible, exciting and even heroic—that is, until she began interviewing people one-on-one in cities and towns across the American Midwest. Sitting in homes, attempting to interest consumers in their first (free) taste of hummus proved to be surprisingly difficult.

Among the first things my colleague found out was that for the uninitiated, the most common perception of hummus was a brown, boring, vegan, "hipster" food, one associated with aging hippies, acid trips and tie-dyed T-shirts. Most interview subjects told her they seldom if ever touched the stuff. The team then interviewed experienced hummus-lovers who ate hummus passionately and regularly. In common, most if not all of these people revealed that they had a memorable "first time." Each had a very close friend—a person they knew well, and trusted—"concierge" them into trying out the dip amid a small gathering of close friends. In most cases, this trusted friend had given them hummus to sample along with a familiar snack they loved, whether it was baby carrots or potato chips, while also emphasizing that hummus was both wholesome and healthy.

This "concierge" insight inspired Sabra to rethink their marketing campaign, and made them prioritize "experiential sampling" in ways they hadn't before. Sabra began to understand the value of its most loyal consumers as future "concierges." This insight, needless to say, would never have come about from survey data, but only as the result of ethnographic research and the search for smaller data.

The Cariocas, I knew from experience, were less a specific demographic than a universal ideal. In common with beachside communities across the world, from Hawaii's North Beach to the surfing communities of Malibu and Seal Beach, California, the Carioca symbolized informal living, physical beauty, wealth, freedom and lack of responsibility—in short, those characteristics we believe that southern Italy embodies.

Two weeks later, my team and I had selected four visible, innovative, well-connected Cariocas whom we appointed as seeders and ambassadors for Devassa 2.0. Our Carioca ambassadors would use their distinct networks to present monthly cultural events—parties, sports activities, fashion shows, music concerts, art openings and charity events—that incorporated the Devassa brand, and gave our newly revitalized beer the opportunity to connect authentically with consumers. Our four Cariocas would have an enormous influence on the public perception of Devassa, their responsibility being to seed, or thread, the brand back inside Rio society at an aspirational level, and from Rio to the rest of Brazil. They were tasked not only to generate interaction through social media, but also to recruit ten additional "amplifiers" who could spread the word about Devassa online and off.

More than a drink or its taste, we tend to remember the stories that surround our drinking. The better a beverage is at inspiring conversation, the more we feel that we, and the drink in question, are integral parts of the same tribe. It is still too early to assess how Devassa 2.0 will fare, but the executive team and I fully expect consumers to congregate around the beer's new narrative—one that combines transformation, desire, sensory appeal and ritual to create an experience honed in Hong Kong, developed in Italy . . . and common to anyone who has ever craved transcendence—that is to say, all of us.

CHAPTER 6
THE CASE OF THE MISSING HAND CREAM

HOW SELFIES SMOOTHED THE WAY FOR AN IN-STORE FASHION REVOLUTION

AS FAR AS PRODUCTS AND BRANDS ARE CONCERNED, THE world is no longer local. Two or three decades ago, tourists could come back from visiting a country 3,000 miles away assured that the souvenirs they'd brought home with them in their suitcases—the Sumatra-Indonesian Barbie Doll, the wooden salad tongs from Botswana with animal carvings, a sweater from French Gap with a neck zipper—were not only one-of-a-kind, but could be someday directly linked back to memory and experience. Today, there are few objects that tourists can store in their suitcases that aren't already available somewhere, from someone, online, detaching the treasures we find while traveling from the context of experience.

Still, just as there's a wide array of Western brands and companies that Russian and Asian consumers would be surprised to discover exist, some stores and brands remain unknown to a majority of Westerners. I've already mentioned Picard, France's frozen-food chain, but it's also safe to assume most US and European natives have never heard of Mr. Bigg's, a Nigerian fast-food chain with over 170 locations across that country serving local delicacies including moin moin and ofada rice.

What about NTT DOCOMO—not AT&T, or Verizon—which controls approximately one-half of Japan's wireless market? Won Hundred is an up-and-coming Danish menswear company, and a Chinese eyewear chain with the breathtaking name of Helen Keller sells frames and sunglasses at 80 Chinese locations.

It's also fair to say that few people outside of Europe are familiar with Tally Weijl, a leading Swiss-French fashion label headquartered in Basel, Switzerland, whose logo is the silhouette of an extremely pink rabbit.

Tally, as its tween and teenaged female clientele calls it, has approximately 1,000 stores in 30 countries including Ireland, Italy, Holland, Poland, Germany, Greece and Russia. Similar to H&M or Forever 21, Tally's low prices are similar to Target's price points. So why did Tally Weijl need to bring in a branding consultant? The chain had a problem—namely unused, unsold merchandise. For years Tally had succeeded again and again in hitting the fashion nerve—the perfect length, the trendiest style, the hottest color—but the company's warehouses still overflowed with millions of dollars' worth of unsold inventory. Nor did the teenaged girls I interviewed in my preliminary Subtext Research seem to enjoy visiting Tally's physical stores. The spaces were dense, cramped and disordered, they told me, and overloud techno music pounded from overhead speakers, as if the fashion and jackhammer industries had merged beneath one roof. It was sensory overload, and not in an exhilarating way.

Why were twenty-first-century adolescent girls so fickle about fashion? Was it a worldwide problem, one caused by customers of all ages reluctant to pay full price for clothes they knew they could buy online instead at a discount? If the Internet had transformed the role of the bricks-and-mortar retailer and the definition of "social"—which it clearly has—were there any new ways of successfully combining the offline and online worlds?

AN ISSUE TROUBLING not only Tally Weijl but all fashion retailers is Fashion Week, which predates the Internet by half a century. Fashion Week debuted in Paris in the late 1940s and, as it still does today, showcases to buyers, customers, industry experts and the media the latest fashions and designs for every season. Fashion Week still takes place twice a year in New York, London, Milan and Paris, and additional unofficial Fashion Weeks occur in Brazil, Germany, Australia and pretty much anywhere else in the world girls and women love fashion and new clothes.

Obviously, segmenting fashion by season generates opportunities for consumer purchasing, which is why over the past few decades, the four fashion seasons have expanded to include subseasons like "prefall," "resort," "swimwear" and "ready-to-wear." For adolescent girls who want nothing more complex than to blend in with their peers while subtly standing out from them, too, the "seasons" concept serves to remind them of the ephemeralness of their enthusiasms, as well as how easy it is to fall behind the curve.

Outsourcing manufacturing overseas has been a boon for Western retailers and designers, with roughly 98 percent of the clothes worn in the West manufactured in China, with the rest coming out of Vietnam, Thailand, Honduras and elsewhere.[1] Less welcome is a multiseason fashion year that obliges designers to keep abreast of trends, as well as to predict the vagaries of upcoming seasons as much as 18 months in advance. (Drug abuse, breakdowns and suicide are common in an industry dedicated to coming up with new, innovative ways of—there's no other way to put it—making a shirt.)

For most retailers, the process goes like this: After receiving specifications on cuts, colors and lengths, factory workers in mainland China manufacture the clothes, which are then loaded onto a container ship for their long transatlantic voyage. Once the clothes arrive at their destination, workers transport them onto trucks, which ferry them to distribution outlets and area stores. In the worst-case scenario, a fashion or style will pivot in an unexpected direction—blue has overtaken black, and the color green, for no good reason, repels buyers—when a container ship is in transit. In response, some retailers will go so far as to ask ships to return to port and destroy their shipments. (Rumor has it Zara, the Spanish-based retailer, and others have begun producing clothing aboard ships equipped with large production lines, allowing for dramatic turnarounds in taste at the last minute.)

Some, though, have found ways to lower the risk of chucking millions of dollars' worth of clothing items every year. The Italian-owned Benetton label, for example, manufactures its entire clothing line in white. Once the clothes are delivered to distribution centers, Benneton's analysts assess what color or length is in vogue, at which point workers dye and cut the company's shirts, jackets, pants and infant apparel to replicate the style and color preferences popular at the time. But Benetton is the exception, not the rule, in an industry that wields less control than it would like.

Like the cosmetics industry, fashion centers around desire, around aspiration, around the concept of transformation. "Enclothed cognition" is a psychological phenomenon that refers to the influences our clothing has on our cognitive and decision-making processes, and the ways we unconsciously adapt our behavior to the people and symbols around us. Do our voices get higher when we're talking to a baby? Do they slow down when we address an elderly person? Do they deepen in the presence of our parents, or get higher around our pets? Does our behavior change in the presence of a police officer, a firefighter or a physician? Most of the time, the answer is yes. (Studies reveal that if we put on a white coat that we've been told belongs to a physician, we pay closer attention to our surroundings, but if we're told the same white coat belongs to a painter, our attention shows no improvement at all.[2])

Enclothed cognition is a variant of a field of scientific study known as embodied cognition, that believes that "humans think not only with their brains but with their bodies,[3]" and that in turn, our bodies themselves can suggest various abstract concepts in our brains that affect our behavior."[4] For example, if you or I carry around a clipboard, in general we feel more important, organized and mindful of what we have to do that day. For unconscious reasons, we associate washing our hands with moral cleanliness, and we also rate people holding a cup of hot coffee as warmer and more approachable than we do people who are holding a glass of iced tea. Also, when asked to focus on an upcoming event, we tend to tilt forward in our seats, as if physically "meeting" our own futures, but we tilt discreetly backward in our seats if someone asks us to reflect on events that have already taken place.[5]

Enclothed and embodied cognition are both nascent fields of psychological study, yet neither will surprise anyone who has ever bought a new article of clothing and believed it would redress issues ranging from poor self-esteem to social phobia. In fact, from the moment we open our eyes in the morning, most of us unconsciously seek out external totems of transformation. Our smartphone. Our first cup of coffee. Showering, shampooing our hair, shaving our legs or faces and changing into our work clothes are all rituals of becoming. At the end of the day, when we wash off our greasepaint and change out of our costumes, we confront who we were all along. On my visits to the United Kingdom, Germany and Scandinavia, I'm always struck by the sheer number of billboards advertising suntan creams and oils intended to darken natives' complexions. But Indonesia, India, Thailand and Brazil offer almost the same number of billboards marketing creams that promise to whiten complexions. Everyone aspires to be something just a bit different than they actually are.

As I prepared for my Subtexting on behalf of Tally Weijl, I came up against two roadblocks. First, I was an older male asking questions of adolescent females; and second, there was a language barrier. Almost none of the teenaged girls I interviewed in Switzerland, France, Austria, Italy, Spain, Turkey, Poland and the Ukraine spoke English. But in the end, it didn't matter, as most of the girls eventually allowed me inside their bedrooms, and bedrooms always convey more information in total silence than most people do using words.

Whenever I enter the bedroom of any teenager, male or female, I carry a checklist with me. Clothing always comes first. Is it displayed openly, or hidden in the closet? What brands are openly displayed, if any? Are there posters or artwork hanging on the wall? How and where is the bed positioned? How central is the bed? Is there a bedspread, quilt or duvet? How many pillows? Where on the bed do you find wear and tear or evidence of heavy use? How close is the bed to the nearest electrical wall socket? How many hours a day do the owners spend in their bedrooms? In addition to these bedroom details, how many selfies do they shoot on average during a 24-hour period? How much time do they spend on their laptops, versus their tablets, versus their phones? What role do music and videos play in their lives, and from where do they access them mostly?

Lastly, I study the parallels between a girl's "home"—her bedroom—and her Facebook "home" page. I like to say that social media is the new bedroom wall. Just as they do inside their own sleeping areas, Facebook users upload artwork and photographs onto their "walls," "like" certain books, magazines and films, and create photo collages and albums. An open Rolodex of their friends is always available for perusal and, of course, users are regularly urged to update their "statuses," a word Facebook means literally.

Social media home pages and offline homes have another critical thing in common: only a small fraction of what we post on social media bears much resemblance to what's really going on in our lives—and our real homes are often edited constructs of who we believe ourselves to be. To add even more complexity to this question, I knew that even though creating a Facebook page has become a rite of passage for a 13-year-old, a teenager's more authentic self is more likely to show up on places most parents don't dare trespass, like Instagram, or across free text-messaging apps like WeChat, Kik and WhatsApp.

First, though, an adolescent girl's identity, aspirations and desires can be found in her bedroom, a place where almost nothing is left to chance.

The bedrooms of adolescents have changed dramatically in only ten years. The centerpiece of any child's room used to be a desk, a chair and a desktop or laptop computer. Today, it's the bed itself. In the past few years, beds have literally expanded, as the result of teenaged boys and girls using them as command posts. Sure, some kids still use desks when doing their homework, but for most teenagers and even college students, the bed is where they read, study, doze, slump, text, post, FaceTime, Skype, listen to music and watch videos, usually simultaneously.

As a result, the concept of light has also changed. All around the world, when we wake up, the first thing most of us reach for is our phone, which has become as much a transitional object as the blankets we carried around with us when we were young. A 2014 survey carried out by YouGov and the *Huffington Post* revealed that almost two-thirds of smartphone users between the ages of 18 and 29 actually sleep "with their phones or tablets in their beds,"[6] implying that our first and final exposure to light during a 24-hour period is the artificial blue light of pixels. The radiance from our phones is almost more potent, and pertinent, than either sunlight or moonlight. A decade ago, there were anywhere from two to five lamps in the average teenaged girl's bedroom. Today, as patches of screen-light illuminate our bedrooms instead, lamps have become nearly as redundant as desks.

Along with light, the concept of "display" has also gone through any number of changes. Chairs still exist, but mostly serve as structures on which to drape or hang clothing. Ten years ago, girls' bedroom walls were papered with any number of posters and artwork. Today, two posters at most hang on the average girl's wall. In many cases, girls may have long outgrown their interest in the subject of the poster, but when asked why they haven't taken it down, they invariably give the same answer: they don't have "time," or they're "too busy." The real reason, it became clear to me later, is that they're holding on to what remains of their childhoods, an idea I'll be revisiting later on.

Boys' bedrooms have undergone a similar number of changes in the past decade, and whenever rooms have transformed, it's safe to say their owners have, too. Generally speaking, adolescent males are becoming more like adolescent females, and the reverse is also true. If today's girls are nerdier, today's boys are needier. Once upon a time, boys would sprawl, the edge of a shoe or a sneaker grazing the chair or couch, but today, boys have taken to curling one ankle around the other. In general they've become more fashion-focused, with trendy shoes and sneakers taking on increasing importance in their lives. Hence the omnipresence of the floor-length mirror, which today as many boys as girls are likely to have.

But what could girls' bedrooms—in Switzerland, Italy, France, Austria, Germany and Poland—tell me about reversing the fortunes of a Swiss-based fashion retailer? Frankly I was puzzled where to start, and a few weeks later, having conducted Subtext Research across eastern and western Europe, I wasn't all that much smarter. Apart from the overall changes in décor I've just noted, and the prominence of the bed, at that point nothing I saw or heard struck me as terribly unusual, which is why I turned things around and asked each girl I interviewed if she wouldn't mind keeping a videotaped and text-based diary, and also whether they were willing to take a dozen photographs that best described who they were (or rather, how they saw themselves).

As far as the videotaped diary was concerned, the rules were simple: The girl was asked to fill out what she did that day, and what she planned to do the next. If she visited a website, she had to write down its name, and the same went for the music she listened to and the videos she watched. At first, the recounting felt cliché and staged—most girls seemed to be reenacting what they saw on shows like *Sex and the City* and *Pretty Little Liars*—but as time went on the videos grew looser and more relaxed: *I am now going to the fridge. Tonight I am going out to meet my boyfriend. I'm now going onto YouTube to listen to Sia's new song.*

Based on their photographs alone, I realized that almost all the pictures the girls had shot revealed imbalances. Ironically, these were often "counterbalanced" on the girls' Facebook pages. The Facebook photo of one girl struggling with her weight showed her profile only, and a gaggle of slender, good-looking friends. The Facebook page of another girl whose parents were divorcing, and who'd confided in me how alone she felt, showed a girl who was literally never by herself. Offline was the real world, it seemed, while dreams lived online. There was another thing, too: Based on their online videos and separate interviews, the lives of adolescent girls revolved around fashion and dressing up. My research revealed that girls spent around 80 percent of their waking hours mulling what they wore that day, what they were thinking about wearing the next day and clothing in general—a somewhat shocking statistic. They were also online anywhere from two to three hours a day visiting their favorite fashion retailers, websites and Tumblr blogs. Swiss girls were preoccupied by British and German fashion websites, as well as Tumblr, Instagram and Snapchat, while eastern European girls tracked Scandinavian websites. Most girls knew the fashion world intimately well, including the names of the top models, and kept an official or unofficial wish list of outfits they wanted to buy but couldn't afford.

This same preoccupation with fashion could be seen with their smartphones themselves, beginning with their covers, which were plastered with stickers and decals, and extending to the apps: color-matching apps, apps that matched lipstick hues to clothing, apps that gave the locations of the hottest clubs in town and apps offering techniques to improve a girl's appearance or make her look slimmer than she was. Not a single girl I met was at peace with how she looked. She either considered herself too plump or too slender, an issue, I might add, that can and should be blamed squarely on the contemporary clothing store. For ease-of-manufacturing reasons, retailers don't produce a wide range of clothes for a range of body shapes, and rather than blaming manufacturers, girls convince themselves that the fault lies with them.

Then there were the selfies. A selfie can sometimes tell me more about a person than anything inside a meticulously staged bedroom. When a girl shows another girl a photo on a smartphone, the first few things she seeks out are, in order of importance: Am I in this picture? How do I look? Who is standing beside me? Does the person standing beside me in this photo lend me a halo effect of popularity, or is standing beside this person a social liability? Selfies, it seemed, were even more important than the event or moment they were supposed to memorialize.

Finally, I put aside an entire week to go shopping with large groups of girls. If there was an H&M near their house or apartment, they would go down there for 45 minutes to an hour, walk around, chat with store employees and ogle the mannequins. They weren't there to buy anything; they were there to immerse themselves in a fashion fantasy, and maybe touch the hem of their own aspiration—it was as if by shopping at a global chain, they had come that much closer to escaping their own local identities. Still, as the girls trooped through store after store, with me trailing behind them, taking notes, I couldn't help but notice that along with observing the clothes, they were also busy evaluating the other girls in the store. Subconsciously, it seemed, girls perceived a clothing store less on what it has for sale, and more on the other women who are shopping there. (The same is often true for prospective female students when they visit college and university campuses.) If the other girls aren't cool or aspirational enough, a girl will take her business elsewhere.

Inside Tally Weijl and other retailers, I observed another intriguing behavior. Girls rarely, if ever, shopped by themselves. Instead, a small crowd of three, four or five girls would appear in the dressing room area. Two of them would stand sentry as a pair of other girls disappeared inside the dressing room to try on a piece of clothing. When one or both girls came out, they were met with a flurry of approving or disapproving comments and opinions. But was this really all that unusual? (The answer turned out to be yes, but at the time this observation didn't feel like anything at all.)

I walked away from my first round of Subtext Research with the distinct impression of how difficult and confusing it must be to be a 14- or 15-year old girl, shy and bold at the same time, dependent on your parents and family, but with your physical development overtaking your chronological age—a confusion that showed up in the teddy bears that kept appearing in bedrooms from Poland to Austria.

Worn and adorable as they were, these teddy bears weren't what they seemed. Many of the girls I interviewed told me they had a boyfriend, and when I asked them about their teddy bears, it was clear in most cases that the teddy bear was a stand-in for the boys in their lives. "Describe your teddy bear," I would say, or "What was the first time you felt really close to your teddy bear?" or "Can you describe a moment when your teddy disappointed you?" These questions weren't as strange as they sound. When girls discussed the boys in their lives, they seldom described them accurately, as I would later find out when meeting the boys; what I heard instead was how girls *wanted* their boy-friends to be, and what their idealized image-making said about the girls themselves.

Teenaged girls inhabited an uncertain area made up of two sepa-rate universes: a Toys"R"Us world of the past, and a sexualized future ecosystem symbolized by stores like Victoria's Secret. Most girls who went into Victoria's Secret told me they felt out of place, and even un-comfortable. At the same time, still living at home, they no longer felt like children. In contrast to boys, their own physical and psychological development placed them in a gray area with no real name of its own. One snapshot I took summed up this duality perfectly and poignantly: a teddy bear sitting on a blanket embossed with a Playboy bunny in a bedroom belonging to a 15-year-old girl.

As well as being preoccupied with how they looked, girls were also hyperconscious of how their friends, and the world itself, perceived them. Being a teenaged girl meant that you were petrified of standing alone, or being left out, forgotten or rejected. Today, everyone knows what a girl does when she is feeling insecure about herself: she posts a new photo of herself on Facebook and awaits a flurry of compliments about her appearance. Once she's regained a dose of self-confidence, she is ready to become, once again, the star of her own life.

IN MY WORK ACROSS BRAZIL on behalf of a beer manufacturer (which I covered in chapter 5), I couldn't help noticing that the bed-rooms of every Brazilian girl featured a display, or collection, of some kind, usually of colorful beer bottles. (Beer drinking is extremely com-mon among Brazilian adolescents.) These collections communicated a message about who a girl wanted to be, or alternately, about the people, or socioeconomic class, with whom she wanted most to be associated. In some cases, the girl in question didn't even like the beer brand she had on display—such as Heineken—but that didn't matter. Heineken cost more than the average beer brand, and Brazilian girls would save up for weeks to afford a night out at a popular club. It was as if by surrounding herself with Heineken bottles during the week, she could somehow move closer to the sort of person she imagined herself being, as well as to the friends she hoped someday to attract.

There was no analogy to those beer cans in the bedrooms I visited in eastern and western Europe. Sure, an Austrian girl might have on display a set of matching pillows, a Polish girl a tray of perfumes, but nothing close to what I had seen in Brazil. Still, knowing that fashion is always linked to aspiration and transformation, I knew I needed to discover where girls kept their "secret display," in the hopes it could help Tally Weijl better understand its consumers. I finally found what I was looking for in an expected place: on girls' feet. Whenever I opened the door to a closet packed with clothing and shoes, I knew I'd discovered the equivalent of a "beer shelf." What's more, girls told me that every single pair of shoes had a purpose, a concrete reason for being. Any girl who owns and wears shoes knows that footwear is a reflection of her mood and attitude, and that shoes, like music, can both reflect and dictate the way someone feels. Based on the Subtexting I carried out, the average teenaged Swiss girl owned 19 pairs of shoes, compared to 15 for a French girl and 13 for a German girl.

That's when I decided to conduct a little experiment. For the next week and a half, every time I flew into a capital city—Berlin, Bern, Paris, Rome, London—I left my hotel and took a long walk. I had no intention of sightseeing. I had a single mission: to track the gazes of every woman on the sidewalk as they passed another woman on the sidewalk. I realized that almost always, the first thing a woman's eyes landed on were the other woman's shoes.

Back on the job, I began photographing the inside of closets, taking photo after photo of the shoes inside. A week later, I returned to the same girls' bedrooms, where I decided to take additional photos of the insides of their closets. Which was when I noticed a strange thing had taken place in only seven days' time. Contrasting the photos I'd taken a week before against the new set, I found that the appearance and even the sequence of the shoes had changed. Only rarely was a pair of shoes in its old spot. This confused me, considering that almost every girl had told me that despite the number of shoes she wore, she seldom put on more than one or two pairs a week. Still, when I brought up this contradiction, most girls shrugged. Maybe they'd tried on the shoes, maybe they hadn't. They couldn't remember.

WHEN YOU GAZE AT ONE THING for a long time, you become blind, and as far as teenaged shoe wear was concerned, I felt as though I'd lost my ability to see things clearly. If I can't understand something, or if something makes no sense, I need to walk away from it for a few days and shock my senses back to normal. In this case, I needed to look elsewhere within the same family ecosystem, but at another end of the spectrum: the bathroom.

Some girls had their own bathrooms; others shared bathrooms with siblings; still others shared family bathrooms. Not surprisingly, most were stocked with standard products like toothbrushes, toothpaste tubes, deodorants, perfumes and lip glosses. What was missing? Anything? No. Nothing was missing. Or was there? It took a few days for the answer to hit me: there were few if any face or hand creams, and when there were, the lotions I saw were water-based. Ten years earlier, the face and hand creams you'd find in most girls' bathrooms were oil-based. Oil-based creams not only last longer, they also cause less damage to skin in cold weather. Yet in only a decade, they had vanished from girls' bathrooms. Why?

Hand creams. Skin creams. Selfies. Hidden shoe collections. It was almost the definition of small data. Alone, none of these things had anything significant to say, but together, they indicated a possible hypothesis. That hypothesis—if I could even call it that at that stage— was, possibly, connected to technology. The moment I realized that oil-based hand and face creams had disappeared from girls' cosmetic collections, my first thought was that face and hand moisturizers make users' fingers fatally sticky. They leave gluey-looking marks on keyboards and space bars. Not only that, but shining skin also creates a reflective glare, which most people would agree is antithetical to the spirit of a good selfie. Most girls are canny enough to know that oil-based creams, text messaging and selfie taking don't mix.

By now I had a theory in mind but I first needed to collect more evidence. Over the next few days, in every home I visited, I asked the same question: would the girls—or their parents—be willing to show me their monthly cell phone statements? Not just the short form, either, or the amount they owed to landline and cell phone providers, but the extended version, the one that enumerated all their mobile phone calls and text messages? Some girls and their parents hesitated; others looked at me strangely; still others asked if this was really necessary. Yet when I explained my theory, most of the mothers were just as intrigued as I was.

Why was I asking? Because a single question lay unanswered, and I knew that monthly cell phone statements could help me zero in on the answer. What, exactly, was going on in girls' bedrooms between 6 a.m. and 6:30 a.m. every morning? Most girls told me they got up early in the morning, and "got ready for school." Based on my bedroom visits, I know they weren't spending time in the shower. How did I know this? From past work I'd done with a European shampoo manufacturer, I know that the bigger the hole in the spout of a shampoo bottle, the more bottles the manufacturer can sell. The reasons why are obvious. When you squeeze a bottle with a large spout, more shampoo than necessary comes out. The bottles thus empty out faster, obliging us to buy replacement bottles. There is, I knew, a direct correlation between the length of a shower and the size of the hole in a shampoo bottle. The bigger the hole, the longer the shower. The smaller the hole, the shorter the shower. I'd tucked this phenomenon away as a curiosity, nothing more, but realized now it might explain more than I'd thought.

WITH THE HELP OF MY ASSISTANT, I spent the next 48 hours poring through phone bills, and when I was done, I knew my hypothesis was right. Phone bills are "big data" seemingly without value, but with the addition of small data, we soon came up with a strong theory. By studying families' cell phone data plans, it was clear that girls were waking up earlier and earlier, despite going to bed later and later. (It's little wonder that sleep deprivation among teenagers is such an issue around the globe.) Most household digital phone use began regularly at around six in the morning, which was the precise time most girls told me they rolled out of bed. Still, it wasn't what you might think. The girls I interviewed weren't prompt do-gooders eager to ensure they made it to school in time, or turned in an error-free term paper. No, they were waking up early and, in the stillness of their homes or apartments, using that time to text their friends one selfie after another.

Speaking approximately, the average girl took 17 selfies every morning. Why? The obvious answer is that thanks to technology, they could. A less smart-alecky answer is that humans are fundamentally insecure people, that at least in early adolescence we want to be like everyone else, and that the fear of expulsion from our tribe is stronger than practically anything else. That said, fashion will always dictate its needs and changes, and for teenaged girls, there seemed to be three points, or angles, of desire. The first began in the privacy of their bedrooms, where they surfed products and fashions online. The second involved planning and strategizing about what they would wear that day and the next. The third angle was now out in the open, and the girls—and the size of the holes in the shampoo bottles—confirmed it when I asked them about it, too.

It appeared that every morning, after waking up, the first thing they did was snap photographs of the clothes and shoes they were considering wearing, and text them to all their friends, who would respond positively or negatively. They spent every morning like this, coordinating their fashion choices, using their peers as stand-ins for Anna Wintour, critics who could weigh in not only about what looked best, but who could also ensure two girls wouldn't show up at school wearing the same shirt, shoes or pair of pants.

Like any members of a tribe, these girls were dressing and color-coordinating their identities in the world. As I found out earlier, their goal wasn't to stand out so much that they might become phosphorescent; their goal was to stand out only slightly. Their parents, naturally, had no idea about any of this, nor should they have. This low-key fashion parade took place behind closed doors, in the stillness of the early morning.

Again, none of us are immune to the pressures of fashion and status, and if nothing else, Facebook and other social media sites have made what is implicit about human beings—what, before the Internet, we used to imagine or theorize about, without any supporting data—explicit. Even the most confident people on earth are insecure when no one's looking. Traveling as much as I do, I spend a lot of time in airport lounges, where I sit surrounded by expensively dressed businessmen tapping away on their laptops or talking on their phones. Over the years I've noticed that many of them turn their boarding cards upside down, or else park them in their lapel pockets, so that you can't make them out. Eventually, I figured it out. These men's gold Visa or American Express cards gave them access to the business and first-class lounge, but in truth they were traveling in economy class. Also? Pore through any businessman's wallet and you will find that any number of club memberships and credit cards expired long ago. Yet these cards are often prominently displayed. No matter our age or gender, we are always sending out conscious and unconscious signals to the world—and the girls I interviewed were no exception.

WHAT DID MORNING SELFIES have to do with the world of adolescent fashion, you might be wondering? How could I take an observation, or a series of discordant observations, and wrap them into a case, or argument, or strategy for helping Tally Weijl?

It bears repeating that the Web has destroyed the concept of "local," not just as it connects to souvenirs, but in how we feel we stack up to others. Before the Internet, we contrasted ourselves to people in our high schools and hometowns, and to friends attending nearby schools. These days, we compare ourselves to many millions more people our age across the globe. Teenaged girls are especially susceptible to falling into this trap, where nothing they wear, or do, is ever good enough unless their friends validate it first.

The extreme coordination required to align clothing daily has made girls' response time shorter. In the old days, girls might have coordinated outfits in the weeks and days before a prom or other significant school event took place. In an Information Era, this level of coordination can easily take place every morning, and it has a direct and consequential effect on retailers like Tally Weijl. After all, comparing and contrasting clothes and shoes forces young girls to add even more items to their existing collections. The need for even more shoes, more shirts, more pants, more lingerie, more sweaters, more coats and more scarves increases accordingly. With multiple fashion "seasons," the adolescent girls of today are forced to refresh and replenish their wardrobes almost constantly.

Tally Weijl had given me a specific mission: to dig up the small data that would not only create and strengthen brand loyalty, but also, in an industry that demands change and reinvention every two months, could remain novel for decades. No retailer in the world catered to young women in the gray area between childhood and their future adult selves. It was uncharted territory. To attract and retain its core demographic, Tally Weijl had to appeal to the teddy bear and the sophisticated Victoria's Secret model at the same time.

COMBINING THE OFFLINE and online world is known across the retail industry as retail convergence. In response, some retailers today have digitally "live" shelves—similar to those electronic speed limit signs that tell you how fast you are driving as you go past them—that customers can swipe with loyalty cards that offer real-time online or in-store discounts, and Waze, the community-based traffic and navigation app, has teamed up with a number of corporations, including Target, to offer geo-location-enabled deals and discounts at nearby stores.

Fashion retailers, Tally Weijl among them, are understandably frightened of losing their hold on the young female shopper who is nonetheless almost never offline. To create our own methods of convergence, the Tally Weijl board and I had to agree on what the word *social* meant in an Information Age. We agreed that offline and on, the biggest advantage of shopping is its social benefits. Shopping gets us out of the house, and stores and malls provide a community, even a small city, of fellow fashion believers. Another thing online retailers cannot do is replace tactility, the human desire to touch and "feel" a shirt or pair of pants before buying it—which is perhaps why Amazon opened its first bricks and mortar bookstore in Seattle in late 2015.

The Internet is also a city that rivals the offline retail world in connectedness, sociability—and place. It gives users access to stores, and brands, and other countries that most of our hometowns would find it hard to compete with. It also offers users social equity and belonging, the approval and disapproval of a peer group whose opinions now define and dominate teenaged girls' lives. At the same time, when we do anything online, including shop, we're alone. My goal was to bring together the authentic sociability of shopping offline with the artificial company that online shopping offers, to create something that, as far as I knew, the world of retail had never seen before.

But when I proposed it to the Tally board, my first concept was a flop. What if we created a dream house, or loft, where a select group of girls could live, I asked the board? We could recruit them via a special in-store contest, or even via a Willy Wonka–like Golden Ticket system. The girls could live in the loft, courtesy of Tally Weijl, and we'd also provide them with perks including a 24-hour chauffeur, a catwalk, a spa and a music studio. We would stream their parties, shows and get-togethers on the Tally Weijl website, in stores, on the brand's YouTube channel and via Periscope, the live-streaming app. In return, the house or loft would serve as a word-of-mouth broadcast center for the Tally Weijl brand.

Everyone liked the idea, to the extent that we began looking for affordable Parisian real estate. A year later, we still hadn't found the perfect property, and in the end the chief designer pulled the plug on the idea, not willing to compromise the Tally Weijl brand by using a less aspirational locale. But two weeks later, the board approved a second concept, and so far it seems to be working extremely well.

The new Tally Weijl—Tally 2.0—was rolled out in 2013, in a pilot store in Vienna. Since then, its success has spread across numerous cities in Europe.

Knowing that adolescent girls are changeable, and not especially loyal to much of anything, I wanted to create a religious temple in the new Tally Weijl. My Subtext Research had taught me that girls today, or at least the ones I'd interviewed, needed something they could believe in, and many no longer had that in their lives. In my experience, once girls uncovered that belief, and found a place where they could come together and even worship as a tribe, they would and could remain loyal to something. My hope was that thing would be the new Tally store.

If the old Tally Weijl was cramped, noisy and abrasive, the new Tally Weijl was spacious, colorful, flamboyant and over-the-top. We hired a well-known English theater director who turned Vienna's flagship Tally store into an event, a circus, a spectacle. On opening night, costumed actors—stilt walkers, street musicians, bearded men in dark glasses and frilly dresses—strolled in and out of the store, sipping pink bubbly water out of champagne glasses. Waitresses in green and purple wigs served trays of cotton candy and pink heart-shaped cookies and oversized lollipops. Inside and outside the store, palm and tarot card readers offered readings as white-powdered circus acrobats bent themselves into curlicue shapes.

An encyclopedia could be written about the gay influence on heterosexual culture and fashion, and the ways in which gay men serve as bellwethers for trends eventually adopted by the mainstream. Two decades ago, for example, men who wore earrings were "gay," and hair gel and moisturizer were also emblems of the gay male world. Today, of course, any number of straight men sport an earring and use facial creams. Where, and how, does the gay male influence on heterosexual culture begin? The answer is complex, but as far as fashion is concerned, the tastes of gay men often influence young girls who, seeing how good something looks on a gay man, persuade their boyfriends to try it out. Working with Tyra Banks on developing a new merchandising line that built on her strong public awareness from *America's Next Top Model,* FABlife and Victoria's Secret, I spent a day studying her database to uncover the brand's core demographics. The line was directed at teen-aged girls, or college-age girls, but I was also surprised to learn that the target audience of many lingerie lines was gay males in their early and late twenties. The reasoning was simple and time-tested: if the line found favor with a younger homosexual population, who found it stylish, or provocative, or elegant, it was only a matter of time before a gay male recommended it to his younger heterosexual female friends. Moreover, many gay men are extremely opinionated; if they dislike a brand or store, find it corny or tacky, they will come right out and say so. Their opinion, in short, acts as a kind of quality control. If a young, observant gay male likes something, it's probably all right, which is why the crowd flocking at Tally's on opening night had a big percentage of young gay men in attendance, whom we hoped might serve as fashion arbiters for younger female consumers.

Earlier, I brought up the question Steve Jobs asked Disney CEO Robert Iger: "If a store could talk, what would it say to the people entering it?" Tally Weijl 2.0—which was chic, trendy, colorful, and simultaneously child-like and sophisticated—had a lot to say. Instead of talking down to them, I wanted Tally to communicate directly to the girl who loved her teddy bear while also keeping her gaze trained on a future international catwalk. Our vision, one that reflected the mind-set of both the brand and its customers? *Eat dessert first.* Tally Weijl's new flagship store itself was a sexy, girlish, phantasmagoric explosion of raspberries and greens, lime-green rugs and pink-red ottomans, all atop a floor of authentic wooden pallets. The deliberately retro-looking décor included reupholstered chairs from Ireland and Scotland, cozy and traditional and at the same time jazzy and diva-like; its mix of fanciful and functional assured teenaged consumers that they were still within a safe family environment, but also suspended in a world of fantasy and theater. We also created what I called the "Best Friends Area," an area of the store that included a giant bed where girls could rest, relax and catch up on text messages. We even provided cell phone cords and chargers to ensure there was no conceivable excuse for a girl to leave Tally Weijl—at least not until she had finished shopping.

Studying thousands of selfies reminded me that today's teenaged girls have a strong need to be the stars of their own lives. Which explained the cameras angled from the ceiling in every room in every store, creating the illusion that each and every Tally shopper was the leading lady of her own life. Everywhere on the store's walls were framed representations of Tally Weijl's bunny logo. There were polka-dotted bunnies, bunnies in cameo lockets, Victorian-era bunnies and bunnies that looked as though Andy Warhol had painted them.

I'd also made it a point to introduce storytelling inside the store. A pair of brightly colored shoes was positioned alongside a small book-case, dominated by a large hardcover book entitled *Safari*. Why? In some core way, Tally Weijl consumers were on their own private safaris, searching for an ideal pair of shoes. The concept of a safari validated their mission, while giving them implicit permission to explore every last square inch of the store.

But I'm saving the best for last.

Over the years I've spent hours observing dressing rooms, notic-ing how girls in pairs squeezed themselves into tiny cubicles only to leave empty-handed; noticing how their boyfriends would stand out-side, waiting, clearly irritated about the unending Try-On-Take-Off, "What do you think?" sessions. Tally Weijl's new dressing room area was itself a candyland, with each dressing room painted a different shade of red, green, orange, yellow and blue. Outside, I created a "park-ing lot" area, where boyfriends could keep an eye on their girlfriends without coming across as impatient or intimidating. But inside was where the magic—and convergence—happened. With the support of the Tally Weijl board, I'd engineered what I called a "Clicks and Mor-tar" dressing room. To explain: In every dressing room, I'd positioned a large, Internet-equipped, floor-to-ceiling mirror that, at the tap of a finger, transformed itself into a giant, live computer screen. A girl who had gone inside a dressing room, alone or with a friend, to try things on could now type in her Facebook name and password, go onto

Facebook, connect with her closest friends in real time, model shirts, pants and shoes before a live camera, initiate a "voting session" and— item by item—request and receive instantaneous feedback about what looked good on her and what was a near miss. In short, the new Tally dressing room was an online and offline version of the secret morning rituals I'd learned about just two months before.

In Tally, we had succeeded in creating a fashion temple—a lounge area and destination equipped not only with phone rechargers but also with the fastest Internet connection in Vienna. Since the launch of Tally Weijl 2.0, the brand has mostly overcome its fashion crises, revenue is up dramatically and the number of Tally Weijl Facebook fans has quadrupled; but more important, the role of one bricks-and-mortar store has been redefined and reinvented. Today, adolescent Austrian girls line up to enter Tally's dressing rooms, extending a private at-home 6:19 a.m. experience among friends into the rest of the day, building the Tally brand, as well as their own starring brand, by texting selfies to Facebook friends. One girl I spoke with called the new Tally "breathtaking," while another who earlier had given the store a "3" now awarded it a "9," adding, "It's now so over the top that you have to see it." The store, in short, deserved a big hand (with or without cream).

CHAPTER 7
SLEEPING WITHOUT A BEDSPREAD

CHARRED PAPER, TOY CARS AND PIXIE DUST HELP DECIPHER THE MEANING OF "QUALITY" IN CHINA

ALMOST WITHOUT EXCEPTION, WESTERNERS WHO TRAVEL to third world countries return home with the same impression. They report that in spite of having fewer resources and material possessions, residents of places like Guatemala or Peru or the Philippines seem to be dramatically "happier"—kinder, friendlier, more giving and hospitable—than people who live in the West. To me, this reveals just how irrelevant the Western concept of "happiness" is to anyone living outside the first world. If you ask people who are born with very little whether or not they are happy, most will reply they are neither "happy" nor "sad." They are simply living their lives. Their priorities are, in no particular order, working, putting food on the table and taking care of their families.

Writers and philosophers from Buddha to Herodotus to Aristotle have been writing and thinking about happiness for centuries. Yet it's worth remembering that, rather than an inherent characteristic or aspiration of being alive, the Western happiness industry is, according to the *Harvard Business Review,* "an artifact of modern history."[1]

The idea of happiness as an expectation didn't begin to flower until 250 years ago, in the years following the Enlightenment. Before that, even in the West, life generally verged on the austere. It was only in the mid-nineteenth century that the pursuit of happiness gradually evolved into a legitimate goal, and unhappiness became a blight to be avoided.

The happiness movement gained strength throughout the nineteenth century, as jobs moved outside of the home and, according to *Harvard Business Review,* "Wives and mothers were urged to maintain a cheerful atmosphere in order to reward their hardworking husbands and produce successful children."[2] Happiness has evolved today into a singularly Western, and especially American, phenomenon—even a mandate. After all, it was an American sound engineer who created the television laugh track and an American company, McDonald's, that came out with the Happy Meal.

Ironically, our insistence on being happy all the time almost guarantees unhappiness, if only by creating the fear that you're not measuring up to other people's levels of contentment, wealth or well-being. The Internet, of course, hasn't helped. Earlier I wrote that the level of transparency in a country has a direct and negative correlation to a nation's level of happiness. Nor can a country's wealth or stability be said to contribute to its overall contentment. The *World Happiness Report,* an annual study published by the United Nations Sustainable Development Solutions Network, measures a nation's overall earnings, living standards, employment, physical and mental health and cultural stability. In 2014, Switzerland, Iceland and Norway were the top-three "happiest countries."[3] This same year, a Gallup Poll came at the subject from another angle, by asking adults in 143 countries if they'd had "positive experiences on the day before the survey." These ranged from laughing, smiling, feeling well rested, being treated with respect and even doing something interesting. No Scandinavian countries made the top 20, and nor did America. Instead, the poll was dominated by Latin and Central American countries including Paraguay, Nicaragua, Panama, Ecuador and Guatemala.[4] At the bottom of the list, reporting the lowest "positive experiences," were Middle Easterners and Africans. The Gallup pollsters made it a point to say that "low positive emotions" didn't necessarily correlate with "high negative emotions." Russians, for example, report some of the lowest positive emotions in the world, as well as some of the lowest *negative* emotions. Why? According to one source, "Gallup has previously reported that people in this region simply don't report many emotions at all—positive or negative."[5]

My definition of happiness? The number of specific days a person remembers over the last year, which often coincides with the number of times he or she passed through a Transition Zone—went on vacation, had a baby, took a child to college for the first time, rode a bicycle, went hang-gliding for the first time. Rather than being measured linearly, happiness should be perceived as a congeries of "moments."

What about other Western concepts like "freedom," or living an environmentally "green" lifestyle? Let's take China as an example. Most Chinese people are aware they live under the grip of a state-controlled media. According to NPR, government restrictions are sometimes invisible, with websites often failing to load or "technical error" messages appearing on the screen; thus, many Chinese don't even realize the Internet is being censored.[6] As for those who do, an almost ten-year-old poll conducted by the Pew Research Center's Internet and American Life Project and a group of Chinese academics revealed that "almost 85 percent of those surveyed say they think the government should be responsible for controlling the Internet."[7] A majority of Chinese citizens subscribe to the Confucian belief that a government is mandated to exert its authority by showing parental care for its citizens. Citizens, in turn, owe it to their government to respect and obey rules and mores. Yes, in a perfect universe, everyone would have a microphone, an opinion and an audience, but is it worth it if their actions or behavior damage social norms or stability for the whole collective?

As challenging (and rewarding) as it sometimes is to travel the world uncovering desires and coming up with a new brand or product solutions, it is harder still asking people if they are happy, especially in a nation like China that is gradually adapting Western values and definitions in much the same way I found that "green" and "organic" had made their way into India. Until the late 1990s, China teemed with bicycles and bike riders. Bikes weren't a "green" response to China's pollution levels—which were already troublesome back then, though not nearly as bad as they are today—nor was bike riding linked to virtue or to "competitive altruism," the term used to describe the status humans glean from their superior social consciousness. Circa 1995, most Chinese simply couldn't afford a car. Bikes were the only way to get around, and the car was a status symbol linked to a distant Western definition of happiness. Today, you see many fewer bikes in China, and the Chinese automobile industry is the biggest in the world. I am merely speculating, but I would argue that once the Chinese were able to access the same films, music and television series the rest of the world watched—albeit 24 to 48 hours later, and on pirated websites—and once they saw what they were "missing," they became less "happy."

That's why it was both a test and an opportunity when a major Chinese automobile manufacturer asked if I could help them "brand" the concept of a Chinese automobile, both locally and internationally. What was the ingredient that European car brands had that "Made in China" cars lacked? If Chinese cars shared almost exactly the same features and options as European-branded cars, why did Western cars outsell them, even in China, by a three-to-one ratio?

Embedded in this question was a problem I'd come up against before when working in China: an overemphasis on rational thinking and a disregard for the emotional ingredients that go into brand building. The reasoning among Chinese companies goes something like this: a product is a brand. A brand is a logo. If a logo is prominent, then consumers, sales and profits will follow. An almost comical illustration of this logic took place in 2001, when 72 hours after the first Apple Store opened its doors in the United States, the first-ever "Apple Stores" made their appearance in China. Chinese Apple store employees wore robin's-egg-blue, logo-embossed T-shirts that precisely mimicked the ones worn by Apple's American employees. There was only one problem: Chinese Apple Stores had no affiliation with Apple and sold dishwashers, vacuum cleaners, refrigerators and other household appliances rather than computers. Again, this is a core problem I come up against whenever I work in China, where the functional, or Blue Script, matters far more than the emotional, or Green Script, and companies and products pay the price.

Every successful brand stands for something more than itself, and that thing is emotional. A great brand promises hope, the contagion of coolness, or desirability, or love, or romance, or acceptance, or luxury, or youth, or sophistication, or high-quality technology. By way of illustration, imagine if you could choose between two cars that are precisely the same in all ways—the same color, the same engine, the same design, the same quality—except for one minor detail: the first was made in Denmark and the second was manufactured in Greece. Which one would you pick? I'm guessing most people would select the Danish model, associating it with Danish values like craftsmanship and close attention to detail. Next, imagine that you were asked to choose between two bottles of the same expensive perfume. The label of the first read Paris, Rome and Beverly Hills. The label of the second read Albany, New York, Manchester, England, and Bong Bong, Australia. Which bottle would best encapsulate the emotional values you hoped the fragrance might convey?

Cities and countries are no different from any other brand, and before I took on the automotive project I had to face the fact that China had a serious national branding problem, even among its own natives.

AS AN ILLUSTRATION OF TWO successfully branded destinations, let's look at London and Paris. To non-natives, London evokes various words and feelings, among them *Big Ben. Rain. Winston Churchill. The Beatles. Buckingham Palace. Twiggy. Tea and Scones. The Clash. Prince William and Kate Middleton. The Rolling Stones. Harry Potter. Cricket.* Similarly, Paris evokes *Romance. Love. Wine. Cheese. Baguettes. The Eiffel Tower. The Louvre. The Seine. Edith Piaf. Jean-Paul Sartre.* Regardless of what everyday life is actually like there, from a branding perspective, both London and Paris are Too Big to Fail.

This is seldom the case when I'm called in to brand a country or city—otherwise, why would you even need a marketing consultant? A country's "brand" is an aggregate of its wars, music, sports, climate, leadership, location, tacit traditions and national character—its entire social, political and cultural history—which blur and intersect over time. In the case of London, *Big Ben* and *rain* cannot be teased apart any more than *love* and *food* can be separated in Paris. Reputationally speaking, if there is anything to learn from a country that is Too Big to Fail, it's what I call the Power of Less—which, in today's overcrowded Information Age, matters more than ever.

Like any other powerful brand, the best-branded countries and cities of the world can be distilled into one or two words. When we think of Richard Branson, we think *rebellious;* Oprah Winfrey, *compassion;* and Apple evokes *Innovation.* Countries are no different. Those that lack a one- or two-word association, or that are young, or in flux, or at war, or in social or economic crisis, or whose reputations were never clear to begin with, face a big challenge: How do they begin to establish a brand? The question was one I confronted almost twenty years ago, when I first visited Dubai.

Though it had been growing slowly since oil was discovered there in the 1960s, Dubai in 1997 more closely resembled a dream, or concept, of a city, than it did an actual city. There were maybe three or four tall buildings, no shops, no highways, no beaches, no skyscrapers. Arguably, Dubai as people know it today began with a concept dreamed up by Majid Al Futtaim, who, inspired by a ski resort he'd seen in Japan in the mid-1990s, decided to construct his own indoor ski slope, Ski Dubai, in the middle of the Arabian Desert. Featuring an indoor mountain with five slopes and a quarter-mile-long run, Ski Dubai was an immediate success and taught Mr. Majid and other local developers that a bold, innovative approach can transform—or in this case, create out of thin air—a country's reputation. Ski Dubai set off an unspoken competition among Dubai's builders and entrepreneurs: Who could break the most rules the fastest?

Today, Dubai is a global business hub and a wildly popular tourist attraction. The city has around 600 buildings, skyscrapers, malls and hotels, with a population of around 2 million. Ninety-six percent of Dubai residents are foreign-born, and Dubai *kharfours,* or supermarkets, feature foods and beverages customized for 16 or so different nationalities (there are over 100 different varieties of rice alone). Most of Dubai's foreign-born residents work in the city's financial and construction industries, attracted by the absence of corporate income taxes and a 2002 land reform law that allows foreigners to buy local real estate.

Like Las Vegas, Dubai is the twenty-first-century version of a Pop-Up City, a city renowned for its seeming mission to be the first, the tallest, the fastest, the biggest, the most ornate and outrageous city in the world. Dubai has the tallest skyscraper in the world, the Burj Khalifa, and "the world's most luxurious hotel" in the Burj Al Arab Jumeirah, a seven-star hotel that sits on its own man-made island overlooking the Arabian Gulf (seven stars, maybe needless to say, is a rating, and a star system, that exists nowhere else in the world). Dubai has the world's largest mall, flower garden and Formula One stadium. Dubai's Emirates airline is the first airline to offer on-board suites, showers and minibars, and its Business and First Class lounges connect directly to waiting airplanes. To combat the desert climate, Dubai was the first country to install cooling systems on its beaches and inside its swimming pools. Here and there across Dubai are vending machines that deliver bars made out of solid gold. Does anyone actually buy a gold bar from a vending machine? It's unlikely, but it's the thought, and the brand, that counts.

A few years ago, I was in Dubai giving a speech about "country branding" to a big group of tourism and marketing officials. At one point, I pointed out that the world's most powerful country brands could be broken down to one or two words. Afterward, over dinner, one of the female guests asked me what Dubai's "one word" brand was. The question flustered me. Country branding takes years, decades, sometimes even a century, to establish, I told her, and despite its accelerated growth, Dubai was still very young. When she persisted, I finally gave in. The word I came up with was the result of visiting and working in a city that in 17 or so years had evolved from a sandy oasis to Oz. The word, for better or for worse, was *plastic*.

Recall that our brains form a somatic marker when two things that have nothing in common come together, positively or negatively. If it takes a country years to establish a brand, Dubai shows that with the strategic use of somatic markers—a ski resort in the desert, a seven-star hotel, vending machines that spit out gold bars—successful country branding can be done in a much shorter period of time.

Let's take another example. For decades Australia was known by a handful of words and images: *Kangaroos. Koala bears. Boomerangs. Aborigines.* There was nothing wrong with these things, except that kangaroos, koala bears, boomerangs and aborigines were only indirectly related to one another, linked by their exotic "other"-ness.

The resurrection of Australia as a worldwide tourist attraction probably began in the mid-1980s with the release of the film *Crocodile Dundee*. The movie had as its protagonist a bushman who told time using the position of the sun (well, kind of) and who, with dry, imperturbable machismo, faced down two knife-wielding New York muggers by producing a bush-machete with the words "That's not a knife—*that's* a knife." A subsequent marketing strategy was, and is, linked to the fact that the Australian summer solstice takes place in late December, meaning that summer arrives in Australia just as winter appears in most Western countries. In response, Australia rolled out a handful of marketing strategies that culminate around the winter holidays. Around Christmastime, Australian broadcasters shoot video footage of bronzed men and bikini-wearing women adorned in Santa Claus hats along Sydney's Bondi Beach, a stretch of ocean popular with surfers, skateboarders and volleyball players. The week between Christmas and New Year's Day is slow, and Australian broadcasters offer this footage for free to news outlets worldwide. Except for a few cities in Samoa and New Zealand, Australia is also the first continent to greet the

New Year. Sydney is a photogenic city, and its annual fireworks display frames both the Sydney Bridge and the Sydney Opera House, footage that is also offered free of charge to news stations worldwide.

If it takes years for a city's or a country's brand identity to crystallize, it can also take a long time for a country to overcome a negative somatic marker. Vietnam, for instance, is renowned for its beaches, parks, museums, shopping and physical beauty, yet several generations of Americans can't help but link Vietnam with a disputed, protracted war. Colombia, in South America, is one of the world's most beautiful—and peaceful—countries, but it is still trying to shake its global reputation as a country synonymous with kidnapping, murder and drug violence. Why, I sometimes wonder, doesn't the Colombia tourism board take advantage of one of its most positive associations—coffee—and partner with Starbucks to create an in-store campaign devoted to Colombian coffee beans? Alternately, as I wrote earlier, Medellín is home to the longest escalator in the world, built into the side of a mountain. Why doesn't Colombia market its escalator in the same way Dubai trumpets its indoor ski slope?

Again, the power of film should never be underestimated. New Zealand, a largely unbranded country, saw its tourism industry increase by 50 percent after the 2001 release of Peter Jackson's *The Fellowship of the Ring*.[8] Today, New Zealand's customs service stamps "Welcome to Middle Earth" on the passports of incoming tourists, and the government also issues postal stamps with the names of Tolkien characters on them. Some nations, like Taiwan, negotiate directly with Hollywood, hoping to find story lines that can help transform their image, in the same way the 2010 remake of *The Karate Kid,* partially filmed in China, helped to overturn the popular image of a polluted manufacturing center into that of a magical, mysterious, historically fascinating country.

Still, few people associate contemporary China with the Xia, Tang or Song dynasties, the Silk Road or Confucianism. What comes to mind instead is more likely than not a series of negative somatic markers, including the unsmiling face of Chairman Mao, communism, the

Tiananmen Square protests and state-run censorship of the press, the Internet, religion and reproductive rights. Widespread publicity about the working conditions at Foxconn's manufacturing facilities—which manufacture the West's best-known products from Apple, Hewlett-Packard, Dell, Cisco, Vizio, Microsoft and others—hasn't helped things. By now most Westerners are aware that their most beloved gadgets—iPhones, iPads, Kindles, Wiis, PlayStations, Xboxes and others—are built by poorly paid, ill-treated Chinese workers in working conditions so substandard that Foxconn erected suicide nets after 14 employees jumped to their deaths in 2014. "Made in China," then, is a three-word fragment it would be difficult to transform. I wouldn't be able to do it with one job, but I would do what I could.

ON MY FIRST VISIT TO SHANGHAI, when I checked into my hotel room on an upper floor of the Park Hyatt, the floor-to-ceiling windows were enclosed by smooth drapes the color of wax, or chalk. Seconds later, I realized that what covered my window weren't drapes at all, but smog so dense and restrictive that nothing at all was visible from my 88th-floor window. The bathroom tap water had a chemical taste, and when I went outdoors, the air had a faint tang of metal.

China is responsible for more pollutants than any other country in the world, with two-thirds of China's biggest cities falling short of minimal environmental standards.[9] Among the first words every Chinese child learns is *wuran,* or pollution. The word means "dirty contamination," though the Chinese state media prefers *wumai,* or "haze," with its implication that the conditions are short-lived and occasional. Regardless of what word you use, wuran is real, its effects physical, psychological and constant. Wuran sticks to the back of your throat. It invades your larynx, turns the inside of your nose black and makes your eyes tear up and itch. On Shanghai's most overcast days, residents press rags, cloths and handkerchiefs against their noses and mouths whenever they go outside. Nearly a quarter of all Chinese infants are born with pre-existing allergies, and a former Chinese health minister reported once that anywhere between 350,000 to 500,000 Chinese people a year die prematurely from air pollution.[10] According to the *New York Times,* "Only 1 percent of the country's 560 million city dwellers breathe air considered safe by the European Union."[11]

On the worst wuran days, a red flag hangs ominously at the front of local schools, and students stay indoors. So pervasive is the concern with airborne pollutants that the British School of Beijing and other international schools have built airtight domes equipped with hospital-grade air filtration systems around their campuses.[12] Some runners participating in the 2014 Beijing Marathon dropped out of the race early, with "some saying it felt like running through bonfire smoke."[13] Not surprisingly, the biggest product trends in China are water filtration devices, air-quality phone apps, face masks, anti-nausea pills and high-end air-conditioning systems. The biggest pollutant is coal, which China burns more of than the United States, Europe and Japan combined, and whose sulfur dioxide and nitrogen oxide emissions reach as far away as Japan and North and South Korea. The second culprit, according to the *New York Times,* is the increasing number of cars, heavy traffic conditions and low-grade gasoline.[14]

China, as I wrote earlier, is the largest car market in the world, with an annual production that exceeds that of America and Japan combined. Overseas car brands are obliged by Chinese law to partner with domestic Chinese automakers for local production, and most Chinese-made cars are the result of joint ventures with international brands. In 2010, a Chinese automaker, Geely, bought Volvo—today, many Volvo models are manufactured in China—and four years after that, the state-owned Dongfeng Motor invested more than a billion dollars in Peugeot-Citroën.

Herewith the problem. Global automakers and brands, including Hyundai and Buick, compose two-thirds of China's car sales. This leaves branded China-made automobiles with a local market share of only one-third. Even the Chinese believe that local car brands are inferior to American and European brands, which is why, as a rule, Chinese automobile manufacturers earn most of their revenues by exporting cars to other developing countries, where low prices matter more than brand or legacy. For Chinese car buyers, Western brands stand for two things: aspiration and trust. By way of analogy, an Apple iPhone costs around $600, of which roughly one-third goes back to China, making the iPhone more or less a Chinese product, despite the fact that Apple has its headquarters in Northern California. The iPhone is a source of national pride for the Chinese, while at the same time, the company's American roots add an exotic appeal that would be lacking if the iPhone's provenance was exclusively Chinese. A Western-branded product guarantees that a phone, or a car, isn't just real, but that it also *works*.

By contrast, the Chinese are historically skeptical about Chinese-made products, from cars to infant formula, especially premium-priced ones. The pollution infecting everyday food, in particular infant formula, means that Chinese tourists visiting Australia line up in supermarkets to bring back home international formula options—a phenomena that has become such a problem that many Australian supermarkets restrict the number of cans consumers can buy at one time. Thus, whenever the Chinese can purchase an extra seal of trustworthiness—a European or American logo—it increases their confidence that what they bought is high quality. Unlike, say, an iPhone, "Made in China" automobiles didn't exude any aspirational qualities. What was the point of being a successful Chinese businessman if you ended up driving a Chinese car? China is a proud country. Chinese residents needed to show the world who they were, and few things shore up a person's identity more eloquently than the car he drives.

Before thinking about improving the quality of Chinese cars, I had to begin Subtexting what "quality" meant for the Chinese. This was a difficult question to answer in a country that deemphasizes emotion, and whose natives are more or less stony-faced. In situations like these, I find it better to observe people from an undercover perspective, a skill set I developed when a team of Australian customs officers from Sydney let me shadow them for a week. What I learned over those seven days was what *not* to look for. The staff taught me not to be focused on or distracted by what people did, but to keep close watch on what they *didn't* do. Customs eventually let me join the five-member security team tasked with opening and closing thousands of purses, backpacks and carry-ons, in order to correlate people's behavior and the contents of their suitcases. In time, they told me, I would be able to predict what passengers had inside their bags before they even opened them. And before I knew it, I could.

On an earlier trip to China while working for a retail client, I asked executives whether they would let me spend 48 hours inside their CCT camera security room, a pipeline of sorts into the DNA of Chinese body language. How do Chinese consumers behave when they're alone? How do they act when they're considering buying something? Finally, how do they act when they are stealing?

Inside the CCT booth in Beijing, I spent two days monitoring both in-store purchases and thefts. People would pick things off shelves and tuck them under their coats, pockets or handbags. More intriguing still were their tics in the moments leading up to the theft. Invariably they would scratch the sides of their arms. Cut to ten years later, when I asked a cross-section of Chinese men to sit inside their dream cars. As they took seats inside the car, I noticed they scratched their hands up and down, back and forth, on their pants, before placing their hands on the wheel. During this time, not one showed any emotion, or even smiled. Their cultural training dictated that their facial expression remained blank and indecipherable.

Later, when I interviewed them outside the car, they unconsciously repeated this same behavior. To me, the scratching was an old childhood tic, an absent, unstudied gesture the men used to comfort and reassure themselves in a time of stress. The men knew they were doing something wrong. They were in a car that wasn't theirs. They were revealing their childhood dreams. They wanted to make sure no one else noticed. In China, I would later learn, almost every other bodily gesture or expression has been tamed, trained and controlled out of existence, except, perhaps, for this one. I took note of it, and then it was time to venture inside Chinese apartment buildings.

MORE THAN HALF THE CHINESE POPULATION lives in, or close to, an urban area. Across Beijing, Shanghai and many other cities, you'll find many thousands of functional, anonymous high-rise apartment buildings. As a rule, Chinese apartments are built to last 25 to 30 years, versus 70–75 years in the United States.[15] They are poorly constructed, with negligent safety standards, tiny rooms and minimal personality. The walls are white and blank, and the flooring is plastic. Almost every piece of furniture is wrapped in plastic, which couldn't help but remind me of my work in Saudi Arabia—except that in China, there were no Eiffel Towers or London Bridges, just one object after another—lamps, tables, chairs—enshrouded in the tightest possible coating of plastic.

When you do the work I do, you quickly learn that the more "personal" an item is, the more it reveals the truth about someone. Among the most personal things we own and use are those we put inside our bodies, or place inside our mouths, or that our bodies absorb—food, drinks, pills, toothbrushes and even the weather. On the basis of this equation, a banana is more "personal" than, say, a pair of shoes, in the same way a frozen TV dinner is more personal than a coat, a hat or a pair of gloves. In this case, the most critical clue about Chinese behavior—and how the Chinese assessed the quality of a product, or service—began with the sight of a lone toothbrush.

Generally speaking, when toothbrushes stand in a holder, or a cup, or jar, their owners tend to be less sexually active than not. If and when their owners *are* romantic, their sex lives tend to be highly structured and less hospitable to spontaneity or innovation, a scenario that over the years I've come to call "Appointment Sex." In Russia, only three out of ten toothbrushes were standing, and I found a similar ratio across France and Italy. It's worth adding that the owners of toothbrushes whose heads face down are more sexually active, more impulsive and altogether less constrained to schedules. Yet in the first seven or eight Chinese apartments I visited, the toothbrushes were standing, either in cups or holders. Three weeks later, as I set out my photos on a bulletin board, I totaled up the figures. Nine out of ten Chinese households appeared to be under the leash of "Appointment Sex."

It wasn't just Chinese toothbrushes that caught my attention, but the bristles, too. Their wear and tear indicated normal everyday use, but with a difference: the normal indentation that ran down the midpoint of the bristles, dividing them equally, was missing. Did Chinese toothbrushes as a rule lack indentations? No, having visited local drugstores and markets, I knew Chinese toothbrushes resembled toothbrushes sold everywhere else in the world. Were the toothbrushes for display rather than for everyday use? No: the worn handles indicated that the toothbrushes were used regularly.

Tooth-brushing rituals are the same across the world. Over the years, I've noticed interesting, oddball global behaviors around this subject, independent of culture, religion or age—including the fact that based on my own polling, 4 percent of the world's people brush their teeth in the shower. Shower brushers, I've noticed, too, tend to be more creative than most, and generate most of their ideas while under the nozzle or in contact with water. Still, the length of time we take to brush our teeth, and the pressure we exert as we grip our toothbrush handles and press the heads against our gums and teeth, vary from country to country. What, then, had happened to the indentation on the bristles? Several Chinese consumers let me watch as they brushed their teeth, and the answer showed up immediately. Across the West, people press the bristles of their toothbrushes hard again their teeth. It's as if they believe that the more pressure they apply, the more likely they are to end up with whiter teeth and brighter smiles. In Shanghai, it was a different story. The Chinese parted their lips, applied toothpaste onto the bristles, and held the toothbrush in place before their teeth. Then they brushed. Not with the bristles, as Westerners did, but by rapidly fluttering their hands and arms up and down. The toothbrush itself barely moved.

If nothing else, this gave me my first fragment of small data about sensory perception in China. Reminding myself that the toothbrush itself was a Chinese invention dating back to 1498, I took the liberty of noting this clue as one likely embedded in China's DNA. It was a good foundation on which to begin creating a hypothesis.

On to the shower, where the first thing I glimpsed was a soap bar. So? In contrast to body wash, a popular trend throughout the 1990s, a soap bar acts as a buffer between our hands and our bodies that, in turn, may also point to reduced levels of sensuality. Not by itself, of course; people have been using soap bars and having feverish sex for centuries. But coupled with the standing toothbrushes, it added to a theme I was observing, focused around the concepts of momentum and speed. Once I made my way into Chinese bedrooms, I knew I was on the right track.

Any amateur detective will tell you that it's more difficult to notice the absence of something than its presence. Still, just as every Chinese shower had a soap bar, not a single bed wore a bedspread. Sheets, yes, a light blanket, yes, pillows, yes, but bedspreads, no. There were virtually no exceptions to this rule, either. By itself, the absence of a bedspread wasn't terribly unusual, but considering the high levels of protection across China against everyday wuran—fabrics pressed against people's mouths and noses, stand-alone bubbles around schools and sports centers—the absence of bedspreads surprised me. Put another way, if a bed is akin to a human hand, where was its protective glove? Human skin, after all, comprises three layers. The epidermis, or visible layer, flushes our skin with color while continually generating new cells. Beneath the epidermis is a thicker layer, the dermis, which produces sweat and oil, and also connects to our blood vessels. The third layer of our skin is a shelf of subcutaneous fat, which modulates skin temperature and links the dermis to muscles and bones. Like the skin on the human hand, a bed is also an arrangement of layers, with the bedcover on top of the mattress, followed by sheets, blankets and occasionally a quilt or duvet. These things all have a role to play in the process—the slow seduction—of falling asleep, or preparing for romance or sex. Nor was this a general cultural discrepancy; from research I'd done in Japan and Thailand, I knew that bedspreads were commonplace elsewhere in Asia.

Chinese toothbrushes. Tooth-brushing habits. Soap bars. No bedcovers. Together, they pointed me toward the same conclusion, or rather the same words: *Direct. Quick. Now.* This was confirmed two or three nights later when one of my host families invited me to a local restaurant, in the town of Manzhhouli in the inner part of Mongolia, near the Russian border. The restaurant had a reputation for excellent food and service, though you would never have known it from its cold, naked lighting. My host family and I took our seats around a table in whose center was a revolving stand—a Lazy Susan of sorts—and when one of us ordered a dish the waiter set it down on the stand.

It was a memorable meal. The family ordered quickly, and the food appeared nearly at once. They spun the wheel as if playing a game of roulette. Everyone ate as if competing for a prize that would be awarded to the first person who finished. There were no pauses, breaks, respites or conversations lasting longer than a minute. Less than 45 minutes passed from the time we sat down to the time we stood up to leave.

It seemed that the Chinese had a radically different definition of the meaning of *sensual*. Elsewhere in the world, *sensual* was synonymous with softness, luxury, slowness and anticipation. Was there any time, or place, when the Chinese *weren't* in a hurry? Then there was the matter of Chinese cars themselves. They were less like cars than apartment annexes. Inside most were functional elements that mirrored a household interior, from garbage bags, to mini-kettles allowing drivers to boil water for tea while in transit using a 12-volt power system, to—in one case—a mini-refrigerator. Chinese families regularly brought food along with them, too, which they ate while driving or riding in the backseat.

I decided to carry out an informal experiment. Over the next few days, I visited three or four local museums, including one devoted to jade, one of China's most valuable and revered stones. Visit any museum in the world, and you'll quickly realize how slowly museumgoers walk as they meander through galleries and exhibits. (Arguably, we walk with a reverence that complements the quality, prestige and reputation of the art surrounding us.) Once, in Paris's Monet Museum, I clocked the velocity and speed of museumgoers over a 72-hour period. Visitors moved at around three miles per hour; that is to say, at an average speed. But at Beijing's local jade museum, the approximate speed of museumgoers was four, almost five miles an hour. Japan is a brisk, no-tarrying culture, too, but the Chinese walk even more quickly than the Japanese do.

To the concept of speed, I now had to add another word: *transition.* Even when a transition was involved—eating a meal in a restaurant, going to a museum, tooth brushing or taking a shower—the Chinese never slowed down. Their cars were mini living rooms and mini kitchens. Even the experience of moviegoing seemed to be on a fast-moving timer. Some cinemas have curtains that part tantalizingly slowly as the overhead lights dim to reveal the movie screen. Not Chinese cinemas. In the nearly half-a-dozen Beijing movie theaters I visited, the curtain flew open like a flasher on a subway.

There was only one kind of occasion where the Chinese paused, and that was during one of their most important holidays.

I WAS IN BEIJING when a family I was interviewing invited me to attend the national ceremony known as Qingming Jie. Qingming Jie, otherwise known as the "Tomb-Sweeping Festival," takes place every spring, two weeks after the solar equinox. On Qingming Jie, the living devote the day to the memory of their ancestors. They fix or beautify cemetery stones and stroll around graveyards and columbariums, snacking on *qingtuan,* or green dumplings, while savoring the warmth and colors of springtime. Some fly kites in the shapes of animals from well-known Chinese operas, and others burn incense or pop firecrackers. Most pray and offer food, tea and wine and also burn replicas of small cars, iPhones, iPads and Louis Vuitton handbags made from joss paper, bound packs of common paper that resemble legal tender. Chinese people believe that even after they have died, the deceased may still need these things in the afterlife. As kites shaped like pigs and goats and snakes fluttered overhead, papery phones, purses and cars were consigned to the flames.

As I observed people arriving and making their way toward the graveyard, both their body language and their behavior changed. The pace of my host family slowed down. Family members spoke to one another carefully, and with greater emphasis. Was it simply the gravity and ceremony of Qingming Jie?

With their permission, I began videotaping my host family both at Qingming Jie and afterward. Back in my hotel room, I Small Mined the footage. I tracked and measured people's walking speeds, beginning from when they left their cars to when they passed through the graveyard entrance, at which point they slowed down even more. My host family in particular intrigued me. Even after leaving the graveyard and making their way back toward their car, they didn't resume their usual walking speed. For the rest of the day, they walked, drove, cooked and spoke to one another more slowly.

China has many similar festivals, including Beijing's Five Gods of Wealth Temple Fair, where the Chinese flock to worship gods symbolizing prosperity, burn incense, pray for luck and buy sheets of intricately designed paper decorated with the Chinese characters for good fortune and happiness; and the Lantern Festival, where red lanterns, many in the shapes of animals, are raised high in the air to symbolize the shedding of past identities and the adoption of new ones. These national festivals, it seemed, were the only times the Chinese slowed down. Other than that it was all speed, all the time.

Velocity, it turned out, was one of the keys to understanding China. Speed represented an imbalance, an exaggeration. To me this implied several things, chief among them that the opportunities for transformation in China were rare, almost nonexistent.

By "transformation" I mean those moments that oblige us to "become" something or someone else, or that influence and affect our behavior based on what we're touching, or holding, or seeing, in the same way that Qingming Jie obliged Chinese families to decrease their walking speed and even speech. From Qingming Jie, I took away another clue as to what lay close to the Chinese national character. The joss money they burned represented what they held most dear: material goods. Which meant, as I knew already, that Western values were slowly making their way into the country.

The concept of transformation in the early twenty-first century intrigues me, in part because smartphones and computers are chipping away at our opportunities for escape. The fewer opportunities for transformation we have in our lives, the more we crave it. A car is a transformation zone. So is a coffee shop. So is a ferry that takes you from the mainland to an island, or going to a movie, or taking a long bike ride. Drinking, taking drugs and even meditation are all transformation zones. Yet in a digital era, the opportunities for transformation are diminishing. Thanks to our phones we are never altogether present and never completely alone. When we go by ourselves to a coffee shop, we are, in fact, accompanied by a digital device. Do we ever shut down our computers or smartphones anymore, other than to reboot them? *What's the point,* we ask ourselves, *since we'll just be turning them back on in the morning?* Thanks to our phones, most of us "go to work" when we open our eyes every morning, only to stop "working" when we go to sleep. The only time we power off our laptops is when we're in transit. We are in the same season, and emotional climate, all the time, one that's neither work nor leisure, neither at our desk nor officially off-duty.

From experience, I knew that the Chinese shared the same dearth of transformations as the Japanese. For decades, the Japanese have struggled with issues created by density. Tokyo trains are crowded, the sidewalks are congested, and even at home, space and privacy barely exist. Where, then, do Japanese people find space, and where had I first glimpsed the Chinese predilection for speed? In two places: Disneyland in Tokyo and Paris, where I found myself consulting for France's Disneyland Resort Paris in the early 2000s.

Opened in 1992 in a suburb of Paris, Euro Disney was an immediate target for controversy and criticism. Some French critics found it a symbol of American cultural imperialism and consumerism, with one even calling it a "Cultural Chernobyl."[16] Euro Disney faced labor strikes, then a recession and, with turnout lower than expected, financial difficulties. The "magic" for which Disney was known world-wide seemed to be missing, which is when the management team contacted me to see if I could help reverse the park's downward spiral.

After interviewing a selection of Euro Disney park-goers, I soon discovered that the "missing magic" could in fact be distilled to an absence of transformation. I couldn't help but notice that this apparent flatness was coincident with a decrease in churchgoing across Europe. When I visited Catholic and Protestant churches in Germany, France and Italy, I came away convinced that what religion had historically given believers—faith, transformation—was no longer enough. In Europe at least, parishioners made their way through church portals at around the same pace they strolled through a market or store. The fact of being in a sacred place no longer slowed people down, which meant that religion was no longer creating the necessary degree of embodied cognition, or space, for worship, or contemplation, or reverence.

This insight—that a decline in churchgoing creates the need for other outlets to address the need for transformation—was what moved me to re-infuse superstition into the Euro Disney experience.

My inspiration was, of all people, Tinker Bell, the winged fairy from J. M. Barrie's *Peter Pan,* and the superstition we brought back was Pixie Dust. We handed out small bags of colored powder to Disneyland cast members who, in turn, handed them to visitors who were then asked to close their eyes, make a wish and scatter the Pixie Dust into the pond beside Sleeping Beauty Castle. As a ritual, it required only a fast scattering of yellow and red and blue powder into a body of water. Still, the effect was powerful. Not only did thousands of Euro Disney visitors begin tossing Pixie Dust into the pond, but I soon noticed the differences in how visitors of different nationalities did so. For example, after gripping the Pixie Dust, Americans tossed it into the pond with their eyes half open and half closed. Japanese tourists took only a minimal amount, tossing it into the lake with formal elegance. Of all the nationalities I observed, Chinese adults and children grabbed the largest handfuls possible of Pixie Dust, which they then hurled into the pond as quickly as possible. It was, I remember thinking, as though they were desperate for a transformation to take place, to enter an otherworldly zone that took them well out of themselves.

EARLIER I WROTE THAT ONE of the strategies I used when turning around Lowes supermarkets was to give customers permission to act like children again. We all have multiple ages inside of us. The first is our actual physical, chronological age. Then there's our inner age, the age we feel emotionally inside. I call this "emotional age" our Twin Self. It's a phenomenon I make it a habit to remember whenever I'm running a board meeting. The conference room may be filled with businesspeople in their 50s and 60s, and to avoid feeling like a kid who someone managed to sneak into the corporate offices, I focus on what I take to be their approximate inner age—for most people, this age is anywhere from 18 to 26—at which point whatever fear or trepidation I might have felt disappears.

Who among us, at 50 years of age, "feels" 50? Almost no one. A good rule of thumb in brand building is to communicate, always, to a consumer's Twin Self—and more than anything else, I realize that this was among the strategies that could help solve the Chinese car challenge.

What determines someone's inner age? In my experience, our inner age is directly connected to the first time we felt liberated and on our own. It could be when we left for college, or moved into our first apartment, or bought our first car. I opened up my own advertising agency when I was 12 years old, and not surprisingly, most of the time, I still see the world from the perspective of a 12-year-old. A 47-year-old man I know once told me his inner age was 40. When I asked him to explain, he told me that only when he met and married his wife, and the two of them moved into their dream house (right around his fortieth birthday), did he feel truly liberated. Have you noticed how businesspeople sometimes carry around a backpack? It's a sign of their Twin Self rejecting the typical props of the business world, and clinging to what it felt like to be young.

I've used the Twin Self concept any number of times in my work, most notably when I was consulting for iRobot, the manufacturers of the Roomba, the high-tech floor vacuum cleaner. Founded in 1990 by three roboticists from MIT's Computer Science and Artificial Intelligence Laboratory, iRobot is a New England–based robotics company that creates autonomous home robots—the Roomba, and for hard floors, the Scooba—and also manufactures police and military robotic units that have been deployed by the US military in Iraq, Afghanistan and elsewhere. By 2002, iRobot had sold 10 million Roombas, but when sales leveled off without explanation, the company brought me in to create an integrated branding strategy to reposition the Roomba—a rechargeable black disc that slides across the floor of a house, sucking up dirt—as a high-tech alternative to the vacuum cleaner.

Once I began my Subtext Research, a few things became clear, among them the fanaticism of the Roomba's core fans. Once Roomba users "experienced" the Roomba, they became lifelong brand ambassadors. Each had an intimate relationship to their Roomba, treating it almost like a member of their families. Many gave their Roomba names: Whitie, Big Red, Spot. The word *cute* kept coming up. Consumers loved how the Roomba zoomed across the floors of their house, until it crashed into a wall or a chair. One woman had recommended the Roomba to at least 20 of her friends, adding that she often steered even casual conversations toward iRobot and Roomba.

If most psychologists agree that identity is a construct, then we're all engaged in three processes simultaneously: Expressing who we are; expressing who we believe, or hope, we are; and finally, expressing who we want other people to think we are. No one rolls out of bed fated to dress, or act, in any one way; each of us is a deliberate self-creation. Nowhere was this more obvious than when I interviewed Roomba owners in their homes and apartments across New York and New England.

In a suburb outside Boston, Massachusetts, I found myself talking to a 35-year-old man named Jim. A few minutes into our conversation, I noticed that Jim had his own hydroponic plant system installed on an outdoor balcony, clearly visible from the living room. Jim told me how much time he spent cultivating his balcony garden, though he admitted to me it yielded only three or four tomatoes every year. In another home, Sam, an engineer, had set out all his technological devices on a coffee table, in precise rows. He had 9 remote controls, 73 diodes and 11 tightly coiled cables. In one corner of the room he kept a portable rolling minibar with its own built-in brew station designed to make homemade beer. Sam later confessed to me that he seldom drank beer and didn't even like the taste. Maggie, a 56-year-old woman, had a knitting pattern hanging off a sewing machine. "It's almost done," she told me. Eventually she admitted to me that she hadn't gone near her sewing machine in 15 years. Why was it so prominent in her living room, then? Maggie laughed; she had no answer.

The bigger point was how the apartments of countless male Roomba owners were laid out intentionally and strategically. One man, Richard, kept a basketful of toys in one corner of his living room. Only once or twice a year did his three-year-old nephew come to visit, which is why it made even less sense to me that he would showcase children's toys in his permanent collection—though I later found out he had his reasons. Two days later, I visited another apartment, this one belonging to a 29-year-old Roomba fan named Stuart. In his bathroom there hung any number of notes and placards announcing, in French, the name of certain items. The sink. The toilet. The shower. Was Stuart studying French, or memorizing grammar? No he wasn't. Then what explained the French signs all over his bathroom? "I want to learn the language," he replied. But when I pressed him further, I found out the real reason.

It's as if the insides of our homes, and even our cars and handbags, all feature a small variation on public image—a piano, a guitar, a vintage tattered American flag—in order to provoke an emotional response in others, and signal that their owners are more than what they do for a living, more than who or what they appear. I call this phenomenon "Breaking the Frame."

I first noticed this in Japan, when I saw that a middle-aged woman had hung a small key ring on the handle of her elegant handbag. I later realized how common it was, in fact, for local consumers to display a

small twist of individuality in a controlled, efficient, structured, homogenous country like Japan. Japan, after all, is a country where if your
meeting is at 1 p.m., you show up in the waiting room at 12:45 at the
latest. The bonsai trees are impeccably manicured. The sushi presenta-
tions are small, aesthetic works of art and, as I wrote earlier, getting
your purchase gift-wrapped can take up to 30 minutes. Japan is also a
society where natives repress their emotions, with many feeling unable
to express either their creativity or their imagination.

By "owning" a single word—*time*—Switzerland can be just as repressive, at least on the surface. Swiss trains enter and exit train stations
at schedules down to the second. If Swiss dinner guests plan on showing up five minutes late, they will call and alert you first. In response,
many outsiders would say that the Swiss are conservative, routine-ori-
ented, unimaginative and even dull. My experience there tells me otherwise. For one thing, based on my analysis of toilet water there—yes, I
even analyze toilet water—Zurich has one of the highest levels of drug
consumption in the world. Zurich was also the first and only city I
know of to construct street-side mobile booths where prostitutes could
entertain their clients, as well as the first city to launch public vending
machines that sold condoms. Today, among other things, Zurich is
home to some of the planet's wildest raves, and it is a popular destination for the world's most popular deejays. In short, while Zurich, and
Switzerland, may be known for straitlaced efficiency, they have found
their balance elsewhere.

Japan has found its own way of Breaking the Frame. In Tokyo,
after a morning spent doing business, many men and women change
out of their office clothes and costume themselves in the uniforms of
animated characters. They then eat lunch while interacting with other
men and women dressed as animated characters, then change back into
their office garb and return to their offices. Japan is also the site of cat
cafés, where for 100 yen, people spend their lunch hour playing with
kittens and older felines. Underneath the roles society asks them to
play is an alternate life they are forbidden to play or express: *Breaking
the Frame.*

In Japan, of course, many people express the concept known as *cute*. *Cute* would play a big role in the relaunch of the Roomba. Whenever I interviewed people about the Roomba, at first most would tell me about its functional benefits. The Roomba saved time. The Roomba freed up its owner from household responsibilities. Thanks to the Roomba, the house was cleaner, not just in the obvious places but in hard-to-reach corners.

But the body language of my interviewees gave them away. As they spoke, they moved their hands, and scratched the backs of their heads and their forearms. It was the exact same behavior I'd noticed in China when I asked Chinese men to sit behind the wheel of a car. It told me one thing: the Roomba may have had a slew of functional benefits, but its true, visceral appeal was to the owner's Twin Self—in this case, the child inside who had never gotten what he or she wanted growing up.

In the course of Subtexting on behalf of iRobot, I repeatedly found myself interviewing men and women who held highly structured, disciplined, administrative jobs with establishment titles. They were lawyers, insurance claims adjusters, sales representatives, middle managers. At home, though, once they changed out of their office clothes, they revealed another side of themselves. To compensate for their standardized, regulated day jobs, most had created a small, rebellious quirk—a way of Breaking the Frame—that couldn't help but remind me of plants trying to break through pavement—sprigs of hope, individuality, freedom. Not least, every one of them owned a Roomba.

Here, though, is where the story gets interesting. Most of us own a vacuum, or at least a broom, a dustpan or a box of Swiffers. Even if we decided to trade in our vacuum cleaner, broom and dustpan for a Roomba, we would no doubt store it in a closet, along with our other unsightly household gear. Or would we? As far as Roomba owners were concerned, the answer was no. In most homes and apartments, the Roomba was partly concealed, partly exposed. One half of the Roomba was visible, as if it had decided to hide—in a closet, under a bed—but changed its mind at the last moment. In most homes and apartments, there was ample room and space to store a Roomba, which meant that its passive-aggressive placement was intentional—a major clue, in fact. On the surface, the Roomba may have been about cleaning, efficiency and time savings, all wrapped up in a high-tech robotic package, but that wasn't why consumers loved the Roomba. No, the Roomba was a way to Break the Frame of the institutionalized lives they led during the week. In common with Trollbeads fans, they were allowing a brand to announce to the world that they were interesting, different, imaginative, quirky and even cute.

Another interesting fact about many Roomba owners? Many of them had a pet who'd recently died, or else they were on the verge of getting one, and it was between these two points that the Roomba came into their lives. The Roomba represented a bridge connecting the past to the present, an earlier identity with a future one.

There was one final secret reason why young, unmarried males bought a Roomba: to get women into bed. It took me awhile, and numerous interviews, to figure this out. Absolutely, these young men loved keeping up to date with the latest technology. Yes, the Roomba was a time-saver, allowing them to vacuum and do other things at the same time. But the Roomba was also a major pick-up device, especially for Jim, the man who kept a boxful of baby toys in his apartment. When I asked Jim to list off in their order of importance the four aspects of his apartment most likely to appeal to visiting females, he didn't even have to think about it. His dog; the baby toys; the frayed flag he had hanging over his bed; his Roomba. As for Stuart, the man who plastered his bathroom with French translations for "The Sink," "The Shower" and "The Toilet"? For him, the French was (as with Jim's dog, baby toys and dilapidated flag) a ruse designed to seduce visiting females, considering that French is linked to Paris, which, in turn, is associated with love and romance.

But I didn't realize where iRobot had gone off course until I was headed to the airport for my next job, which was Subtexting for Pepsi. So far, what I had found out about the Roomba puzzled me. Clearly, the machine did a lot more than vacuum floors, and I suspected that

I'd caught repeated glimpses of the emotional foundation that might ultimately reunite the Roomba with its fans.

People often ask me if I hate flying and the long hours I spend aboard planes. The answer is that I enjoy the flights more than I enjoy the long security lines, the crowded airports and the occasionally condescending TSA agents. I also can't help observe how people change once they board a flight. If you want to understand aspiration, you might consider asking flight attendents, as I have, about their constituents. Contrary to assumption, the most haughty, demanding passengers are neither in the First Class cabin nor in the Economy zone. No, every flight attendant I have ever asked tells me it is the Business Class passengers who are by a long shot the most difficult.

As I sat in my seat, I began wondering, not for the first time, why food generally tastes worse when you are airborne. Does it have something to do with the airflow, the minimal cooking facilities, or the fact that airliners are cutting back wherever they can? I also observed that when I was wearing my earphones, my food seemed to taste better than it did when I removed those same earphones. I played around with my headset by adjusting the volume, switching off the noise-reduction feature, but it made little difference. Without a doubt my food—and even the soda I was drinking—*did* taste better when I was wearing my earphones.

My upcoming work for Pepsi focused around strengthening their brands in the wake of changes in social media consumption. While doing Subtext Research throughout the world, I couldn't help but notice that in only five years time, consumers had begun gazing at screens in entirely different ways. That said, despite the variety of new platforms ranging from tablets to phones to binge-watching websites like Netflix, the television set endured. Among other reasons, its continuing popularity could be credited less to what consumers watched on TV, or to the larger screen, and more to what they heard. In my experience, we *listen* to the television more than we actually watch it.

Still, the question of airline food and flavor kept nagging at me. Over the next couple of weeks, I peppered catering company employees with questions. Did they know whether sound altered humans' perceptions of food at an altitude of 35,000 feet and, if it did, rather than sound making food taste worse, could sound possibly improve the flavor of foods or beverages? Later, I found out that at several thousand feet, our sense of taste and sense of smell are the first to weaken, thanks to drops in humidity and air pressure and even the role of background noise.[17] BBC News once reported that people eating to a soundtrack of loud background noise rated food as being less salty, less sweet and even crunchier than those who ate in silence.[18]

All of which made me wonder: Rather than Pepsi focusing on changing the visual appearance of its brands, wouldn't it make far more sense for the company to concentrate on "owning" the *sense* space? When you consider most if not all television commercials for foods or beverages, there is seldom any sound. No frying. No sizzling. Rarely will you hear the sizzle of a steak on the grill, or the *glug-glug-glug* of a soda filling a glass. Wouldn't it be smart if Pepsi could "own" the actual sound of its soda trickling over ice cubes?

When I brought up this idea with company executives, their response was enthusiastic, even though it made them ask the obvious question—namely, why had sound gone missing from their television commercials for decades too? Almost immediately Pepsi began experimenting with what would ultimately become its trademarked sound.

If it weren't for Pepsi, it would have taken me much longer to grasp iRobot's core issue. From Pepsi, I learned that just as a pair of earphones can persuade us that the meal we're eating on the plane is flavorful; sound can also change our perception of product performance. (When consumers vacuum using a silent vacuum cleaner, most will tell you it's not working. This same high degree of irrationality perhaps explains why when we vacuum the rug only to see a tiny thread on the floor, we pass the vacuum head over it stubbornly and repeatedly, even though it would be much easier to pick it up.)

Human irrationality led me to ponder the following question: By altering, or even eradicating its sound, had iRobot damaged the very heart of its brand? I wasn't talking about the brand's logo, design or efficiency, but the sounds that it made. By sending out the subtlest emotional message to Roomba fans, was the silent treatment compromising this particular love affair?

The technology team had gotten rid of the sound, inadvertently destroying the brand's "cute" factor. It's no coincidence that one of the founders of iRobot and the Roomba was a big fan of the *Star Wars* franchise. Over time, as iRobot scaled from its modest 1990 beginnings, the dash of cuteness inspired by R2-D2, the so-called "astromech droid" from the films, had vanished. By the time the company called me in, no one knew what the Roomba was anymore. When I asked the technology team to disassemble a Roomba, they did, and once the parts lay before me on the table, I asked them what was missing. No one could answer. "It no longer talks," I said. "It no longer says 'uh-oh' or 'dood-dood.'"

In the course of my Subtexting, most Roomba owners told me how much they liked the noises their Roombas made. When it grazed the wall by accident, the Roomba said, "Uh-oh." When it backed up, it said "dood-dood," similar to the sound a truck or backhoe makes as it runs in reverse. But in the hands of iRobot's crackerjack technology department, all sounds had been eliminated. The Roomba was now another faceless chunk of high-quality technology—sleek, impeccably designed, efficient and boring—with all its humanity bred out of it. Instead of helping Roomba owners Break the Frame, it had become another dreary extension of their already technologically overloaded workweeks.

The Roomba team had engineered all the whimsy out of the product. When you opened the Roomba, the first thing you saw were the words: *Warning: Do Not Return This Unit to Retail.* And *Please Read Instructions Carefully Before Use.* If hard-core Roomba fans were looking for ways to Break the Frame, and if the Roomba served as a silent communication device intimately linked to identity (and in some cases, romantic success), this was a losing strategy.

My mission? To re-infuse the "cuteness." When I asked Roomba fans what other brand reminded them most of the Roomba, most told me it was BMW's MINI Cooper, which everyone will agree has cuteness down to a science. When you order a new MINI Cooper, among other communiqués, BMW promptly sends you updates from England, digital links about the MINI and a reflective decal. When a new MINI is aboard a container ship, bound for its destination, the company's communications continue: *The Mini is enjoying its cruise and relaxing, and can't wait to see you!* MINI owners who've had their cars serviced at a BMW dealership have their cars returned with a sign on its wheel saying, *I Missed You.*

Inspired by the MINI Cooper, I asked iRobot's research and development team to set aside the Roomba's high-tech functionality and to do whatever they could to bring back the Roomba's emotionality and humanity. I asked them to bear in mind one simple fact: the Roomba may be a wizardly piece of technology, but it was also a toy, a baby, a pet, a conversation piece, a displacement for its owners' identity and, for some young men, a way to get women into bed. Sure, it may have swept up the most difficult-to-reach places in a home, but that was probably the least of its talents.

I HAD THE ROOMBA on my mind when I addressed the issue of tackling a "Made in China" automobile. Again, on the surface, the Chinese are unemotional or, at least, it is culturally taboo to express a range of emotions in public or private. Another critical point was that in contrast to the West, where women and children have a strong say in what car a family buys, in China the men purchase most new cars. Most businessmen are unwilling to buy a "cute" car, or a "cute" anything for that matter. (Japan, as I mentioned, has "cute" sewn up, and the Chinese, who don't exactly love Japan, know this. *Cute* tends to be "small," too, and the Chinese have a cultural preference for the splashy, the oversized and the exaggerated.)

That said, the concept of "cute" was slowly migrating into China, a phenomenon that can be traced back to China's one-child policy. "The Little Emperor Syndrome" is the popular term used to refer to the single Chinese son or daughter who receives inordinate amounts of love and attention from parents and other family members. My Subtext Research revealed that more and more Chinese parents were seeking out their children's opinions and perspectives. I had to bear in mind not just contemporary China, but also the evolving Chinese car industry. This meant that the future Chinese car had to operate on several tracks simultaneously. In order to appeal to the male Chinese driver, it had to be brash, masculine and powerful, while also appealing to his Twin Self, in this case, to a child denied toys when he was growing up. In a culture that lacked opportunities for "transformation," a Chinese automobile had to create a new, special mood, the illusion that a driver had entered a zone distinct from his everyday life. Not least, the car's styling—its lighting, how fast or how slowly the doors slid open and closed—had to reflect the unspoken Chinese preferences I'd observed over the course of my Subtexting.

Think about a song you love, one that has been covered in the years since by other artists, for example, "Something" by George Harrison. Since the song appeared on the Beatles' *Abbey Road* album in 1969, it has been sung by James Brown, Frank Sinatra, Tony Bennett, Ike and Tina Turner, Joe Cocker, Neil Diamond, approximately 150 musicians in all, making it the Beatles second-most-covered song next to "Yesterday." But arguably, no matter how superior or inferior all the others versions are, I can guarantee you that Harrison's original recording remains most people's favorite version. Why? The simple answer: it was the one they heard first. We prefer what we saw, heard or sensed first, whether it's the color of our childhood bedrooms or the lake, pool or ocean where we first learned to swim.

Our perception of what "quality" means is no different from our earliest exposure to music or to color. For Chinese cars designed for Chinese consumers, I focused both on male drivers and on the children who would someday grow up to buy cars. But if the Chinese car company was intent on exporting its cars abroad, I had to determine what "quality" meant elsewhere in the world. What better place to conduct my investigation than in two hubs of global car production, Germany and the United States?

OBVIOUSLY, YOU CANNOT INTERVIEW children using the same methods you use to talk to adults. Most children find it difficult to put their feelings and desires into words, which is why I've found that playing games with them often reveals greater insights. I carried out my study in Beijing, Berlin and Michigan, surrounded by a roomful of children accompanied by their parents. Before us were several boxes of LEGOs. With the goal of understanding the difference in how children in various countries manifested "speed"—which directly correlates with "quality" in the automobile sector—I asked them to show, build, construct and in general improvise around the concept of speed. Then I sat back with my notebook and watched.

All three nationalities—Chinese, American and German—built enormous cars. There were no surprises there. What did surprise me was when German and American children demonstrated "speed" by dragging their fingers across the floor. In contrast, the Chinese children showed no interest in finger demonstrations, but instead flung a LEGO piece against the nearest hard surface. Once they finished building their cars, both the American and German children, as invested in defense as they were in velocity, created bumpers, safety fences, garages and other protections around their cars to safeguard them against danger. One German child even constructed a rocket ship with a smaller survival capsule hugging the main frame, in the case of an emergency landing.

I next encouraged the children to play a game centered on "crashing." Here, the differences among the three nationalities showed up at once. The Chinese children showed no hesitation about carrying out one full-on collision after another. Bumpers, garages and safety rails seemed to bore them. When the Chinese kids played a game of chicken with their cars, neither car slowed down at the other's approach. The Germans and American children by contrast were far more cautious. Their LEGO cars slowed prior to impact. For them, the concepts of "speed" and "crashing" were both regulated and controlled.

The children couldn't put it into words, nor should they have, but it was obvious to me that an exaggerated focus on security, safety and protection had affected an entire younger generation. Both the Germans and Americans had intuited an "adult" definition of speed that ran counter to their own natural childhood behavior.

What did this all mean? When I Small Mined all my data, this insight about speed confirmed that "quality" in China was perceived as fast, no frills, almost breakneck, and would remain the same for the next generation of car buyers, too. I'd seen this same thing in how the Chinese brushed their teeth, in the bars of shampoo soap, in the absence of bedcovers and in the way people ordered, and were served, food in restaurants. Relatedly, the Chinese perceived light—light that other nationalities would find overly direct, naked and even confrontational—as "high-quality," as it was in the restaurant where I shared a meal with my Chinese host family. With the exception of the country's religious and memorial festivals, there was a striking nationwide absence of build-up, foreplay and anticipation. Culturally speaking, China went straight to the point.

I next commissioned a global study of doors.

Yes, doors. My assistant and I traveled the world taking short films of department store doors, subway doors, bus doors, elevator doors and basically any kind of door we could find. When we filmed Japanese commuters boarding a train, and the door began closing, we took notes. Did the door spring back as if bitten? Did it close slowly, then accelerate for the next few inches? Did it move slowly and patiently? We also filmed escalators. How fast or slowly did they ascend? I carried out another experiment in homes around the world, this time asking people which part, or zone, of their kitchen, or bedroom, or bathroom best represented "quality." Few Americans would ever discern quality in a drawer opening or closing, yet almost every northern European told me that a drawer that begins slowly, accelerates and slows down again is of higher "quality" than a uniformly fast-moving or slow-moving drawer.

Bizarrely, enough, the variation in these differences in how we perceive quality can be traced back to our grandparents' era. In the 1930s and '40s, doors in northern Europe were larger and heavier than they are today, as slow to open as they were to close. Without knowing exactly why, the perception of "quality" in how things open and shut has been handed down to subsequent generations.

Knowing that the Chinese car company had plans to go global, I created a "fast versus slow" translation kit for feelings and sensory signals to create the perception of "quality" in every country where they planned to expand. In France, for example, there is a widespread cultural emphasis on transition and on ceremony. France may have an ongoing love affair with frozen produce, but even when buying frozen food, the French will buy the ingredients for a three-course meal, and do the same when visiting McDonald's. They will buy a starter—perhaps chicken nuggets—work up to a hamburger and French fries, and end things with a dessert. The French expect a similar three-part formula in the way their car doors open and close. Americans are accustomed to an instantaneous feedback loop, and have little patience with a product that doesn't come to life immediately. An American tourist traveling abroad who switches on a Bang & Olufsen television in his hotel room will likely perceive the set as broken, not realizing it takes roughly seven seconds to turn on. Apple is one company that has solved this issue smartly. When a consumer powers on an iPhone, the silvery Apple logo appears, alerting users that the phone is on. Knowing the phone works, a consumer is happy to wait an additional 30 seconds before the phone is officially ready for use. I have no doubt that Apple engineers could tinker with the insides to make the phone turn on more quickly. Instead, they've designed the iPhone to give users both instant gratification and a sense of anticipation, which they interpret to mean that the phone is both technologically sophisticated and high quality.

China, of course, was different. Department store doors snapped open quickly. Elevators and escalators shot up. The trains were cannonballs. At the same time, outside of religious festivals, there was no space allotted for transition, or transformation. Even the Chinese cars I studied were more like extensions of apartments than automobiles. Which is why one of my first mandates for Chinese automobiles to appeal to Chinese markets was that the doors open and close fast.

The next question—importing the concept of the Twin Self in the car design—was more challenging.

The Twin Self has two elements, both of which are linked to desire: what we had once, but lost, and what we once dreamed about having but never possessed. Males across the world not only have a younger person inside them, they also have a third party, which any number of superheroes and action stars reflect. What is the fundamental appeal of books and films such as *The Godfather* and the *Bourne* and *Matrix* franchises? What explains the popularity of Batman, or Superman, or Spider-Man, or the X-Men films, or the success of the American television series *Breaking Bad*? The answer: they all feature as their protagonist a normal, everyday, even somewhat mild male who evolves into an animal or, at the very least, a powerful, menacing, occasionally cold-blooded killer who plays by his own rules. It was this aspect—the driver with a Twin Self, who is also in possession of a masterful, powerful alter ego—that I recommended we incorporate into the overall design of our "Made in China" car.

Another element we incorporated into the car's design was a transformation zone. Alongside a team of designers, we created a special internal ambience akin to the change in acoustics you hear when entering a sound studio. We used ambient light that snapped on when the doors opened and snapped off when the doors shut. The result: amplified masculine symbols, including a deep resonance to the sounds the doors made when slamming shut. We also made it a point to elevate the car seat, to give the driver a sense of omniscience and control. Knowing that Chinese children had a say about car buying, and were equally stimulated by power and mastery (and cuteness), we created a dashboard that resembled a flight deck. From watching ESPN, I'd learned about the power of information bombardment. ESPN strafes its viewers with an almost hysterical amount of data and details. Scrolling boxes. Panels. Bars. Graphics. Multi-angle camera perspectives. When exposed to a surfeit of data, men tend to feel more masculine and in command. Do most men bother to decipher these boxes, panels, bars and graphics? No—but that's not really the point. My mission was for

Chinese drivers to perceive their cars as fast, powerful and male, even if they weren't. More to the point, the doors opened and closed quickly, in a fast, straight line, and the same went for the electronic windows. My mission was to appeal to the child inside the driver, the driver himself, and his children.

Today, thanks to its new "translation kit," the Chinese car company is better able to translate "feelings" into sensory clues. A sliding passenger-side door in Europe, for example, opens very slowly, reaches a midpoint one or two feet in, then zips the rest of the way open. When the door is shut, the overhead light fades slowly. By contrast, the side doors on the "Made in China" car open and close furiously fast.

It's too early to tell how our Chinese car manufacturer is doing, but they've far surpassed their sales from last year, and the brand has dramatically increased its revenues across China. More to the point, the company is more hospitable than it has ever been to the emotional aspects of branding. Has the "Made in China" brand made forward progress? Yes, but there's still a lot of work left to be done. Someone asked me whether the Chinese predilection for speed will eventually migrate across the rest of the world, helped along by our own digital habits. I told him no, that in fact I believed that the opposite is true. As always, and whether they know it or not, human beings seek balance. The faster we go, the slower, in some respects, we will become. It may not always be conscious, but unconsciously we are all seeking to redress acceleration with idling, velocity with patience, chatter with quiet. How do I know this? Because small data is everywhere, if we know where to look.

CHAPTER 8
A GLIMPSE BEHIND THE SCENES
INCORPORATING SMALL DATA INTO YOUR BUSINESS AND LIFE

WHAT POLARIZED THE INTERNET BEYOND ANYONE'S IMAG- ination was a simple—or maybe not so simple—striped dress.

The dress, worn by a guest at a wedding ceremony held on the remote Hebridian island of Colonsay, was posted on Tumblr by a member of the wedding band, who asked her followers for their opinion: was the dress blue with black lace fringe, or white with gold lace fringe? "I was just looking for an answer because it was messing with my head," said Caitlin McNeill, a 21-year-old singer and guitarist.[1] Unfortunately, the answer led to even more disagreement. To one set of eyes, the dress appeared to be blue-black, and to a second it appeared to be white-gold. The dress photo soon migrated to Facebook, Twitter and Buzzfeed, which published a poll, "What Color Is This Dress?" that at one point attracted more than 670,000 people simultaneously, breaking all previous Buzzfeed records for traffic.[2]

Never mind that the original dress, in fact, was blue and black, and retailed for £50 at Roman Originals, a UK fashion chain.[3] The robust debate revealed that the differences in how we see color are based entirely on how our brains process visual information. Individual differences in color vision are fairly common, it turns out, and can be attributed to the 6 million or so tiny cones in the back of the human eyeball, known as photoreceptors, that process color in different ways, depending on our genes. Quoted in CNN.com, Dr. Julia Haller, the chief ophthalmologist at WillsEye Hospital in Philadelphia, said, "Ninety-nine percent of the time, we'll see the same colors . . . But the picture of this dress seems to have tints that hit the sweet spot that's confusing to a lot of people."[4] Another expert concluded, "This clearly has to do with individual differences in how we perceive the world."[5]

That humans are prone to seeing the world in different ways—while still being more similar than we ever imagine—is what this book is about.

BY NOW YOU KNOW I'm Danish by birth—that is to say I'm not American, French, Spanish, English, Scottish, Irish, Brazilian, Australian, Swiss, Kenyan, South African, German, Italian, Russian, Chinese, Japanese, Vietnamese, Filipino, Austrian, Greek, Guatemalan, Chilean, Argentinian, Colombian, Mexican or a native of any other of the world's 196 countries. More importantly, as a forensic investigator of emotional DNA, I've somehow managed to come up with brands or innovations not *despite* of my outsider's status, but *because* of it. Familiarity, in fact, is at best counterproductive, and at worst, paralyzing.

A few years ago, when Pepsi asked if I would help them improve the public perception of their soft drink, of course I said yes. But only a few days into the job, I had to acknowledge that my perspective, my senses and my instincts were all compromised. Pepsi—its taste, its bubbles, its cans, its bottles, its advertising—was just too familiar. I had no distance from the brand, no frame of reference about desire, or craving, my own or other people's. I couldn't think straight. I couldn't get inspired. I couldn't do my job.

My solution was to get rid of all the Pepsi cans from my refrigerator and kitchen cabinets, so I could better observe and analyze my own responses to craving. I asked friends who were liable to offer me a Pepsi when I visited if they wouldn't mind doing the same. Physically and psychologically, the next six weeks were an ordeal. I got head-aches, found it hard to function normally and, at night, dreamed about Pepsi. The good news is that when the six weeks was up, I had managed to stimulate a response in myself and the other Pepsi drinkers I knew. I had become, again, a stranger to the everyday, an alien to the commonplace.

Working with Pepsi wasn't the first time I've carried out Subtext Research on myself. The best insights always begin with ourselves. Having interviewed 2,000 or so consumers across the world, it seems only fitting to turn my methodology inward. As self-confident as I may come across sometimes onstage, when I go home to my hotel room at night, I still have a stubborn need for confirmation and validation. It all goes back to my own childhood insecurities. I can suppress them, or pretend they don't exist, but they're always there. Over the years I've looked on with interest, and sometimes dismay, at how the brands I surround myself with reflect my own confidence (and occasional lack of it).

The first, of course, is LEGO. (Growing up, I didn't just build my own LEGOLAND, I also slept in a LEGO bed.) The second brand is Aeronautica Militare, a fashion line I wrote about earlier in this book.

Growing up, I wasn't entirely sure what Aeronautica symbolized. I knew only that I liked its patches and wanted to buy one of its shirts. At the time I didn't know that Aeronautica had any military significance, which, consciously or unconsciously, can be irresistible to a child anxious to find a sense of belonging and identity. Aeronautica and its logos are visually arresting, and it came as no surprise to discover later the well-documented correlation between an oversized logo and a high level of insecurity. Today I still have a few Aeronautica shirts hanging in my closet—an attempt, no doubt, to hang onto my own Twin Self, in this case, a kid who craved a shirt he wasn't able to buy.

The third brand? Royal Copenhagen, an elegant porcelain brand founded in 1775, whose debut collection included plates and bowls for the Danish royal family. Most families with children living in Denmark during the 1970s, '80s and '90s, including my own parents, owned one or two pieces of Royal Copenhagen china with its signature blue, hand-crafted lines. Growing up, I associated the brand with high-end restaurants, royalty, heritage and tradition. Later, when I could afford to, one of the first things I did was to buy a set of Royal Copenhagen plates. Why? Subconsciously, I can't help but think I wanted to "complete" my life in a way my parents never could. By buying Royal Copenhagen in a culture governed by *Janteloven,* the Scandinavian moratorium against standing out, maybe I was also telling the culture I had succeeded in my life—that I was *someone.* It was a moment when I realized the degree to which brands fill in the missing holes of our identities, whether we acknowledge it or not.

Along with a well-cut suit and a necktie, a luxury watch is almost mandatory in the business world, and I eventually allowed a fourth brand, Rolex, to "say" something about myself. One day, when I was at a meeting, flashing around my Rolex, I noticed a well-dressed older man studying my watch intently. He seemed bemused rather than impressed. Finally he approached me. He couldn't help but notice my watch; in his experience, only Russians and Chinese wore Rolexes as conspicuous as mine. Also, was I at all aware I was wearing the women's model? No, I said, ashamed, I wasn't. Twenty-four hours earlier, my Rolex had been my proudest possession. Now I was mortified. I ended up giving it away and buying the "right" one, which I still wear today.

Along with the Rolex, for years I also carried around an American Express Centurion Card, known as "the Black Card." I told myself I'd chosen the card because of its functional benefits, including a concierge and travel agent, personal shoppers at Saks and Gucci, and assorted worldwide hotel privileges, when in fact I was seduced by its emotional appeals. Three or four years ago, when American Express told me they weren't willing to honor the points I'd accumulated over the years, I let my membership go. I replaced my Amex with a Visa that offered more than double the points. Yet I still felt a huge sense of loss. What had I just given up? Status. Belonging. The feeling that I was special. What would merchants, waiters, hotel clerks and my friends say when I took out my Visa? The answer: nothing. They wouldn't notice. The validation and worth the Amex Black Card had given me was suddenly very obvious.

The brands we like, and buy, and surround ourselves with—and by now you know I define a "brand" as anything from the music on our playlists to our shoes, to our sheets, to our toothpaste, to the artwork hanging on our walls—have the profoundest possible things to say about who we are. As brands, our professional job titles are really no different. For example, over the years many people have come to me for job advice. Should they quit their job at the Fortune 100 company and launch a consultancy out of their home? Lost in all the talk about salary, benefits and commuting time are the emotional consequences of a job change, or the vulnerability the people are liable to feel once the logos on their business cards are gone.

The fear of losing their "branded" identities is as good an explanation as any to me why CEOs and senior executives spend almost no time at all in their own stores or interact with the consumers who keep them in business by buying their razors, sodas, seafood, shirts, granola, frozen foods, perfumes and pharmaceuticals. Even executives who participate in focus groups observe the proceedings behind one-way mirrors, in air-conditioned rooms equipped with snacks, cold drinks, monitors and mute buttons. What they miss, again and again, are those moments when they might uncover something new and valuable about themselves or their brand.

In some instances, I've found that executives don't even use their own products. A case in point was Ansell, the world's second-largest manufacturer of medical and industrial gloves and condoms. Recently, Ansell's executive team invited me to speak at the company's annual retreat in Sri Lanka, the headquarters of all Ansell's condom production, to discuss "the future of condoms." As I entered the room, I noticed that most of the executives were in their 40s, 50s and 60s. This was striking only to the extent that Ansell is in the business of making and selling condoms, a product generally favored by a younger demographic. It soon became obvious that everyone there was accustomed to using standard, clinical descriptions of their product, like "prophylactic" and "protective solutions." That's when I told the room we were going to carry out a small experiment. I handed out a condom to everyone in the audience, and then switched off the overhead lights. "We're now going to do something you've never done before," I said. "It's *sex* time! With no lights on!" and I asked people to open their condoms.

I hadn't intended to shock anyone, but it was obvious I had. I heard a lot of crackling and rustling in the darkness as Ansell executives and employees attempted to tear open the package's double seal. When I turned the lights back on a minute later, not a single person in the audience had managed to open the package—in conditions that duplicated how most consumers access condoms.

This is why I do everything I can to ensure that company executives experience their stores—and products—in the same way consumers do. During my interactions with Tesco, the British multinational grocery retailer, the CEO introduced "Mission Feet on the Floor," a program in which every executive was required to work on the floor of one of its grocery stores for several days at a time. To help them understand how Tesco's food tasted compared to its rivals, executives were also invited to an offsite location and asked to prepare and cook all of Tesco's premade sandwiches, salads and hamburgers, as well as the foods of their competitors. In Colombia, I once consulted for a bank chain notorious for its slow customer service and long lines. I asked bank officials to pretend they were customers. It was an exercise in frustration, and even rage. Some executives waited up to an hour in line, while others were punted from teller to teller in order to secure a simple signature. When it was time to present my findings, I told the executive team that from now on we were implementing three new rules: No one should have to wait longer than three minutes for customer service; customers should be asked to sign a piece of paper only once; and there would always be a parking space available. A year later, it was the premier bank in South America for customer service.

Bear in mind that none of these examples had much, if anything, to do with big data, which can only take us so far. After all, humans dissemble, consciously or unconsciously. Most of us aren't aware of our habits and desires. In a 2015 discussion at the Cannes Lions Festival between Tom Adamski, the CEO of Razorfish Global, and Will Sansom, director of content and strategy at Contagious Communications, Adamski went so far as to say that digital media, and big data, has contributed to a global decrease in brand loyalty. Why? In Adamski's words: "Brands are not treating us as individuals . . . Brands are still relying on archaic—and quite frankly, flawed—segmentation processes that market to demographics. But they don't market to me."[6]

Big Data rarely helps to identify the "needle" in the stack
Illustration by Ole Kaarsberg

If companies want to understand consumers, big data offers a valuable, but incomplete, solution. I would argue that our contemporary preoccupation with digital data endangers high-quality insights and observations—and thus products and product solutions—and that for all the valuable insights big data provides, the Web remains a curated, idealized version of who we really are. Most illuminating to me is combining small data *with* big data by spending time in homes watching, listening, noticing and teasing out clues to what consumers really want. After all, at age 14 when LEGO first hired me, I *was* that consumer, a kid enamored with the company's building blocks. By observing my own behavior, and that of my friends, I was able to give LEGO executives insights on their product and company that any number of quantitative surveys could not—just as, in sharp contrast to what big data was telling them, the observations of an 11-year-old German boy were able to help reverse LEGO's slide into bankruptcy.

Intriguingly, we are now turning the tables on the Internet by circling back and finding human—not digital—insights about ourselves based on our own unconscious online behaviors.

In 2013, for example, using data accumulated from 250,000 people over a period of ten years, a study appeared in the *Journal of Personality and Social Psychology* examining music consumption tastes as they evolve over the course of a lifetime. Music, it appears, adapts to whatever "life challenges" or psychosocial needs we face as we get older.[7] The study divided music consumption patterns into five "empirically derived" categories dubbed the "MUSIC model"—an acronym that stands for *mellow, unpretentious, sophisticated, intense and contemporary.* Perhaps unsurprisingly, the first significant age of music-listening is adolescence, a time defined by *intense,* which possibly reflects increased hormonal activity or the creation of the teenaged "self." *Intense* intersects with a rise of *contemporary* music, a trend that lasts until early middle age, when two other "preference dimensions"—Electronic and R&B—enter the mix, both of which are "romantic, emotionally positive and danceable."[8] The final musical age of humans is dominated by *sophisticated*—jazz and classical music—and *unpretentious*—country, folk and blues. These latter two musical forms are relaxing, positive and link indirectly to listeners' social status and perceived intellect.[9]

What do the sports we love the most say about us? A study carried out by Mind Lab surveyed 2,000 UK adults and found that bicyclists are "laid back and calm" and less likely than runners or swimmers to be stressed or depressed. Runners tended to be extroverted, enjoyed being the center of attention and preferred "lively, upbeat music." Swimmers, the study concluded, were charitable, happy and orderly, whereas walkers generally preferred their own company, didn't like drawing attention to themselves and were comparatively unmaterialistic.[10]

Are you aware that people with a lot of Facebook friends tend to have lower-than-average self-esteem?[11] Or that the more neurotic Facebook users are, the more likely they are to post mostly photos?[12] Last year, an article in the *New York Times Magazine* analyzed the significance of the passwords we use to get online and access certain websites. The article reported that in the same way we leave a trail of emotional DNA in our wake, we also distill emotion inside our passwords—and that many of our passwords ritualize a regular encounter with a meaningful memory, or time in our lives, that we seldom have occasion to recall anywhere else. "Many of [our passwords] are suffused with pathos, mischief, sometimes even poetry. Often they have rich backstories. A motivational mantra, a swipe at the boss, a hidden shrine to a lost love, an inside joke with ourselves, a defining emotional scar—these keepsake passwords, as I came to call them, are like tchotchkes of our inner lives."[13]

Big data might find it hard to find meaning, or relevance, in insights like these. In every study I mention there is a missing question: How might these findings be combined with small data to affect or transform a brand or business? Subtext Research might reveal that a 16-year-old girl who listens to "intense" music might find it a poor fit with her teenaged identity, and a 45-year-old Englishman who listens to John Coltrane and Chopin might tell you he pines for the intensity of his teenaged years and, in fact, wears a black rubber band around his wrist as a badge of rebellion. But you would never know this until you sat across from these people in their living rooms or bedrooms.

Nor, it seems, could an unnamed banking institution truly comprehend the behavior of its customers even after leveraging a big data analytics model designed to prevent customer "churn," a term referring to customers who move money around, refinance their mortgages, or generally show signs they are on the verge of exiting the bank. Thanks to the analytics model, the bank soon found evidence of churn, and promptly drafted letters asking customers to reconsider. Before sending them out, though, the bank executive discovered something surprising. Yes, indeed, "big data" had seen evidence of churning. Thing is, it wasn't because customers were dissatisfied with the bank or its customer service. No: most were getting a divorce, which explained why they were shifting around their assets.[14] A parallel small data study could have figured this out in a day or less.

Then there are the issues facing Google's new self-driving cars, most of which it seems can be credited to the mismatch between technology and humanity. According to the *New York Times,* last year as one of Google's new cars approached a crosswalk, it did as it was supposed to and came to a complete stop. The pedestrian in front crossed the street safely, at which point the Google car was rammed from behind by a second non-Google automobile. Later, another self-driving Google car found that it wasn't able to advance through a four-way stop, as its sensors were calibrated to wait for other drivers to make a complete stop, as opposed to inching continuously forward, which most did. Noted the *Times,* "Researchers in the fledgling field of autonomous vehicles say that one of the biggest challenges facing automated cars is blending them into a world in which humans don't behave by the book."[15]

As accurate, then, as big data can be while connecting millions of data points to generate correlations, big data is often compromised whenever humans act like, well, humans. As big data continues helping us cut corners and automate our lives, humans in turn will evolve simultaneously to address and pivot around the changes technology creates. Big data and small data are partners in a dance, a shared quest for balance.

EARLIER, I WROTE THAT despite the 7 billion or so people inhabiting the earth, in my experience there are only anywhere from 500 to 1,000 truly unique people in the world. This isn't to put down individuality; instead, it recognizes the degrees of connectivity aligning humans who ultimately can be "divided" by four criteria: Climate, Rulership, Religion and Tradition.

Climate is only indirectly linked to the sun shining overhead, or whether or not your winters are cold or temperate. Rather, it refers to how your environment reflects and also influences behavior and diet.

Scandinavian natives, for example, favor a diet weighted heavily toward richer, fattier foods, whereas the Mediterranean diet is lighter and more oil-based.

Rulership refers to the power, or government, in charge, whether it's Vladimir Putin in Russia, a Democratic or Republican regime in the United States, the Communist Party in China, or the dictatorships of Iran, Jordan, Ethiopia, Sudan and elsewhere. How free are a country's residents? *Religion,* of course, refers to the influence of belief in a country, how dominant or irrelevant it is, and whether a person's belief system lies behind decision-making processes. Finally, *Tradition* focuses on a country's unspoken protocols, whether it is the European habit to ignore other elevator passengers or the American predilection for friendliness. Once you've taken these four variables into account and set aside differences in class, race, skin color and gender, humans are the same no matter where they live.

Until recently, I never considered what I did for a living as a repeatable methodology. But over the past few years, nearly half-a-dozen companies have asked if I could distill my Subtext Research into a training program. In some segments of Nestlé, where I've consulted for years, my techniques, or Subtext Research methodology, have become an integral part of analyzing new products, ideas, innovations and brands. Today, thousands of Nestlé employees spend 48 hours a year visiting consumers in their homes.

I'm often asked the following question: What about sampling bias, where members of a population are unequally represented? With a smaller sample size, how can anyone, much less a company, hope to find a comprehensive solution or answer? If it does, is there any guarantee that your findings will accurately represent a larger whole?

My answer is that a single drop of blood contains data that reveals nearly a thousand different strains of virus. Providing that your sample size is well chosen, there is little difference between a blood sample and the work I do, which is why interviewing 50 respondents (rather than 5 million) is often more than adequate to carry out a solid 7C methodology. Harder for many people, and businesses, to admit is that rather than basing their research on millions of consumers, sometimes all it takes is ten people to transform a brand or business.

Working for Lowes, for example, I began my investigation with my own observations about American culture: the rounded shapes, the lack of physical touch and the homogenous retail landscape. I eventually connected these observations to a hypothesis, i.e., the high degree to which fear influenced American life. When I interviewed Trollbeads fans, one of the first things I picked up was how many of them said they missed the sense of community, family and collegiality they remembered as children and how, for many, Trollbeads was able to assemble a collection of highly personal memories that linked together the passing years.

In every case, something was missing from people's lives: a subconscious desire. By identifying an unmet desire, you are that much closer to uncovering a gap that can be fulfilled with a new product, a new brand or a new business. Remember that every culture in the world is out of balance, or in some way exaggerated—and in that exaggeration lies desire.

The 7Cs in my Framework stand for Collecting, Clues, Connecting, Causation, Correlation, Compensation and Concept. Consider the following as a pocket guide to how to take one, or several, small pieces of small data—a refrigerator magnet, a porcelain frog—and very possibly

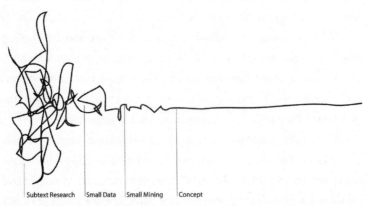

Subtext Research | Small Data | Small Mining | Concept

Subtext Research helps to identify Small Data, which in turn leads toward the creation of a Concept
Illustration by Ole Kaarsberg

transform them into a winning concept. Throughout this book you have been traveling the world with me on an airplane, bouncing from place to place, culture to culture. It's time you came inside the cockpit.

COLLECTING, OR, HOW ARE YOUR
OBSERVATIONS TRANSLATED INSIDE A HOME?

The viral Internet dress photo is a good reminder that none of us sees the world in the same way. Most of us are blinded by the familiar. We surround ourselves with people who are like us, who believe the same things we do. Our Facebook newsfeeds are no different, reflecting our interests, beliefs, concerns and biases.

The first step in the 7C process, then, is to do everything you can to remove the filter that keeps you from seeing what is really going on. My advice? Get a haircut.

Let me explain. The "collecting" step begins with establishing navigation points, on both macro and micro levels. This includes getting perspectives from cultural observers, for example, people who are new to the area, either expats or people who see the community through objective eyes. Ask them: What does the neighborhood, or city, or town, look like and feel like? Are the sidewalks deserted? Are there children playing outside? Are people friendly? Do you ever feel scared, and if so, why? Is there any sense of neighborhood pride? If you see people on the streets, do they meet your eyes or look away? Is the garbage picked up regularly? What makes a city or town come together? What divides it? Why? Visiting Brazil, I quickly found out that the nation is preoccupied with football and religion, and divided by restrictive class levels. There was a tension implicit in these layers. *Did Brazilians need to escape?* This tentative hypothesis was one I would eventually shape and refine.

Now, seek out a hairdresser or one or several other "local observers" who can help you establish a baseline perspective, and who inhabit a more or less neutral space within a community. It doesn't have to be a hairdresser; it could be a bartender, a mailman, or a church, community or sports club leader. Whoever it is, cultural and local observers are privy to information most people are not. They can tell you what's really going on. They are more or less unbiased. They can also point you to their own networks of friends and acquaintances.

The navigation points you gather from local observers will help you to frame your initial observations and create a hypothesis before you enter a consumer's home. In turn, your initial hypothesis will help you create "tracks," or topics of interest or focus, to follow once you begin interviewing consumers. Only rarely will one of your first six tracks be the final one, and half of them will later be disproven or tossed away. Think of them as stepping-stones that lead to bigger and better stepping-stones that lead, finally, to a concept.

At this collecting stage, you are trying to capture as many different perspectives from as many trustworthy sources as possible. If you have any doubt whether these local observers are useful, or reliable, social media is a fast, easy way to confirm their degree of integration into a community. People active in social media are, by nature, extroverted and confident. Take notice of how often they post; their degree of curation; the relevance of their content; and whether or not there is a touch of swagger or exhibition to their postings—all of which combine to create an ideal local observer. Bear in mind that local observers often have both a public and a private Facebook profile, making it easier to contact them. During your preliminary phone call, by asking the same questions you asked of cultural observers, you can quickly discover if their perspectives are useful or not.

If you are working on behalf of an existing brand, I also recommend interviewing the brand's past, current and potential future users—a group that ideally should reflect 50 percent of the total aggregate of respondents.

CLUES, OR, WHAT ARE THE DISTINCTIVE EMOTIONAL REFLECTIONS YOU ARE OBSERVING?

Remember, you are an investigator whose goal is to create a narrative, a cohesive story that hangs together. For this reason, nothing you see or hear is irrelevant or wasted. Imagine that you are equipped with a hypothesis and entering someone's home for the first time. (Your hypothesis may be true, half true or false—you don't know yet.) Think of a residence as a place that is home to an infinite series of small voices that owners are broadcasting in every room. Are the voices congruent, or are they out of tune? What unconscious, seemingly random pieces of small data are hanging from the walls, hiding inside "off-limits" zones like the refrigerator and the kitchen cabinets? Everything in the home, from the art on the walls to the insides of bathroom cabinets, is positioned where it is for a reason.

Here, I regularly call upon a model to divide the assorted "selves" that make up the average consumer. First is the idealized self we project onto the world, the one focused around how we'd like others to see us (which, I might add, is often very different from who we actually are). This manicured, public self is similar to the one we assemble on our Facebook pages and Instagram accounts. Components that also fall under the category of "idealized self" are the objects we collect and display in our homes, from photographs to heirlooms to tchotchkes. Over the years, I've observed that our collections form a timeline of our lives, a secondary calendar that offers a valuable perspective on who we are—or believe we are—and where we've been. The most common "recharging station" for reflecting on what we have accumulated is the living room, and for adolescents, backpacks and laptop covers.

That said, the places where our idealized selves conflict with our actual selves tend to be private: our refrigerators, kitchen cabinets, wardrobes and—in the case of men—garages and online folders.

Often, it is what is *missing* that forms the cornerstone of a successful hypothesis. Take Denmark, for example, with its countless "conversation kitchens" and untouched, unused Brio tracks. On the surface, most Danish homes are "perfect" in appearance. Get closer, and you will realize that room after room is, in fact, staged, and the country's stress levels are among the highest in the world. Relatedly, take note of a small symbol that may, in fact, overwhelm every other clue. In a small residence inside a Brazilian favela, I saw a flower in a cup inside a beer can on a shelf. In a gritty environment, it stood out as a badge of hope.

As LEGO found out more than a decade ago, the question "What are you most proud of?" can yield surprising and transformative answers. It could be an old guitar; a handmade quilt; a contemporary painting; a set of vintage wineglasses. Ask respondents if you can look through old photo albums or iPhoto collections. Explore the refrigerator and the kitchen and bathroom cupboards before moving into the bedroom and the bedroom closets. Determine how people want to be perceived by the rest of the world by asking them to show you their favorite piece of clothing. Determine the age of their Twin Self by paying close attention to the musical playlists on their smartphones, computers or streaming music services. Do they subscribe to any iTunes television shows or movies? If applicable, what films and TV shows are in their Netflix queues? (In this way, you can determine their shared cultural references.) What evokes the strongest emotion in them? Is it pride? Is it the memory of a loved one? Is it a pet? Is it a child? Finally, I ask people to answer two questions: *What is most important in your life?* and *What worries you the most?*

Don't be discouraged if at first you don't find what you are looking for. Such is the nature—even the definition—of detective work.

CONNECTING, OR, WHAT ARE THE CONSEQUENCES OF THE EMOTIONAL BEHAVIOR?

By now, you probably have half-a-dozen or more pieces of small data in front of you. You may find yourself, as I did with Lowes, in a culture that prohibits touching, and whose downtowns empty out at 5 p.m. every afternoon and where there is a striking absence of community and belonging. In the case of Trollbeads, by this point I had discovered that the brand's fans were aware something was missing from their lives; and that consumers attracted to Roombas were staging their homes using a technological gadget as a conversation piece.

Ask yourself: Are there any similarities among the clues you have accumulated? Are the clues beginning to tilt in one direction? If you had one, are you beginning to validate your initial hypothesis?

Remember that a clue might be physical (an extravagantly patterned shirt that doesn't fit with the rest of a respondent's wardrobe) or emotional (a respondent is obsessed with U2). You are seeking an emotional gap—*too much* or *too little* of something. As is the case with many homes in Denmark, if you enter a home where nothing is out of context, you know you've struck gold. If you are on the right track, the body language of respondents will often show unease or outright discomfort, in which case you will know you are onto something.

The next step is to Small Mine—distill and analyze—the clues you've accumulated
Illustration by Ole Kaarsberg

CAUSATION, OR WHAT
EMOTION DOES IT EVOKE?

For Lowes customers, the routines of their lives had become a self-ful-filling prophecy. Trollbeads consumers were experiencing a sense of deep insecurity, whereas Roomba customers found the product a way to fill a vacuum of loneliness and insecurity. It's now time to gather your findings in your office or place of work, and begin the process of Small Mining.

Generally, I mount a time line consisting of photographs and observations on a large bulletin board. It is here that your wall reflects the emotional DNA that you have found, as well as the correlations you've identified along the way. Place all these observations and photographs together and seek out the commonalities.

Ask yourself, "What emotion will this evoke in a human being?"

At this point, it's essential to put yourself in the shoes of respondents. If you were he or she, how would you feel? What would you want? This isn't a particularly easy question to answer, especially in cultures alien from our own. If it is too challenging, it might be a good time to call, or revisit, the cultural or local observers you interviewed before beginning the clue-gathering process. Present your observations to them. Ask them what *they* think.

CORRELATION, OR, WHEN DID THE
BEHAVIOR OR EMOTION FIRST APPEAR?

In the correlation stage, we seek evidence of a shift, or change in a consumer's behavior, otherwise known as an entry point. When did this change take place? Did it happen when she got married? When she had her first child? When she got divorced? An entry point, or person-ality shift, can be expressed via clothing, or by adopting a new set of friends, getting (or losing) a partner, sending children off to college or any other major milestone or career transition.

As I wrote earlier, we are too close to ourselves to observe what is familiar. For this reason, often during the Small Mining process, we need to reset our own perspective by reaching out to one of the respondent's friends or family members. Contact this person so that he or she can help validate, or add to, your thinking during the latter part of the interview.

COMPENSATION, OR, WHAT IS THE UNMET OR UNFULFILLED DESIRE?

Having found evidence of a shift, it's now time to distill it to its most emotional essence: desire. What is the desire that is not being fulfilled? What is the best way to fulfill it? With Lowes, the answer was to create a strong sense of belonging within a physical setting. Trollbeads fans needed to reconnect and rediscover what it felt like to belong to a group; and Roomba fans needed a way to show the world their humanity.

Often, by poring through people's photo albums, you will find the answer. As you review the pages, look for the happiest moments in people's lives. Use them as reflections of a time, or a moment, when people felt most in harmony, on top, at peace and emotionally fulfilled.

Inside these two poles—where people felt emotionally fulfilled versus where they are right now in their lives—is where you will find desire. Does the desire you have identified complement the cultural and local observations, as well as the clues you observed inside respondents' homes?

CONCEPT, OR, WHAT IS THE "BIG IDEA" COMPENSATION FOR THE CONSUMER DESIRE YOU HAVE IDENTIFIED?

Take your observations home and mull them over. As I wrote earlier, my best ideas come as a result of swimming laps in hotel pools. I fundamentally believe that "creativity" involves combining two ordinary things in a completely novel way. LEGO Mindstorms—the company's brand of customizable robots—involved merging LEGO building blocks with a computer chip. Uber involved combining a private car service with a social media network. In my own work, Lowes 2.0 came as the result of combining a supermarket with entertainment and community, while Tally Weijl 2.0 mixed and matched social media with the traditional dressing room.

Ideas, remember, are less likely to germinate under pressure. They come together when we least expect them. So swim, bike, garden, walk along the sand.

I'M OFTEN REMINDED of the most memorable interview I have ever conducted. The reason it was so revealing, I realized later, was that I got the time of our appointment wrong and showed up an hour before I was supposed to. When I rang the doorbell, the respondent, a middle-aged woman, greeted me at the door. She had just gotten out of bed, her hair was uncombed and she was wearing a loose blue bathrobe. She didn't look at all pleased to see me. I apologized repeatedly for getting the time wrong, and told her I would come back in an hour, but she insisted I come in anyway.

What followed was the most honest interview I've ever conducted. The woman had had no time to get ready. She'd had no time to prepare her face, or clean her house. I was seeing her, for all intents and purposes, naked. Accordingly, there was no point in deception, no point in telling me what she assumed I wanted to hear. Two hours later, I left her house reminded of the sheer hours of our lives we spend putting on masks to greet the world.

Based on the findings of a recent qualitative survey carried out in Switzerland, in fact, most of us have up to ten discreet interdependent social identities—identities, the study concludes, which are often in conflict.[16] Let's imagine a middle-aged bank teller living in Pensacola, Florida. He is a father, a son and a husband. He is a Floridian. He is a bank employee. He is also a bicyclist and a recreational runner, and at night, drinking with his friends, he is "the funny one." He is also a vegetarian, an amateur guitarist, and on weekends he helps coach soccer at his daughter's high school. Then there are his online identities, including his Facebook, Twitter and Instagram selves. Most surprising is that the man's ethical mind-set, honesty, sociability and even level of social engagement changes from personality to personality. Imagine that in his professional role, for example, he may be primed to dissembling, or outright deceit, while simultaneously, as a dad, he finds dishonesty repellent. My role—the role of anyone trying to make sense out of small data—is to understand not just one single personality, but all of them.

Which is why in the end the secret behind any ethnographic research will never be found in any methodology, even mine. It begins with yourself. Who are you? What are you like when you're by yourself? When you post a status update on Facebook, or "like" a piece of music, what are you telling the world about yourself? When you buy a pair of pants, or a new brand of shoes, when you hang a set of bamboo curtains across your window or cherry-pick photographs to tack onto your refrigerator, or leave out a bottle of facial moisturizer in your bathroom, what are you communicating? In our small data, now and forever, lies the greatest evidence of who we are and what we desire, even if, as LEGO executives found out more than a decade ago, it's a pair of old Adidas sneakers with worn-down heels.

ACKNOWLEDGMENTS

A CHINESE PROVERB I ONCE HEARD SAYS THAT PEOPLE get three opportunities in their lives—and that if they take advantage of them, they might very well receive another three. I've somehow managed to grab a larger-than-normal share of these opportunities in the course of my life, and while not every one has panned out, I must confess that at least in my case, this proverb makes sense. Twenty years ago, a colleague asked me why so many opportunities seemed to float my way. I told her that, in fact, we're all exposed to an equal number, that it's more a matter of recognizing opportunities when they're in front of us and, crucially, converting them into action.

The ability to spot options and possibilities comes not only with age and experience, it also takes place when we open our minds. In this case, I'm not talking about politics, or religion, but, rather, about letting down our personal guards, leaving behind our well-appointed offices, and moving in with strangers, all the while not revealing anything about our backgrounds, achievements or talents. In this situation, we become no more and no less than observant human beings, people whose only mission is to observe how other people live. It is only when we experience what it feels like to have nothing that we can realize and appreciate the true value of our personal brand.

That said, I've been (undeservedly) lucky throughout my life to work alongside individuals more talented than I am, and to borrow their wisdom, piggyback on their insights and gracefulness—and pass their abilities off as my own(!). This is why you are reading this book, and why I have so many people to thank. The individuals listed below have one thing in common—they have an unusual ability to spot, and grab, opportunities. Without them, this book wouldn't have been what it is.

It was in Zambia, of all places, that Malcolm Gladwell planted the first seed that led to *Small Data*. Malcolm helped me shape my initial thoughts, guided me throughout the process, and gave me the type of feedback that only "a Malcolm Gladwell" can give. Malcolm, thank you so much.

I'm truly grateful for the outstanding efforts of Peter Smith, my writer, and James Levine, my agent at Levine, Greenberg, Rostan Literary Agency. Together, on the basis of one or two scattered notes, a few phone conversations, a suitcase full of experiences and a dinner in downtown New York, we crafted what would ultimately become the idea behind *Small Data*. It's hard to believe the number of iterations we've been through to create what I hope in the end comes across as a simple concept! Jim and Peter were instrumental in helping me see clearly even when I began losing the ability to make out the essence of what this book was about.

Peter, I'm greatly appreciative of your work—we've now worked together for a decade—and you continue to surprise me. Along the way I've learned a secret word in publishing: When people truly feel a book is outstanding, they typically use the somewhat humble word "*Terrific!*" Well, Peter, you're terrific, and an amazing talent. Jim, I can only repeat the same about you. I'm proud that you're my agent, and that you and I have also worked together for more than a decade. Thank you.

With Jim comes a large, experienced team. In particular, I would like to point out one person who has helped spread my words to the rest of the world: Elizabeth Fisher. Beth has also ensured that my previous books have been released in languages I barely knew existed, and she has my lasting gratitude.

Mark Fortier, of Fortier PR, belongs to this same stable of people I've worked with for more than a decade. Mark is simply outstanding at what he does, and I don't say this lightly. Of all the public relations agencies I've worked with across the globe—and there have been a few of them!—Mark is by far #1. Mark, thank you.

Throughout my book I refer back to a mysterious, ever-present, ever-energized and even at times *shivering* assistant, Oliver Britz. (I know he hated my using this word about him in one of the chapters of this book—and in truth, Oliver almost never shivers.) He is, however, an enormously talented individual who travels the world with me, and has an almost supernatural ability to connect with other people. (During our Subtext Research, people regularly fall in love with him.) Today, Oliver is engaged to be married to a woman he met during an interview—the ultimate tribute to the powers of Small Mining! Thank you, Oliver, for being who you are, and keeping up with my extreme speed, demands and expectations. You're a true star.

Not least, there's one other person from Lindstrom Company who for over twenty years has been, and continues to be, instrumental in building my brand: my assistant, Signe Jonasson. Signe is my gatekeeper, my eyes, my ears, my coordinator, my source of energy and my friend. Thank you, Signe, for keeping up with me, even though you've probably never had a holiday in your life since the day we started working together.

A special thank you to Chip Heath, who not only embraced the idea of *Small Data* the second I mentioned it to him, but offered to write an outstanding foreword. Finally I'd like to give a shout-out to my "chief researcher" Bobbie 7, who has searched, searched and searched—and found what I was looking for every time.

The team at my publisher, St. Martins, has been wonderful. Admittedly I'm not easy to work with. We produced almost a dozen book covers before managing to agree on one. And, yes, I even managed to change my mind about the title halfway throughout the process, creating nightmares for everyone. Thank you all very much for your dedication to *Small Data,* especially my editor, Emily Carlton, Christine Catarino, Laura Clark, Gabrielle Gantz, Alan Bradshaw and the entire St. Martin's sales force, which has done outstanding work giving birth to *Small Data.*

If you've watched and enjoyed any of the Small Data videos, or my website, I'm sure you realize it comes as a result of a hard (and I mean *hard*) work by everyone who works behind the scenes at Juice Group, with whom I've worked for more than a decade. Juice came about by coincidence when its owners, Jonathan and Lara Greenstein, unable to secure a visa in the United States when working for clients, moved "temporarily" to Vancouver, Canada. A decade later, Vancouver is still their home, and Juice is thriving. Jonathan and Lara, you're absolutely amazing . . . or let me rephrase this; your effort is absolutely *terrific!* Along with Jonathan and Lara, I also want to thank Ben Regan, Mark McDermott, Terry Tsiao and Jonathan Kwok

Considering that a lot of the work I do is somewhat pioneering— or at least breaks new ground now and again—sometimes I hit a wall when giving names to some of my new techniques. Of all the word-smiths I've worked with, without a doubt I can state that Anthony Shore—who runs his own naming agency, Operative Words—is #1 at what he does, namely, coining new words. He has come up with several of the ones you've read about in this book, including Subtext Research, Subtexting and Small Mining. Anthony is an amazing guy.

Jack Morton Worldwide has been an instrumental partner in the release of *Small Data*. Early on, some people found it difficult to wrap their heads around the concept, but Jack Morton understood what I was trying to do immediately, which tells you a lot about the agency. A special thank you goes to Craig Million for his dedication, and for making so much else possible, and thanks also go to Julian Pullan, Josh McCall, Bill Davis, Rob McQueen and Abigail Walker.

Out of all the clients my company works with, I'd like to single out one: Lowes Foods. (Remember them? The guys who do the Chicken Dance?) To buy into crazy ideas in the first place tells you a lot about Lowes, and its executive team, and I have to say that hands down they are the most amazing client I've ever worked with, with many executives becoming as close to my heart as family members. A special thank you goes to Boyd George and Brian George, who first laid down the chal-lenge of transforming the stores. Boyd is one of the most humble people

I've ever met and, despite his seniority, as sharp as a Japanese blade. For his part, Brian manages to understand and appreciate creativity, while simultaneously running, guiding and motivating his team. Huge kudos to them both. Heather George, another family member, is a true talent, and I feel we've known and worked together forever. Unlike most people in our industry, Heather really, truly understands consumers, store managers, merchants, vendors, as well as what creativity is (and isn't). She's not only an outstanding individual, she's also a dear friend.

Without Tim Lowe, the president of Lowes Foods, we ran the risk of completing a successful operation . . . except the patient died. Passionate and engaging, with a deep understanding and knowledge of retail, Tim has one of the highest energy levels I've seen in any client. Thank you, Tim, as always, for everything.

There are so many other people at Lowes I want to thank that I honestly don't know where to begin, but let me just mention a few: my favorite architect, Gary Watson, Kimberly George, Anita Joffe-Smithwick, Chris Van Parys, Michael Moore, Kelly Davis, Debbie Williams, Jason Ramsey and countless more. Thank you to everyone at Lowes, MDI and Alex Lee.

Buzzfeed, Frank Cooper, and Tami Dalley have both been key partners in spreading the gospel about *Small Data*. Frank and I go back many years, to Pepsi days, and he and his team have shown a remarkable skill in spreading the word about this book. The same goes for Mike Barbeau who, along with his team, has an outstanding ability to spread positive word of mouth. Neal Schaffer belongs to a very small group who truly understands the social media space. Thanks to all of you for putting *Small Data* on the social media map.

A ton of other people have either directly or indirectly influenced elements in this book, including Frank and Tiffany Foster, Georgia and Philippe Garinois-Melenikiotou, Fatme Khalife, Tracy Luckow, Philip Kotler, Tyra Banks, Paco Underhill and Nicholas (Goldfish) Simko, who spent time with me in Siberia.

Then there are the people who inspired me over the course of this project, either by sharing thoughts with me, reading the manuscript, conducting an interesting study or simply exposing to me a perspective that made a difference. In no particular order I'd like to thank: Tony Tsieh, Jeff Weiner, Ryan Holmes, Deepak Chopra, Danny Sullivan, Tim Ferriss, Gary Vanyerchuk, Martin Shervington, Sarah Hill, Michelle Killebrew, Muhammad Yunus, David Edelman, Meg Whitman, Denis Labelle, Dr. Jane Goodall, Dharmesh Shah, Beth Comstock, Thomas Friedman, David Sable, Chris Brogan, Michael Hyatt, Jeff Bullas, Don Peppers, Charlene Li, Rand Fishkin, Pam Moore, Nicolas Bordas, Peter Shankman, Steven Pinker, Richard Florida, Mike Allton, Jay Baer, Brian Solis, Steve Rubel, Neil Patel, Mark Schaefer, Jonah Berger, Chad Dickerson, Josh Leibowitz, Erica Hill, Niall Ferguson, Lee Odden, Jonathan Becher, John Jantsch, Yifat Cohen, Robert Cialdini, Andrew Hunt, Matt Heinz, Joe Pulizzi, Joseph Stiglitz, Michael Brenner, Michael Gold, John Rampton, Shawn Collins, Chris Ducker, David Skok, John Lee Dumas, Lee Odden, Jonathan Salem Baskin, Brent Csutoras, Heidi Cohen, Bill Tancer, Anita Newton, Matthew Barby, Craig Rosenberg, Brian Massey, Jon Haidt, Tom Fishburne, Roger Dooley, Pamela Wilson.

As you can see, even though "Martin Lindstrom" may appear on the cover of this book, it has truly been a collective effort to make these pages as inspiring and—I hope—transformative as they have become. Thanks everyone.

NOTES

INTRODUCTION

1. John Ashcroft, "The Lego Case Study," John Ashcroft and Company, http://www.the legocasestudy.com.
2. Brian Solomon, "Everything Is Awesome: Lego Leaps Barbie for World's Largest Toy Maker," *Forbes,* September 4, 2014.
3. Gwendolyn Seidman, Ph.D., "Do We Lie More in Texts or Face-to-Face?" *Psychology Today,* November 23, 2014.
4. Internet Live Stats, http://www.internetlivestats.com/internet-users/.
5. Maeve Duggan, Nicole B. Ellison, Cliff Lampe, Amanda Lenhart, & Mary Madden, "Frequency of Social Media Use," Pew Research Center, January 9, 2015, http://www .pewinternet.org/2015/01/09/frequency-of-social-media-use-2/.
6. YouTube Statistics, https://www.youtube.com/yt/press/statistics.html.
7. "Big Data, for Better or Worse: 90% of World's Data Generated over Last Two Years," Science Daily, May 22, 2013, http://www.sciencedaily.com/releases/2013/05 /130522085217.htm.
8. Marc de Swaan Arons, Frank van den Driest, Keith Weed, "The Ultimate Marketing Machine," Harvard Business Review, July-August, 2014.
9. Nick Bilton, "When the Cyber-Bully Is You," *New York Times,* April 29, 2015.

CHAPTER 1

1. "Most-Used Emoji Revealed: Americans Love Skulls, Brazilians Love Cats, the French Love Hearts," Swiftkey.Blog, April 21, 2015, http://swiftkey.com/en/blog/americans -love-skulls-brazilians-love-cats-swiftkey-emoji-meanings-report/.
2. SwiftKey, "SwiftKey Emoji Report," http://www.scribd.com/doc/262594751/Swift Key-Emoji-Report.
3. "Global Gender Gap Index 2014," World Economic Forum, http://reports.weforum .org/global-gender-gap-report-2014/rankings/.
4. SwiftKey, "SwiftKey Emoji Report," http://www.scribd.com/doc/262594751/Swift Key-Emoji-Report.
5. Robert Haas, "Meditation at Lagunitas," *Praise,* HarperCollins Publishers, 1979.

CHAPTER 2

1. Karl Ove Knausgaard, "My Saga, Part 2," *New York Times Magazine,* March 11, 2015.

2. "The First Lady on the First Family," excerpt of Michelle Obama appearance on *Ellen,* https://www.youtube.com/watch?v=dbYEEBrjOAA.

3. Amanda Macias, "This Chart Shows How the Rest of the World Doesn't Even Come Close to US Military Spending," *Business Insider,* April 19, 2014. http://www.businessinsider.com/us-military-spending-chart-2014-4?IR=T.

4. Drew Desilver, "A Minority of Americans Own Guns, but Just How Many Is Unclear," Pew Research Center FactTank, June 4, 2013.

5. "What Is Cards Against Humanity," https://cardsagainsthumanity.com.

6. "Mobile Technology Fact Sheet," The Pew Research Center, http://www.pewinternet .org/fact-sheets/mobile-technology-fact-sheet/.

7. Daniel Wood, "US Crime Rate at Lowest Point in Decades. Why America Is Safer Now," *Christian Science Monitor,* January 9, 2012.

8. Nick Bilton, "Steve Jobs Was a Low-Tech Parent," *New York Times,* September 10, 2014.

9. Ibid.

10. Nate Cohn, "Big Drop in Share of Americans Calling Themselves Christian," *New York Times,* May 12, 2015.

11. Ibid.

CHAPTER 3

1. Gardiner Harris, "Poor Sanitation in India May Afflict Well-Fed Children with Malnutrition," *New York Times,* July 13, 2014, http://www.nytimes.com/2014/07/15/world /asia/poor-sanitation-in-india-may-afflict-well-fed-children-with-malnutrition.html #slideshow/100000002994895/100000002994992.

2. Gardiner Harris, "Holding Your Breath in India," *New York Times,* May 29, 2015.

3. Vivekananda Nemana and Ankita Rao, "In India, Latrines Are Truly Lifesavers," *New York Times,* November 13, 2014.

4. Gardiner Harris, "Websites in India Put a Bit of Choice into Arranged Marriages," *New York Times,* April 24, 2015.

5. "Why Tensions Are Soaring in Mother (in Law) India," http://www.thestar.com/ news/world/2014/02/17/why_tensions_are_soaring_in_mother_inlaw_india. html.

6. "The Curse of The Mummyji," *Economist,* December 21, 2013, http://www.economist .com/news/christmas-specials/21591745-curse-mummyji.

7. Ibid.

8. Madison Park, "Top 20 Most Polluted Cities in the World," CNN, May 8, 2014, http:// www.cnn.com/2014/05/08/world/asia/india-pollution-who/.

9. Bruce Grierson, "What if Age Is Nothing but a Mind-Set?" *New York Times,* October, 22, 2014.

10. Ibid.

CHAPTER 4

1. Gina Kolata, "Obesity Spreads to Friends, Study Concludes," *New York Times,* July 25, 2007.

2. Ibid.

3. Cynthia L. Ogden et al., "Mean Body Weight, Height, and Body Mass Index, United States, 1960-2002," Division of Health and Nutrition Examination Surveys, Centers for Disease Control and Prevention, October 27, 2004, http://atlanta.cbslocal.com/2015 /06/15/cdc-average-american-woman-now-weighs-as-much-as-1960s-us-man/.

4. Jan Hoffman, "Parents' Denial Fuels Childhood Obesity Epidemic," *New York Times,* June 15, 2015.

5. Sarah Boseley, "Mexico Enacts Soda Tax in Effort to Combat World's Highest Obesity Rate," *The Guardian,* January 16, 2014, http://www.theguardian.com/world/2014/jan/16/mexico-soda-tax-sugar-obesity-health.

6. Deborah Amos, "Saudi Girls Can Now Take Gym Class, but Not Everyone Is Happy," http://www.npr.org/sections/parallels/2015/03/10/391878690/saudi-girls-can-now-take-pe-classes-but-not-everyones-happy.

7. Shirley Wang, "As World's Kids Get Fatter, Doctors Turn to the Knife," *The Wall Street Journal,* February 14, 2014.

8. Mary Kaye Schilling, "Get Busy: Pharrell's Productivity Secrets," *Fast Company,* November 18, 2013, http://www.fastcompany.com/3021377/pharrell-get-busy.

9. Jan Brogan, "When Being Distracted Is a Good Thing," *The Boston Globe,* February 27, 2012.

10. Tom Vanderbilt, "The Crisis in American Walking," *Slate,* April 10, 2012, http://www.slate.com/articles/life/walking/2012/04/why_don_t_americans_walk_more_the_crisis_of_pedestrianism_.html?wpsrc=fol_tw?wpsrc=fol_fb.

11. Peter Cohan, "Weight Watchers Winning $61 Billion War on Fat," *Forbes,* November 14, 2012.

CHAPTER 5

1. Leonard Reissman, *Class in American Society* (New York: The Free Press, 1965), p. 178.

2. Simon Romero, "Rio's Race to Future Intersects Slave Past," the *New York Times,* March 8, 2014, http://www.nytimes.com/2014/03/09/world/americas/rios-race-to-future-intersects-slave-past.html.

3. Jonathan Watts, "Why Brazil Loves Nip and Tuck as Told by the Country's Leading Plastic Surgery 'Maestro,'" *Guardian* (UK), September 24, 2014.

4. Antonio Prata, "Brazil's Shaken Optimism," *New York Times,* June 23, 2015.

5. Lisa Baertlein, "Los Angeles Water Sommelier Wants Bottled Water Treated Like Wine," Reuters, March 2, 2015.

6. Susanne Ault, "Survey: YouTube Stars More Popular Than Mainstream Celebs Among U.S. Teens," *Variety,* August 5, 2014.

7. Laura M. Holson, "The Feng Shui Kingdom," *New York Times,* April 25, 2005.

8. Dan Levin, "Adidos and Hotwind? In China, Brands Adopt Names to Project Foreign Flair," *New York Times,* December 26, 2014, http:/www.nytimes.com/2014/12/27/business/international/adidos-and-hotwind-in-china-brands-evoke-foreign-names-even-if-theyre-gibberish.html.

9. Caroline Wyatt, "'Paris Syndrome' Strikes Japanese," *BBC News,* December 20, 2006.

10. Caroline Wyatt, "'Paris Syndrome' Strikes Japanese," *BBC News,* December 20, 2006.

11. Antunes Anderson, "God Has a New Home: A $300 Million Mega Temple in Sao Paulo," *Forbes,* July 30, 2014, http://www.forbes.com/sites/andersonantunes/2014/07/30/god-has-a-new-home-a-300-million-mega-temple-in-sao-paulo/.

CHAPTER 6

1. Bradley Blackburn, "Clothing 'Made in America': Should US Manufacture More Clothes?" *ABC News,* March 10, 2011, http://abcnews.go.com/Business/MadeInAmerica/made-america-clothes-clothing-made-usa/story?id=13108258.

2. Sandra Blakeslee, "Mind Games: Sometimes a White Coat Isn't Just a White Coat," *New York Times,* April 2, 2012, http://www.nytimes.com/2012/04/03/science/clothes-and-self-perception.html.

3. Sandra Blakeslee, "Mind Games: Sometimes a White Coat Isn't Just a White Coat," *New York Times,* April 2, 2012.

4. Sandra Blakeslee, "Mind Games: Sometimes a White Coat Isn't Just a White Coat," *New York Times*, April 2, 2012, http://www.nytimes.com/2012/04/03/science/clothes-and-self-perception.html.

5. Ivan Oransky, "Holding Hot Coffee = Warm and Fuzzy Feelings," *Scientific American*, October 23, 2008, http://www.scientificamerican.com/blog/post/holding-hot-coffee-warm-and-fuzzy-2008-10-22/.

6. Alena Hall, "7 Reasons to Banish Your Phone from the Bedroom," *Huffington Post*, November 3, 2014.

CHAPTER 7

1. Peter N. Stearns, "The History of Happiness," *Harvard Business Review*, January–February 2012, https://hbr.org/2012/01/the-history-of-happiness.

2. Ibid.

3. World Happiness Report 2014, John Helliwell, Richard Leyard, Jeffrey Sachs, Editors, http://worldhappiness.report/wp-content/uploads/sites/2/2015/04/WHR15-Apr29-update.pdf.

4. John Clifton, "People Worldwide Are Reporting a Lot of Positive Emotions," Gallup, http://www.gallup.com/poll/169322/people-worldwide-reporting-lot-positive-emotions.aspx.

5. John Clifton, "Mood of the World Upbeat on International Happiness Day," Gallup, http://www.gallup.com/poll/182009/mood-world-upbeat-international-happiness-day.aspx.

6. Laura Sydell, "How Do Chinese Citizens Feel About Censorship?" NPR, July 12, 2008.

7. Ibid.

8. Carol Pinchefsky, "The Impact (Economic and Otherwise) of Lord of the Rings/The Hobbit on New Zealand," *Forbes*, December 14, 2012.

9. Brook Larmer, "How Do You Keep Your Kids Healthy in Smog-Choked China?" *New York Times*, April 16, 2015.

10. Malcolm Moore, "China's 'Airpocalypse' Kills 350,000 to 500,000 a Year," *Telegraph* (UK), January 7, 2014.

11. *New York Times* quoted in ibid.

12. Oliver Wainwright, "Inside Beijing's Airpocalypse—a City Made 'Almost Uninhabitable' by Pollution," *Guardian* (UK), December 16, 2014.

13. Ibid.

14. Joseph Kahn and Jim Yardley, "As China Roars, Pollution Reaches Deadly Extremes," *New York Times*, August 26, 2007.

15. Christina Larson, "The Cracks in China's Shiny Buildings," *Bloomberg Business*, September 27, 2012, http://www.bloomberg.com/bw/articles/2012-09-27/the-cracks-in-chinas-shiny-buildings.

16. Jeff Chu, "Happily Ever After," *Time*, March 18, 2002.

17. Katia Moskvitch, "Why Does Food Taste Different on Planes?," BBB.com, January 12, 2015, http://www.bbc.com/future/story/20150112-why-in-flight-food-tastes-weird.

18. Ibid.

CHAPTER 8

1. Jonathan Mahler, "The White and Gold (No, Blue and Black!) Dress That Melted the Internet," *New York Times*, February 27, 2015.

2. Ibid.

3. Pamela Engel, "Here's the Dress from a British Retailer That Started a Debate on Social Media—It's Clearly Blue and Black," *Business Insider*, February 27, 2015, http://www.businessinsider.com/the-roman-originals-black-and-blue-dress-2015-2.

4. Elizabeth Cohen, "A Scientific Tale of Two Dresses," CNN, March 2, 2015, http://www.cnn.com/2015/02/27/health/science-of-gold-blue-dress/.

5. Ibid.

6. Joe Mandese, "Extinction Event: Why There May Be Far Fewer Brands at Cannes 2025," *MediaPost Live!,* June 22, 2015.

7. A. Bonneville-Roussy, P. J. Rentfrow, M. K. Xu, J. Potter, "Music Through the Ages: Trends in Musical Engagement and Preferences from Adolescence Through Middle Adulthood," *The Journal of Personal and Social Psychology,* 2013, October: 105 (4): 703-17. Doi: 10.1037/a0033770. Epub2013, July 29, http://www.ncbi.nlm.nih.gov/pubmed/23895269.

8. Ibid.

9. Ibid.

10. "What Your Favorite Sport Says About You," British Heart Foundation, April 1, 2015, https://www.bhf.org.uk/news-from-the-bhf/news-archive/2015/march/what-your-favourite-sport-says-about-you.

11. Jong-Eun Roselyn Lee, David Clark Moore, Eun-A Park, Sung Gwan Park, "Who Wants to Be 'Friend-Rich'? Social Compensating Friending on Facebook and the Moderating Role of Public Self-Consciousness," *Computers in Human Behavior* (Impact Factor: 2.69. 05/2012; 28 (3): 1036-1043. DOI: 10.1016/j.chb.2012.01.006, http://www.researchgate.net/publication/257252915_Who_Wants_to_be_friend-rich_Social_Compensatory_Friending_on_Facebook_and_the_Moderating_role_of_public_self-consciousness.

12. Eftekhar Azar, Chris Fullwood, Neil Morris, "Capturing Personality from Facebook Photos and Photo-Related Activities: How Much Exposure Do You Need?" *Computers in Human Behavior,* Volume 37, August 2014, pp. 162–170, http://www.sciencedirect.com/science/article/pii/S0747563214002696.

13. Ian Urbana, "The Secret Life of Passwords," *New York Times Magazine,* November 19, 2014, http://www.nytimes.com/2014/11/19/magazine/the-secret-life-of-passwords.html.

14. Nicole Laskowski, "Seven Big Data Failures to Watch Out For," SearchCio, Tech Target, August 12, 2015, http://searchcio.techtarget.com/news/4500251611/Seven-big-data-failures-to-watch-out-for.

15. Matt Richtel, and Doughery, Conor, "Google's Driverless Cars Run into Problem: Cars with Drivers," the *New York Times,* September 1, 2015.

16. Von Bettina Höchli, Karin Frick, Mirjam Hauser, "We-Dentity: Wie Das Netzwerk-Ich die Wirtschaft und Gesellschaft von Morgen Verandert," University of Zurich, Gottlieb Duttweiler Institute of Economic and Social Studies, GDI Studie #42, @ copyright GDI 2015.

INDEX

IF YOU LIKED THIS BOOK YOU MAY LIKE . . .

A $7,000,000 Neuromarketing study of our brand and the influence of brands.

How the power of our senses has an amazing influence on our purchase decisions.

A million dollar experiment showing how powerful word-of-mouth can really be.

Visit MartinLindstrom.com for more . . .